The Journey
of A
Lifetime

By

Rayola Kelley

Hidden Manna Publications

The Journey of a Lifetime
Rayola Kelley Copyright © 2024

GENTLE SHEPHERD MINISTRIES
www.gentleshepherd.com

ISBN: 979-8-9893588-5-4

Except where otherwise indicated, all Scripture quotations in this book are taken from the King James Version of the Bible.

Hidden **M**anna **P**ublications
P.O. Box 3572
Oldtown, ID 83822
www.gentleshepherd.com

Facebook:
https://www.facebook.com/HiddenMannaPublications/

ACKNOWLEDGMENT AND RECOGNITION

We wish to convey special thanks to Crystal Garvin and Jeannette Haley for the proofreading and editing of the material in this book.

Finally, I want to acknowledge the faithfulness of our great God to see each of us through each challenge in our incredible journey through this present age. He has always been patient to teach me valuable lessons, ready to show His mercy in my failures, and His wisdom when powerfully intervening in my life. He has preserved my life in Him and enlarged my testimony regarding His willingness and majesty to meet me in each challenge and test.

Contents

Introduction

This book contains two books in which author, Rayola Kelley, shares insights about her spiritual journey. Her first book, *From Prisons and Dots to Christianity*, presents a powerful look into the process that must take place to bring a believer to perfection in Christ. By revealing the inner struggles that often take place in this process, it allows the reader to see into the author's heart, life, and mind. It shows how such a process is capable of firmly establishing God's servants according to His life and purpose for them.

The author clearly shares the personal struggles she encountered to find her place in Christ. She addresses the obstacles and attitudes that served as hindrances in her journey to come to this place of spiritual rest, service, and satisfaction. Although these hindrances initially seemed unfair and oppressive to her, she eventually learned how they actually served as disciplines that helped her discover her abiding place in Jesus Christ.

Once these hindrances were allowed to have their way in her life, she finally learned the reality of Jesus. Such reality reveals that Christianity is not a religion or simply a lifestyle. Christianity is the reality of Jesus' very life coming forth in a person. It is His life that serves as the light of man. It is His mind of humility and example of servitude and obedience working within believers that enable them to see and hear what the Spirit is saying. And, it is within His heart of love and grace that His followers manifest Him to the world. Clearly, it is Jesus' life manifesting through those who love Him that allows His powerful light to penetrate into the darkest recesses of their souls. This light will reveal that people are not only miserably lost, but that hope, grace, salvation, and purpose can be found at the foot of an old rugged cross.

In the author's second book, *So You Want To Be In Ministry,* she gives insight into the real shaping and molding of God-ordained ministries. Often formed in travail, established in fiery ovens, tested in the challenging harvest field of humanity, proven on the spiritual battlefields of adversity, and brought forth from the grave of death and obscurity, they serve as an example that true ministries of God just do not happen. They are not the result of good intentions, overzealous strength and passion, or winning abilities. Rather, servants of God and their ministries must be prepared and personally shaped by the hands of the great Potter to be used for His glory and purpose. Every aspect of the servant's life and every way of service will be subject to the birth pangs of new life, the purging from the old, the bitterness of failure, the defeat in battles, and the despair of the dying out process for the servant, along with their service in order to come to a place where they can become pliable in God's hands.

So You Want To Be In Ministry is the story of how God brought two woman of God, Jeannette Haley and the author Rayola Kelley, together as a ministry team in 1989. You will see the culmination of the adventures and challenges these two women faced together as God forged them into a seasoned ministry team. Their call to front line ministry in the trenches with lost, hurting humanity not only made them seasoned servants and soldiers in God's kingdom, but it allowed them to see the heart of God in relationship to the real battle that is raging in the spiritual realm for the souls of people.

This book simply "scratches the surface" as to the experiences and depths these two servants of God have encountered, but what it highlights reveals the reality of godly ministry. Such ministry is not about standing in front as a great and popular orator, building up religions kingdoms that will impress the world, or presenting a successful front to attract more "followers"; rather, it is about becoming an extension of Jesus to lost and wounded souls. It is about becoming His mouthpiece that proclaims the Gospel, His hands that reach out in mercy and compassion, and His feet that walk in obedience to the will of God. It is about becoming a mirror that truly reflects Jesus' lowly disposition as a servant, His meek attitude of submission to the Father, and His divine truth and glory as the One who came from heaven to be a sacrificial lamb that serves as the way of God that will lead to everlasting life.

So You Want to be in Ministry is a candid book that readers will not easily forget. The lessons, revelations, and reality of what constitutes genuine ministry is presented in a concise way, allowing the reader to see that real ministry is not marked by worldly successes or numbers, but by the life of God being worked in and through the believer for His purpose and glory.

FROM PRISONS

AND DOTS

TO CHRISTIANITY

Book One

INTRODUCTION

This book is about a personal search. It has been a long search that is not limited to a particular group of people, gender, race, or culture. It is a search that all encounter in their lifetime, but few take up the challenge to discover the truths or secrets surrounding this exploration. Those who do accept the challenge are greatly buffeted along the way. As a result, many give up in disillusionment, discouragement, and depression.

This search has to do with finding the meaning of life. My search to understand my reason for being here started with my need to be a someone. The desire to be a someone is the need to make and leave an impression in this world. Later, I realized that it was not an impression I wanted to leave with this world, but the need to make a difference to ensure my life counted for something.

My search to discover the reason for my existence started a process that would expose every aspect of my personal character. It began with me realizing I was imprisoned by various unseen sources. Others could not see my prisons, and I could only feel their oppressiveness. They kept me from moving forward to discover the answer to my nagging question. Each prison had its own particular brand of enslaving devices or bars that kept me in a limited area of personal growth.

My prisons began to evaporate when I encountered the Jesus of the Bible. Chains that bound me began to fall to the wayside, while unseen bars that held me began to dissipate. The brick walls that enfolded me crumbled before the feet of my new found Friend. The initial freedom I experienced was indescribable.

Eventually, I ran into another type of bondage. This bondage was different from my past prisons. It seemed relatively harmless, but it was subtle and powerful. In the scheme of things, its power rested in its ability to change my focus or vision from that which was important. This bondage was like small dots on a piece of paper. These dots were nothing when put in perspective, but they had a way of drawing one's focus away from what is real and important. I discovered that these dots caused me to take detours or walk in circles. Life was beyond these small dots, but my focus had to change before I could discover the real purpose of life.

Each prison that evaporated and each dot that faded in the glorious light and life of Christ allowed me to come to terms with the purpose and meaning of life. It could be summarized in one word—Christianity. Christianity is a walk that leads to Calvary. It is a life of self-denial, death, and resurrection power. This life leaves a mark on all who encounter it. It has the power to make an eternal difference. In fact, Christianity is nothing more than the living expression of Jesus Christ being reflected in this world.

As I considered my search, I realized that I had made it more difficult. However, this difficulty was not in vain. Because of it, I can now share my journey with others. My prayer is that those who read this book will come to understand the spiritual process they will encounter by the struggles before them, but that in spite of the intensity of the process, they will continue on until they finish the course that has been especially prepared for them by the great Potter (2 Timothy 2:19-21; 4:6-8).

1

FOUNDATIONS SHAKEN

When does life begin? I am not talking about physical life. The life I am referring to is when a person has some sense or awareness that there is more to life than existing on a physical plane. Perhaps, there is a reason for one's existence. However, this purpose cannot be realized until the person's destiny is fulfilled.

I had a keen awareness that I had some destiny when I was in high school. This awareness was vague, but occasionally it would nudge at me and stir up my curiosity to ponder the purpose for my life, especially when my foundations were being shaken. Initial foundations consist of a person's fantasies, hopes, expectations, desires, or dreams. Obviously, concepts surrounding the ideas of success and accomplishment find their springboard in such foundations.

These foundations create pinnacles in a person's life. In the beginning, as well as at the end of my senior year of high school, I reached such a pinnacle. To explain this pinnacle, I must go back to the summer of 1965. I had been greatly hurt and rejected by classmates when I was a fourth grader. It had been a difficult time for my family.

My parents were divorced and my brother and I were exposed to a devastating transition that was hard to swallow. We tried our best to adjust, but found ridicule and rejection from the classmates of the elementary school we attended. Isolation and class prejudice comprise a bitter and overwhelming cup to drink from when you are only nine years old.

After fourteen months of this struggle, my mother remarried, and I saw a chance to take on a new identity. It was in the midst of this new life, new home, and new hope that I decided that I was going to prove to the world that I was of value. From that point on, I worked hard to excel as a person and student.

It was in the summer of my junior year that I was selected to participate in Girls' State. Surprisingly, I recognized that some of my former classmates from the fourth grade were in attendance as well. To my disappointment, the victory of my success was short-lived. These young people may have left a negative impression on my tender life, but I had left none on theirs. They didn't care if I existed during that time and cared even less who I was at the present.

My next reality check was my paternal grandmother. I was always aware that she favored my brother. I interpreted her preference as a form of rejection. This rejection caused me to make another determination. I would also prove to her that I was of worth. After hard work, I barely slid into the salutatorian position of my senior class in the small school I attended. I could hardly wait to flaunt my accomplishment before my grandmother so she could see that I was of value. To my disappointment, she did not attend my graduation to hear my speech. It seemed as if all my work was futile. The victory was lost in what appeared to be the uselessness of it all, causing the disappointment that manifested itself in bitter tears that were hard to swallow. It seemed as if a terrible joke had backfired on me.

These incidents proved to me that life's pinnacles fall short of expectations. They often leave an empty feeling or a bitter taste. Their victories are short-lived, and appear useless in the bigger picture. Pinnacles may have their upside, but they also have their down side. My conclusion to the matter was if life simply consisted of pinnacles, it has no real lasting meaning. In the end, such pinnacles leave you without purpose and hope. As one would say, "Is that all there is?"

My foundations had been shaken, but they still remained intact. I was much wiser because I discovered that there had to be more to life than pinnacles. Like all new graduating seniors, I had zeal and hope. The world lay before me, and it would be a matter of time before I would conquer it and find my destiny.

I failed to realize that this immature view of the world was nothing more than a fantasy. This fantasy could come crashing down around me at any time. As I considered my options, I chose the United States Navy. My reasoning behind my choice sounded patriotic and noble. But, underneath my fake nobility, I knew I was running from my present unpleasant circumstances in hope of finding my destiny.

At the time, I was unrealistic, ignorant, and foolish. I had learned how to play the game and win favor with certain people. Since I foolishly concluded that I knew how to play people, I reasoned that I could actually control my world. This foolish perspective is prevalent with eighteen-year-olds. In fact, I saw myself as being very wise. Later, I learned that I was not being wise, but blinded by personal conceits.

The military did more than teach me how to march. I discovered the harsh reality that the idea of being in control of one's world was a fantasy. My experiences in the military also revealed the shallowness of my character. This caused my life to escalate out of control. As my world fell apart at the seams, I found myself drowning in confusion and uncertainty. I began to see aspects of my character that made me realize that I was anything but honorable and noble.

This harsh reality created a fear that swallowed me up in depression. As I considered life, I could see no purpose for it. In summation, life seemed to be a big joke. I toyed with suicide, but figured in my present state I would mess up any attempts, and somehow live through the whole ordeal to only suffer more.

Obviously, I was in a precarious mental state. The whole situation seemed hopeless. Where could I turn since the horizon before me was bleak? My ordeal seemed eternal. Life appeared to be a cruel satire that was too great to endure.

My foundations were not only shaking and shifting, but they were crumbling before me. I was drowning in a cesspool of failure, and I could not stop myself. I had been raised in the Mormon Church, but I was a jack Mormon. I did not believe all of their religious rhetoric, and realized I was a Mormon simply in name and association, but not in heart or mind.

Although I was being somewhat conditioned to be a good Mormon girl in primary and the youth group, I harbored doubts about the church's claims and beliefs. Some of these doubts were a product of my mother's skepticism about some of the church's teachings. This struggle caused confusion. Some of the Mormons who influenced my life seemed genuine, but I also saw the perversion that lurked within my own family.

I knew that religion was a personal matter, and I could not be content until I came to terms with the personal doubts that constantly raised their head. After all, could I leave such matters up to my family who often appeared hypocritical because of their own struggles? Could I assume that my family was right in their religious preference, or were they simply enslaved by what was familiar? I could easily concede that heritage and family were supposed to hold the secrets and wisdom to real life. Such a conclusion could allow me to hide behind them to avoid personal responsibility for what I believed or who I was becoming. But, was that wise? Underneath it all, I knew that such matters were personal, and somehow, I had to make peace with these issues for myself.

My life was now crumbling before me. In my heart, I could not turn to my religion because it would deem me a failure. After all, my religious indoctrination and understanding maintained that it was up to me to do good, to be righteous, and to overcome. However, life was exposing the depth of my character. I could not find any goodness, nor could I stir myself up to be good or even give the impression that I was good and that everything was under control.

I knew my religion was not the solution, but my situation was desperate. I needed hope. In the midst of this spiritual struggle, I sensed that God was the solution, but in what way? It dawned on me that I had no real knowledge of God. He was some vague notion that had no identity. How could this be? I had heard about God in those years of religious training. Yet, it was as if He were dead and lifeless. In my struggle to figure out why I was ignorant about God, it struck me that the Mormon Church had served as my god. It had become a sick substitute of what and who God is. This church had subtly tried to define God by defining its personal goals and agendas. Yet, the Mormon Church was not God, but an organization that was doing nothing more than indoctrinating people to serve its purposes in the name of God.

Interestingly, I discovered that I was indoctrinated enough that I felt a certain loyalty to the Mormon Church. Clearly, the beliefs and teachings of the church had failed me, but I knew nothing else. I felt anger towards it because it left me with nothing to cling to, but at the same time, it was the only miserable hope I had in regards to my spiritual life. How could I find God without the Mormon Church or some type of religious affiliation? I trusted no other religious affiliation because I was told that the Mormon Church was the only true church. It had been established because

The Journey of a Lifetime

all the Protestant Churches could not agree on religious matters, showing their inconsistencies.[1]

Looking back, I can see where my plight actually caused me to become open to spiritual truths. At the time, the Father was drawing me to His Son without my conscious awareness. The truths about God began to penetrate my life. I had been blinded to the Gospel, but my desperation was causing me to be open to the things of God.[2] This openness was not to religion or a certain denomination, but to God Himself.

My Christian aunt sent me the book *The Hiding Place* about Corrie ten Boom. I could see that Corrie had something with God that was clearly missing in my life. This reality kept cropping up at different times. There was one Christian Navy personnel who used to hand me Chick tracks. I would consume them on the bus to and from the base, and sense my spiritual vacuum. There was a hospital corpsman who enthusiastically talked about Jesus, while cleaning my teeth. He had something so real and genuine that I envied him. And, then there was the civilian who worked in the Navy's legal office who told me about an incident that surrounded one of the Christian evangelistic crusades she had been on in Denmark. Apparently, many of the people of Denmark are amoral. They had planned blatant opposition and mockery against this Christian crusade, but God protected the crusade in a miraculous way. It went off without any incident.

During their outreach, they attended one of the churches. The pastor was talking about how people who do not know Jesus are walking in darkness.[3] Just as He made this statement, the lights went out in the church. The people thought it to be some ploy, but

---

[1] Cult members who discover the fallacy in their beliefs, often reject God altogether because they associate God to their cult or religious affiliation. For more information, see her book, *Unmasking the Cult Mentality* in the author's first volume of the foundational series.

[2] Matthew 16:17; 2 Corinthians 4:3-6

[3] John 3:19-21

when they peered out of the windows, they realized all the lights in the city were out as well. In the shadows of candlelight, the pastor continued to speak about the darkness that unbelievers walk in. Then, he stated that if people really know Jesus Christ as Savior and Lord, they walk in the light. As he said the word "light," the lights came on.

Needless to say, the combination of things made an impression on me. I realized that these people had something I did not. They had experiences with God that drastically changed their lives. They believed Him in such a way that it stirred me up to consider the difference between their knowledge of God and my vague notions about Him.

As I struggled with this spiritual dilemma, I realized that I was in spiritual bondage. This bondage was caused by my ignorance about God and the spiritual darkness caused by my sins. It felt like I was in limbo, lost in a maze of confusion and doubt about everything that was associated with God. I wondered what was true and real. Who was the real God, and would He ever stand up and claim His rightful position in my life?

Through a series of events, I was transferred to Coronado, California. I had been lost as to where I could find the solutions to my spiritual hopelessness. I never dreamed that God had been situating events. As the committed Shepherd, He was looking for me, His one lost sheep.[4] In the recesses of my spirit, I knew that I desperately needed to be found, but how and by whom?

It was at Coronado that God found me, and my search for the solution came to an end. The Lord brought two cousins into my life, Joan and Mary Ellen Munyon. Due to a change of schedule, the one cousin, Joan, who was in the military, drove me to the base as a favor to a mutual friend.

---

[4] Luke 15:3-10

We started talking about God. I offered my expertise on God. As I recall that conversation, I must have appeared to be religious and foolish, but she was gracious to listen to me. One night, my friend invited the cousins over for dinner. Once again, God became our topic. There was a peace in their lives that greatly attracted me to them. As I was observing these two women's devotion to God, I had this strong impression that I needed to go to church with them. I asked them if they would take me to their church. They had to go a considerable distance out of their way to get me, but they were willing to honor my request.

When I walked into their church the first time, I encountered genuine love. I could sense peace and an excitement. I was aware that these people somehow possessed what I so desperately needed. Slowly, the Holy Ghost penetrated my heart with the reality of Jesus' death, burial, and resurrection. It dawned on me that I was a sinner and that Christ Jesus came for me. He died on my behalf on the cross to redeem me from the bondage of sin. He took my sins to the grave, and three days later, He rose to prove victorious over the consequence and penalty of sin—death.

It was a relief to come to terms with my sin. For a long time, I had tried to work my way to righteousness, but I was aware that I had miserably failed. In light of Christ, I realized that such an attempt was a futile exercise. Only Jesus could save me from my plight. Needless to say, I did not understand the implications of grace, but I knew that somehow Jesus had taken care of my spiritual plight on that cross, and with excitement, I embraced it with a simple faith.

The results were incredible. I no longer felt burdened down by sin. Obviously, I had been released from a spiritual prison that I had grown accustomed to, but because of Jesus' salvation, I now tasted sweet liberty. My new-found freedom was indescribable. I knew that I never again wanted to feel those prison bars of sin that had tightened around me. I never wanted to feel the heavy chains of oppression that forever pulled me downward as I tried to move forward. The Son of God had set me free indeed.[5]

I knew that my salvation was real. There was a change that completely came over me. I sensed that I was a new creation, and that I could now discover my destiny.[6] I did not realize that coming to terms with Jesus and His salvation was not an end to my search, but the beginning of a spiritual journey. This journey would take me to the wildernesses of unbelief, bring me into the valleys of humiliation and failure, and lead me up to mountain top experiences that were short-lived and exhausting.

The year 2016 marked my 40th year of being born of Water (God's Word) and of the Spirit. It has been an incredible journey that has been filled with challenges and wonder. However, there is one truth that has been a constant reality with me in this journey—God is faithful. He has faithfully led me through the wilderness. He has taken my hand in the valleys, and has met me on the mountaintops. When I proved to be faithless and fearful in my walk, He proved to be faithful and abiding.[7]

The Lord has grown more precious to me, as I count this world and my life as dung. He has become my reality, as I have deemed my personal conclusions as untrustworthy. He has become my life, as I strive to lose the essence of my life with each decision of self-denial, each step of obedience, and every time I apply the cross to my way of thinking and doing.[8]

It has been a challenging life, but I have begun to understand how Jesus deals with the prisons and eliminates the insignificant dots. His purpose for opening the prison gates and addressing the dots is so that I can have the freedom to walk out my Christian life in victory.

---

[5] John 8:36
[6] 2 Corinthians 5:17
[7] John 3:3 & 5; 2 Timothy 2:13
[8] Matthew 16:24-25; 2 Corinthians 10:3-5; Philippians 3:7-8

When I was born-again, life truly began for me. However, my born-again experience was just the beginning of my new life. Before I could get on the narrow path, I had to experience the defeat of detours.[9] In my immaturity, I found myself taking major detours, but God used them all to teach me some tough lessons.

Are you in a spiritual prison? Jesus holds the keys. Perhaps you are limited by dots that have taken your perspective off of the eternal. Look up, for your hope and redemption sits on the right hand of the Father.[10] It is the heart of the Father that you know the liberty of His Son's deliverance. And, it is the Son's hope that you will embrace the glorious gift of eternal life and discover the spiritual abundance that is available to you.

---

[9] Matthew 7:13-14
[10] Hebrews 8:1

2

DETOURS

My new-found life in Christ proved to be an important pinnacle. I never realized that the Christian life contained such pinnacles, and that I would find the downside of it soon enough. All I knew is that exciting events were happening. My Navy tour was almost over. I had just discovered Jesus along with people who loved Him. These Christians displayed some of His very same characteristics. They proved to be patient with me in my immature state, and were supportive in my growth. Even in the midst of this excitement, I found myself at a crossroad.

I had a month left in the military. I valued some of my experiences in the military, as well as appreciated all of the lessons I had learned, but my most prized possession was meeting Jesus, the Son of God. I knew that I had to make a decision. The military was definitely not the career I was seeking, but where would I go? I had found a church, but I knew San Diego was not for me. I had one other option, and that was to go home.

This was not an exciting prospect for me. I had intentionally left behind personal problems at home when I joined the Navy. Little did I realize that God would bring me back to face those problems, as well as unresolved issues of my past. As I considered my options, I began to explain to the Lord the problems that awaited me at home. My major challenge was my strained relationship with my mother. As I finished my review of the situation, the Lord gently broke through my thoughts. He basically told me to go home and not worry. He would take care of the matter. The burden immediately lifted from me. A peace came over me, and I knew without a doubt that He would take care of everything.

The last week of my enlistment was exciting. Surprisingly, Corrie ten Boom came to San Diego. Joan and Mary Ellen were kind enough to take me to her meeting. I was reminded that the intensity of my search for God escalated when I read Corrie's book, *The Hiding Place*. Now, I was seeing her in person. It represented the end of one stage of my life, and the beginning of a new stage. I was excited in spite of the unknown that was facing me.

It was also in my final week in the military that I had my last supper with Joan and Mary Ellen. I was thankful for their faithfulness to share Jesus with me along with their time, patience, and energy. They would always hold a special place in my life, regardless of whether we kept in touch. After all, they had shared the eternal prize with me in word and action.

The supper I shared with these two special women was a precious time for me. I savored it, and regretted when it came to an end. Obviously, God had graciously ordered my steps, so that I could meet Jesus Christ. I realized the Christians who were part of my past life had never shared His reality with me. I even asked a friend why she had failed to share Christ with me, knowing I was on my way to hell. She told me that she had been in rebellion.

Joan and Mary Ellen had been faithful to share Jesus' salvation and life with me in both word and deed. To complete the night, they prayed for me. As they prayed for me, the Holy Ghost came down in a powerful way. I felt as if I was as light as a feather. I could hardly stand and walk. This was my first encounter with the Spirit of God. I was actually touched by a bit of heaven, and it was glorious.

My last week in the military was a whirlwind that marked my life with the reality of God. Looking back, I can see where God allowed me to experience these events in order to establish a stake by which I could go back to remember how I met Him. I never realized that everything I understood would be torn up as the fallow ground of my heart would be exposed and the shallow depths of my character revealed. I would be brought to the point where I would question my salvation, only to be reminded of what occurred during this time.

My plane trip home was also marked by God's artistic ways. The plane came into Boise, Idaho at dusk. The sky looked as if it was on fire. A sense of His majesty came over me. I was humbled and awed by His incredible ability to color the sky in such an array of colors. It was as if you could almost feel and taste His majesty through His glorious presentation. These colors penetrated every sense of my being.

My parents were there to greet me. I noticed that my mother looked haggard. I never thought much about it until we sat down for dinner. I decided it was time to share my new-found faith with her. I told her how I met Jesus Christ and received Him into my life as Savior and Lord. My mother remained quiet, but there was an unusual look on her face. Later, I discovered that she had come to the end of herself, and in her attempt to cry out for help, she had tried to commit suicide. In the midst of doctors, drugs, and emotional exhaustion, a friend had brought her Matthew 11:28-30. In these Scripture verses, Jesus invited people who needed rest to come unto Him. On our way home, she asked Jesus into her life. It was an exciting beginning for both of us.

One of my reasons for joining the Navy was to pursue an education. In my mind, the next three or four years were already planned out. I had a couple months of rest before I started this next phase of life. In the meantime, I began to attend a fundamental Bible based church.

This was my first experience with one of those insignificant dots—man's traditions.[1] Sadly, the church I attended made Christianity more about doctrine and outward appearance than the transformation of the inward man. This forced my emphasis to veer away from coming to terms with what it means to have a relationship with God, to a pursuit for theological understanding.

Unfortunately, this appealed to one of my weaknesses—that of intellectual conceit. Since I was saved out of Mormonism, I determined never to be deceived again. I set out to know the Bible from cover to cover. The theological discussions I found myself in the middle of greatly encouraged this emphasis. I studied everything in God's Word from dress code to eschatology and the issue of once saved, always saved. The emphasis of these different topics served as both pros and cons. I became acquainted with the written Word, but I was leaving the Living Word behind. Jesus was subtly being demoted to a nice scriptural concept that I could control and manipulate. In the end, I could debate about any theological point, but I could not intimately talk about Jesus.

This pursuit caused me to put my faith in what I knew, rather than in whom I needed to know. My testimony was about my understanding surrounding the truths of Jesus, rather than intimately knowing the Son of God as the Truth. My attitude was that of self-righteousness instead of humility. This set me up to fall into sin, compromise, and idolatry. Later, I learned that my intellectual emphasis was useless in light of what was really important: Jesus Christ and Him crucified.[2]

At the time, I never recognized that this religious activity was a detour that would leave me empty. Since it surrounded the Bible, I failed to realize that Jesus was clearly not the center of my

---

[1] Matthew 15:3-6
[2] Matthew 5:20; 1 Corinthians 2:2; 10:12-14; Hebrews 11:6; Titus 3:8-9;
   Revelation 12:11

pursuit. I was majoring in knowledge about what the Bible said about Him and His teachings, rather than in coming to the knowledge of Jesus Christ. This pursuit would leave me vulnerable. The arrogance behind it would ultimately set me up for a major crash.

Another dot was the world's standards. I assumed that I needed to go to college to get an education to properly function and compete in this world. It never dawned on me to ask God if He wanted me to go to college. This was to be one of many lessons that involved assumptions. Assumptions are also dots. They seem reasonable, but do not constitute reality. They take your eyes off of the eternal perspective, causing you to take detours that ultimately set you up for failure.

My first semester in college went well, but I could see where it was liberal. I could also observe where this liberal education was indoctrinating young people to become utter fools in their way of thinking. In fact, it was not challenging them to think at all, but it was subtly telling them how to think about the world around them, creating a godless, dangerous worldview. At that particular point, I could discern the difference, but I did not realize how vulnerable fallen man is to the foolishness of vain philosophies, whether they be secular or religious.[3]

The second semester proved to be a disaster. Money got tight, relationship problems bombarded me from different directions, and I found myself going against the tide. I went back to the drawing board. "God what is wrong? Don't you want me to get my education?" Once again, His still small voice broke through my thoughts and struggles. "I want you to quit college and go home for I have a book for you to write."

To obey Him was simple enough. There was no love between the liberal university and myself. It was at this time that I

---

[3] Colossians 2:8

encountered misunderstanding and criticism for my decision to obey God. This would be a natural reaction from many throughout my years as a Christian when it came to godly obedience. Needless to say, some thought it was all a matter of a religious imagination that bordered on fanaticism, but I decided I could not be concerned with such matters.

The idea of going home to write a book was exciting. Little did I know that God had to first prepare me. He had to wipe my slate clean of all personal notions so that He could write on it. He had to break me at the point of my self-reliance, which was my intellectual pride. He had to reveal all of my idols and expose the depths of my depravity. It took Him seven years to bring me to a place where He could actually begin the preparation in me to have His way.

Looking back, I clearly see God's grace and faithfulness. He did establish a sound scriptural foundation under me, but this could not keep me from focusing on the dots and taking detours. It would be a waste of time to describe the details of my detours. The truth is, I took every detour that most sincere, but immature Christians zealously take. I majored in religious knowledge, only to discover that I knew nothing that had any spiritual substance or meaning to it. I even got politically involved for the sake of righteousness, only to discover that it was a cause that could not save souls or change the hearts of people.[4]

My pursuits established me in my own righteousness. Self-righteousness blinds you to your spiritual condition. I knew there were a lot of discrepancies in my character. At times, I would determine to overcome the sins that beset me.[5] Occasionally, I would find temporary victory, only to find myself entrapped in the same lies, sins, and cycles.

---

[4] Romans 10:2-3; 1 Corinthians 2:14; 8:1-2
[5] Hebrews 12:1

Each time I found myself in this dreadful cycle, I would try to adjust my way of thinking. Just as I thought I was on top of it, my pride with all of its jealousies and critical attitudes would raise its head. As usual, I fell into the same traps, which left me struggling with my inability to make my life right.

At times, I thought myself better than others because they failed to be part of the worthy causes I was involved with. It seemed as if only a few people realized the importance of these crusades, which made my involvement a nobler cause in my eyes. I was blinded to the fact that these causes were crusades that had nothing to do with the two-fold commission to preach the Gospel and make followers of Jesus.[6]

Nobility of this type allows you to justify personal sins at the expense of other's failures. I would play the outward game of self-righteousness, while hiding my failures and insecurities behind a religious cloak. Judgment was strictly based on whether individuals agreed with my religious way of thinking. If they did, they were then expected to jump on whatever bandwagon I was involved with to prove their spiritual credibility or Christian devotion.

Importantly, my deliverance from the bondage of these indelible dots is not about the summation of my many failures, but about God's faithfulness and power to deliver. These dots were taking my focus off of Jesus and putting it on counterfeits. They were also hiding a prison that God had to expose in order to stop the cycle.

For God to expose this prison, I had to miserably fail in my own power as a Christian. I had to face how I took something pure and defiled it with my own logic. I had to realize that my foolish confidence in self produced unbelief towards God. The harshest

---

[6] Matthew 28:18-20; Mark 16:15

reality is that I actually judged the God of heaven, especially His work in other people's lives.

My foolishness proved to be a prison in which its very bars made up a mindset. This mindset had been greatly influenced by the American mentality. It embraced my fantasies and rights. It knew nothing of abandonment, refused real sacrifice, and put value in the temporary. I had no idea of how embedded this mindset was in the way I thought and perceived the world around me. It took years for God to get me down to the base of it, but at this stage, He exposed the initial level of it. This level is where I served as God, and everything needed to line up to my personal reality rather than my reality coming into line with the immutable truths of God. This exaltation was subtle and seemed so normal to me, blinding me to the extent of my idolatry.

To bring me down to this mindset, I first had to be broken at the point of my self-sufficiency. Brokenness is often associated with hurt or self-pity. Real brokenness occurs when a person sees the extent of his or her sin and how it affects God. This brings one back to the cross, and Jesus' broken and bleeding body. When you see sin from this perspective, it will break your heart and humble your spirit.

God finally brought me to the end of myself after taking many detours. In spite of all of my religious experience, I was empty. There was no joy. How could this be? After all, I had a real encounter with Jesus years before. However, the dots had subtly caused me to take detours. They gave me occasion to take my focus off of Jesus. As a result, I lost my way.

Somehow, I had to find my way back to Jesus. My condition gave the impression that I was in a maze, hitting one dead-end after the other. My frustration and emptiness hit a boiling point. I felt as if I was being crushed under the pressure. I had no means to fight against the feelings that bombarded me in my state of despair. Suddenly, I broke into tears of repentance. In a prostrate position, I confessed all to God. I could feel His cleansing waters flow through my soul. Jesus gently lifted me up and took me into the Most Holy Place. Surprised to see where I was, I immediately sensed God's forgiveness. I knew that I had been cleansed from all my unrighteousness, and now, I could boldly enjoy His presence. It was a glorious time for me.

The joy of my salvation came flooding back into my soul. I had a keen sense of liberty in the Spirit. A peace settled in my heart. I had a knowing that God was going to restore me and use me in spite of myself. The excitement grew as I realized that God was once again more real to me than my very breath. Sadly, I had lost that initial innocence and revelation about the nearness of God. I had exchanged my first love for heavy burdens of religion and theology. Now I was free to discover my Lord.

I felt compelled to tell the world of God's reality, but I felt a hand on my shoulder. I was aware that it was Jesus' hand. This surprised me. I wanted to tell the world about my experience, but He wanted me to realize that I first needed to be established in a relationship with Him. He had been clearly missing in my detours. Obviously, I had failed to invest in a relationship with Him. I knew that it was in a relationship with Him that I would discover balance in my life, authority in my knowledge of Him, and power in my walk before Him.

Jesus invited me to sit at His table. This was a strange experience. I had spent the last seven years busy in various religious activities. To have to sit and wait for the Holy Ghost to impart the Words of life to me was a different experience. At first, I felt nervous. What does it mean to wait? How does one truly receive from the Spirit of God? My mind was running around in circles to try and figure it out.

My first lesson was to relax. This involved ceasing from being in my mind. My faith was to be resting in His character, and to become receptive in my heart and mind towards His truths. As I relaxed before Him, I realized that I could receive from Him. The heavenly manna that was given to me bypassed my understanding and penetrated my spirit. It was during this time that the principle found in the Apostle Paul's words in 1 Corinthians 2:14 became a living reality to me, "But the natural man receiveth not the things of the Spirit of God: for they are foolishness unto him: neither can he know them, because they are spiritually discerned."

My first seven years represented carnality. I was living according to the flesh, thinking in terms of my carnal mind, and missing the point. My pursuits, attitudes, and handling of matters were fruits of my carnality and spiritual immaturity. Spiritual truths passed me by as worldly logic and self-righteousness determined my reality. As a result, I was striving to reach some type of status of personal righteousness, but had become spiritually dull and deluded. I had also failed to exercise godliness in matters. Without walking out godliness, there is no spiritual maturity. As a result, I was unable to properly discern between good and evil.[7]

It was at Jesus' table that I learned two important lessons. The first lesson is that once a truth is imparted in my spirit, I must walk it out in obedience. After all, Christianity is practical. However, many make this walk a spiritual matter that never invades the physical realm. Such a misconception is dangerous. If spiritual truths do not take root in everyday living, they never become reality in our lives.

I also realized that I had to keep God's truths simple in order to walk them out. Past failures often boiled down to my trying to spiritualize a truth or complicate it. This kept His truth at the level of knowledge. God's truths must become wisdom in order to become life. Wisdom is knowledge put into practice; therefore, it must be experienced. Hence, God's truths must be put into

---

[7] Romans 8:5-8; 1 Corinthians 3:2-3; Hebrews 5:11-14

practice or obeyed before they serve as life-changing wisdom from heaven.

The second lesson I learned is that I must give manna away in order to receive more manna from His throne room. I learned this lesson by accident. The truths of God caused such an excitement in my spirit that I could not remain quiet about them. I shared what I had learned from Jesus' table as soon as I found someone who would listen. Needless to say, some became annoyed with me, but others benefited from the truths. I never realized it, but these truths served as tests of faithfulness. Each time I was entrusted with a truth and shared it I knew I would be entrusted with more. Therefore, when I went back to the table of communion, I was always prepared and enlarged to receive more.

My spiritual growth was escalating. The next part of my fellowship with Jesus involved obedience. He laid on my heart the need to share my experience with a group of Christian women. I contacted the head of the women's group at my church. She agreed to allow me to speak.

I calmed my nerves by convincing myself that there would not be many women present. As I was preparing for the day, the Lord began to reveal to me what He wanted me to share. It seemed like a summation of the simple, but profound truths that had been imparted to me at His table for the past year. It was a humbling time for me as I realized the life and power that came from these truths.

The day arrived for me to share these life-changing insights. I struggled with the notion that I would ever be able to share it in a way that would bring God glory. Surprisingly, my former conclusion that the attendance would be small turned out to be wrong. The meeting was held at a house that had a long living room. After the women were seated, they actually overflowed into the adjacent room. When it came time for me to share, I took a breath and opened my mouth.

I was shocked at the beauty, authority, and power behind my words. There was spirit and life to them. It was as though the women were glued to their chairs. Although the room had carpet, I had a sense that you could have heard a pin drop. I had never witnessed such authority and power. I knew the words did not belong to me, but to the Spirit who was empowering them. Obviously, these words were penetrating hearts and minds. For the first time, I realized what had been missing from my past teachings. The teachings had not been manna from the throne room. They may have been scriptural knowledge, but they were not revelation that could challenge the heart and penetrate the mind. The obvious effect of His words visibly served as a testimony of His ability to bless and empower that which He ordains and inspires.

The whole situation humbled me. I was not only awed by it, but became overwhelmed by emotion. In fact, I felt such a great sensitivity to the Spirit. I was aware that the Holy Ghost anointed the words I spoke. They had touched these women's lives with a bit of heaven during the meeting, but personally the effect went beyond the meeting. Throughout the rest of the day and the evening, I was moved in awe by sweet, indescribable emotions that swept over me at different times like a flood.

My days of sharing were just beginning. The Lord had graciously shown me the difference between man's dead-letter presentation of knowledge that only appeals to the mind, and God's empowered words that are inspired by His Spirit. That which is of the mind will only appeal to the mind, but that which is of the Spirit will penetrate the heart. It is the latter penetration that has the capacity to bring forth life.

I was also about to learn other lessons about sharing His truths. The major lesson was the ability to discern between my cause and His inspiration. It took a process to teach me the difference. I had to first test my motivation. Regardless of the truth I was presenting, I had to make sure that I was out of the way. It was a form of regression, where I had to separate any personal causes or opinions from what God wanted to accomplish. I was surprised to discover how much everything was about me and my personal opinions, and not about God's eternal plan. It was a humbling reality.

The change in my life was obvious. Sitting at His table had been a treasured blessing. Walking out each lesson and revelation proved to be a time of growth and renewing of my spirit. Even though I encountered some major adversities, I now had an abiding confidence that I had never possessed. It was a glorious time, but I was about to learn that sitting at the table was also a time of preparation.

Preparation has to do with preparing a person to stand and withstand. Standing is important in the areas of spiritual conflict, personal testing, and separation. I was about to enter a season when I would encounter all three of these challenges.

Another lesson that I was about to learn is that there are seasons in the Christian life. I had experienced the spring of my life when I first met Jesus. The initial Christian growth served as the summer of my spiritual life. There was a short fall where everything was taking on a different form and shape in my Christian understanding. This particular fall was marked by my pursuit after knowledge. My time of independence and rebellion represented winter.

At His table, I had experienced another spring of my spiritual life, but I was about to encounter summer. This particular summer would prove to be challenging. Unlike before, it was not a time of fun, but a time of intense heat. It would cause me to seek the shelter of my God to survive its intensity. Each intense challenge would prove my character and confirm the character of God. In the end, I would come out with a greater awareness of God's ever abiding faithfulness and commitment to separate me unto Himself, as well as to the life He was calling me to.

3

SEPARATION

Spiritual transition and growth bring people to different stages in their lives. I had been enjoying the beauty of Jesus' table, but I sensed that this was a preparation. I had discovered the point of communion, but I knew I needed to go on to discover Him in greater ways. It is one thing to commune with Jesus and another aspect to walk each of these lessons out with Him.

The Christian life is a walk. Although the truths of God had been made real to me, I still needed to discover Jesus in greater ways. I sensed that I had to find Him in the midst of personal challenges. I had to push through the things of the world to discover His faithfulness. I had to choose to believe Him in the midst of fiery trials to refine my faith. This all spoke of temptation and testing. I realized that unless those things I had learned at His table were tested and walked out, they would never bring life or substance to me.

Unknowingly, I put myself in the path of this testing. As I was trying to evaluate my life and my next direction, I decided that it was time that I marry. I sometimes shake my head at my naive conclusion when I examine this period in my life. Who said I needed to get married? Without realizing it, I was giving in to the indoctrination I had received.

All my life I had heard how a woman finds her life and identity in marriage. Although I was aware of the many problems that confront people in a marriage relationship, I perceived myself to be mature enough to handle it. I had some experiences under my belt that I felt would equip me to face many of the challenges. In fact, my greatest asset was my newfound relationship with Jesus. I felt by marrying a Christian man, that we could share in this new life together. According to Ecclesiastes 4:9, "Two are better than one; because they have a good reward for their labour." I could also partake of the mysterious fruit of intimacy in this relationship to discover what made it special, in spite of the many other challenges that plague marriage.

I never realized how much I was operating in assumption at this stage. I assumed that God concurred with my conclusion about marriage. After all, He ordained marriage, and put all of these needs, desires, and emotions in each person to seek out this type of companionship.

This initial assumption was my first mistake. Although I desired God's will, I assumed that marriage was within the confines of His *perfect* will for my life. My failure to seek His will, as to whether He wanted me to marry or not, placed me in His *permissive* will. If I wanted to marry, He would not stand in my way.

In sincerity I asked God to have His way as far as the man that I would marry. Without realizing it, this placed me in His *providential* will. God would choose the man, but it would be to teach me some hard lessons about my personal agendas and His perfect will.

Needless to say, a man came into my life. I was aware of the man's questionable past of adultery and divorce. I wrestled before God about his past. This man had assured me that he was a Christian. I had been clear with him that I wanted to serve God. There were also those who encouraged the relationship, but there were also those who had reservations about it.

Those who had reservations never verbally spoke their concerns, but you could see it in their faces. As I struggled over this issue of his past and present spiritual life, I was reminded of how God had forgiven me of my past failures and restored me into a new life. If this man had truly committed his life to God, he was forgiven and was ready to be restored. Since he was in agreement with my desire to serve God, the obstacles or doubts I had about our marriage seemed to fall to the wayside.

Eventually, my struggle concerning this man receded into peace. I felt that the peace was a signal that it was God's will that I marry him. I must stress that it was not God's perfect will that I marry, but I was being placed in His providential will in relationship to the situation. This implied that even though He was not ordaining my marriage, He would work in and through the situation to bring about His desired results.

Sadly, I did not understand the three different aspects of God's will. I also did not know how to discern or test the spirit. If I had sought God in His perfect will, I would have never married. If I could have discerned this man's spirit, I would have probably run in the opposite direction. My ignorance and inability in such matters served as blind spots or weaknesses in my spiritual life.

In spite of His people's weaknesses, God never falls off the throne or is caught off guard. He foreknew that I would make a fundamental mistake in regards to His perfect will for my life. As a result, He allowed the marriage, but foreordained what He would teach me and work in my life by orchestrating the right circumstances. He would use my husband, my personal failures, and the devastation of the situation to work depth into my character. Through it all, He would test my husband's spiritual commitment and begin to sanctify me unto Himself, as I learned the necessity of consecration.

You probably have figured out by this time, my marriage was not godly, nor did it survive. In fact, it was a disaster. There were a few warning signals before I took my vows. They seemed insignificant at the time, because as far as I was concerned, it was God's will that I marry. I never realized that when small incidents are etched into your mind, it is God's quiet way of giving you a warning sign. In the end, you will not be able to falsely accuse Him of not cautioning you.

The first lesson I learned was about like-mindedness. My husband claimed he was a Christian and that he would respect my desire to serve God. It was not far into our marriage that I discovered a sobering principle. Just because someone claims that he or she is a Christian does not mean he or she is likeminded. To be likeminded means that individuals have agreement in spirit, vision, and purpose. Within a few months of our marriage, I discovered that my husband believed in evolution and agreed with abortion. I was surprised at his liberal views, and realized that he did not share in my fundamental beliefs. This difference put us on different spiritual spectrums. Obviously, we were not coming from the same basis.

The second lesson was that people have different views as to what it means to serve God. To some, it simply means fulfilling religious duties by going to church. To others, it means being involved in the harvest field, reaching out to people and offering them Jesus. Once again, I encountered a clear division with my husband in this area. Although he only verbally expressed his disapproval towards my evangelism a couple of times, my enthusiasm about Jesus clearly embarrassed him. My ways of investing in people began to create strife between us, as well as occasionally spur resentment in him towards me, which manifested in him when he tried to humiliate me.

Another important lesson I learned is that if there is not agreement about a spiritual matter such as marriage, ministry, and vision, flee. I sincerely searched for God's will about this marriage, but it was one-sided. My husband took my word that it was God's will that we marry. He basically sized up the situation from a personal perspective as to whether I would meet his needs. In fact, he even admitted that I would most likely share in his worldly lifestyle, but he did not seek out God for himself. When the marriage came down, guess who received all the blame?

There is a misconception that if something is in God's will, everything will be a bed of roses. Even a God-ordained marriage has struggles, challenges, and testing. It is up to the individuals involved to do that which is right to maintain the integrity of what God ordains. My husband blamed the failure of our marriage on the fact that it must have not been God's will or it would have survived. Therefore, I was wrong and must shoulder all of the blame.

When you deal with couples, there are multiplicities of issues that serve as the culprits behind the death of a marriage. The practice of pointing the finger or passing the buck is common among disillusioned couples. It is as though it is always the other guy's fault, leaving the accuser as a helpless, innocent victim. The truth is, the success of marriage rests with both parties. Sadly, if one party fails to be accountable for personal attitudes and conduct, this deception becomes the tool that tears the heart out of this relationship. According to my husband, he was a perfect husband and I was a miserable failure as a wife.

I am always painfully aware that I will not arrive at the absolute state of perfection until I meet the Perfect One face to face. Until I put off this flesh and enter the door of eternity, there are always going to be incidents of personal failures and room for growth and improvement. Therefore, I freely admit that I was not perfect in my relationship with my husband. Marriage proved that I did not have much of a domestic inclination in me. This does not mean that I did not try to establish it, because I did. Regardless of how non-domestic I was in certain areas, I understood my responsibility and did my best to fulfill it.

There were also struggles in other areas of my life and character because of inexperience and training. No doubt these imperfections served as irritants that rubbed against the man I was married too. However, they also served as handy forms of excuses and justification for him to cover up the real issue that plagued our marriage in order to put the total blame on me. The main core of our problem was that there was no spiritual agreement between us.

Eventually, we became two people who were co-existing under the same roof. I had found my life in Christ before I married him and was determined to hold on to it. I had miserably failed Jesus in the past, but I was not about to consciously compromise my life with Him to try to calm the raging underlying turmoil that was constantly threatening to erupt in my marriage.

A year before our marriage officially came to an end, the Lord showed me that He was about to bring a sword down through our relationship. I knew that the sword meant separation. In my spirit, I knew our marriage was over, but I also had to consider if there was any point where it had spiritually been alive. Yes, it had a beginning to it in the physical arena and took roots in the emotional or soul area, but it was never brought to life on a spiritual level.

Oswald Chambers said that a person's commitment towards God will always cost those around him or her. I had determined early in my marriage relationship that I would never try to be my husband's Holy Spirit. If there were weaknesses or discrepancies in his life before God, it would be up to God to convict him. On the other hand, I was also going to do everything in my power to maintain my life before my Lord.

I learned early in our relationship that I could not share my spiritual life with my husband. It was like throwing pearls before a swine.[1] Occasionally, he would use these precious pearls to

---

[1] Matthew 7:6

humiliate me. Since my life in Christ was so precious, I guarded it and kept it hidden from him. It was in this environment that I learned about the secret chamber, or the secret life that a person must establish in Christ in order to stand. This secret life in Christ became my source of strength that enabled me to endure when my world started to fall apart at the seams.

Even though I guarded my life in God and kept it secret from my then husband, except for what he needed to know, I was still accused of being too religious. A friend of my parents had apparently later talked to my ex-husband. My husband had told him that I was too religious for him. Needless to say, my family friend took his side. After all, how can anyone expect a person to live around a religious fanatic? In a way, it was a compliment, because I knew the truth. I realized that my life and stands for truth had silently spoken volumes, and left its mark.

Our marriage did come down exactly a year after the Lord told me He was bringing a sword down through our relationship. Many events happened during that time. There was a ripping that took place in the emotional arena. When this happens, the emotions go up in the air. It is always unnerving because a person feels vulnerable and totally out of control. This is a fearful and uncertain time.

This is when a person seeks out others. Everything is out of perspective. Even though everything seems real, nothing can be trusted. Accusations are flying as the parties try to maintain some type of dignity through the death and burial of their marriage.

I lived in a small community. This will always create an interesting scenario. Most people remain neutral because of the demands of their own lives, but there are always those who take sides. Those who take sides do so based on attitudes and opinions about those involved. For example, if the individual had something against me, then I was the culprit and my husband the poor victim or vice versa. Personally, I wasn't looking for people to take my side for no one really knows what goes on behind closed doors.

The death of a marriage is a tragedy, and not a matter of who was right and wrong. After all, a dead marriage is wrong in itself. It is up to the parties involved to honestly sort through the maze in order to examine personal faults and learn necessary lessons. For others to make such judgments in ignorance does not point to sound conclusions, but to vain speculations based on prejudices or biases.

I needed someone to listen to me and properly challenge me in my perspective. The emotional roller coaster was unbearable to me. Praise God, He brought a few people along to help me wade through the emotional uncertainty. These people wisely held their personal opinions and counseled me according to the present situation and challenges. My greatest help came from God. The divorce was unpleasant and reminded me of a chess game. The Lord led me through some difficult challenges and brought me through the maze to a point of total resolution.

Surprisingly, years later, rumors still get back to me about my past life in the small community. One woman I didn't even know refused to buy my book because she "supposedly" knew all about me. There was also the man who had been one of my spiritual leaders who said he just knew I was wrong. That surprised me since he didn't have any involvement in my life when I was married. In one of my stops in my former community a certain store clerk leaned over to the other clerk right in front of my friends to give her details about my life. My friends later mentioned that the clerk obviously disliked me.

I am not proud of my divorce, but I do not regret that time in my life. I do not feel it was a waste of time, because I learned so many lessons. It not only proved to be a time of growth, but also of separation unto God that continues to this day.

Looking back, I can see where my life in Christ has been marked by a series of separations. My first separation came by way of a decision. I had been married for over two years. My life was calm with my husband, but there was restlessness in my spirit. I considered my life. I had all the material possessions that I needed or wanted, along with many other luxury items. The luxury items belonged to my husband. Although I enjoyed them, I had no real desire for them. One day, we took a motorbike ride up to a scenic area. It was beautiful as I considered the majesty of God's creation. Suddenly, this overwhelming feeling came over me. My life seemed so useless. The material things that surrounded me held no real value in light of eternity. In fact, they often enslave people and change their focus as to what is important. At this point, I became aware of all the emptiness attached to the things of my life, including my marriage and home. From the depths of my soul, a request came to the forefront. "God, if I can't serve You, take me home right now, because there is no meaning or purpose outside of You."

This request was not a matter of religious devotion, but a reality that had been put into my spirit by God. He did not want me to settle for less, especially since it was within my very being to see my life count for Him. I could ignore this desire, and simply live for self, while accepting the menial, substandard life that comes out of accepting nominal Christianity. I knew there was more, and I would not be happy until I had discovered it. Little did I know this marked the demise of my marriage.

This separation would also include the church I attended, as well as my friends and family. In the end, I was able to relate to Abraham. He was separated from his home, kindred, and family.[2] The separation was necessary for God to separate him unto Himself. Some separations were painful and others proved to be

---

[2] Genesis 12:1-3

a blessing. For me, each separation made me aware of God's abiding presence and faithfulness in my life. I became more cognizant of my need for God to become my all in all.

One of the major separations was from my hometown. I had spent most of my life in this community. I had a history, friends, and memories of this place. I was proud of the beauty that surrounded it and the friendly atmosphere. My divorce changed all of that. I lost my reputation, and my hometown became an undesirable place to me. I no longer felt like I belonged, nor did I have any desire to remain there. I wanted to flee from it as fast as I could.

Looking back, I realize that God brought this change in my perspective for my own sake. The people had not changed, but my life was changing. I never realized how enslaved a person can be to a place or people, when it comes to serving God. People are unwilling to follow God if it means giving up certain aspects of the old life. Although I was willing to follow Jesus to find my place, position, and life in Him, I was not completely free to walk the walk. There were unseen emotional ties that held me to my community. He had to cut and rip these ties to set me free. After all, He did not want me to be Lot's wife and look back and taste judgment. As Jesus said in Luke 9:62, "No man, having put his hand to the plough, and looking back, is fit for the kingdom of God."

When I left my hometown, I didn't look back. I was not sure where I was going, but I knew that Jesus was in the lead; therefore, nothing else mattered. By His mercy, longsuffering, and grace I had survived the separation, but it was now time to embark on a new life. After all, I no longer had a home and my history had been clearly darkened by events.

Each time I pass through my former community, I have a reality check as to how far God has brought me. I also understand that people will always maintain personal opinions regardless of what is true or right. For me, these opinions are a reminder of how I have been set free from personal bias, unfair, and unrealistic opinions that determine my past, limited reality. I now can soar above my reality to discover God's perspective. I can trust Him; therefore, I can leave all matters to Him, for justice and righteousness are His.

The beauty of the different separations is that I was set free to pursue and discover greater depths and life in Christ. Out of this new life that I embarked upon three decades ago, a different history has been written. Through the challenges, changes, and transitions, I found my identity in Christ and realized my purpose in His kingdom. Although some of the incidents I have encountered were frightening and overwhelming, they also proved to be a time of testing, expectation, change, and personal revival.

4

REGRESSION

Another valuable lesson I had to learn was regression. This lesson came to the forefront in my teaching experiences prior to my divorce. The Lord was gracious enough to entrust me to teach some women of my small community. Once a week, we met for Bible Study. The Lord would give me manna from heaven to impart to these women. Some of the lessons were even challenging and overwhelming to me. At times, I got a sense that the Christianity of America fell short of the Christianity that the saints of old lived out in example and power.

These ladies became a big point of training to me. God used them in a mighty way in my life to help me test out some valuable insights that He had given me about human nature. He would also use them to teach me some lessons about personal agendas.

After almost a year of teaching these women, I began to notice that the group had come to some type of spiritual standstill. I really didn't understand it because I knew that God was still giving me fresh manna that was powerfully changing my outlook. I sensed that something needed to change, but I had no direction or leading. As I meditated before the Lord about the incident, He broke through my thoughts. "You must now regress."

"Regression" was a new principle. I had never heard it taught or really preached. This caused me to consider the meaning of this word and look to the Bible for instruction. "Regression" means to decline. The one person in the Bible that definitely declined was John the Baptist. He made this powerful statement in John 3:30, "He must increase, but I must decrease."

John the Baptist was talking about Jesus. He was stating that he now needed to decline in importance and purpose in order for Jesus to come forth. This brought me back to John the Baptist's purpose. He came to prepare the way for Jesus. He was the voice in the wilderness that was sent to awaken people to the fact that the kingdom of God was at hand.[2]

In order to prepare people for the kingdom of God, John the Baptist preached repentance. Repentance was a way of turning people from the darkness of their sinful ways that plagued them to see and encounter the light of the world.[3]

John's voice was loud and clear. His passion for God was unstoppable. His confidence in His message was formidable. He would not waver from his purpose and goal, but in spite of his power and influence, his flame would only burn for a season.

John was preparing the way for Jesus who is the Way. Once Jesus stepped on the scene, John had to give way to the Way. He had to regress in the eyes of the people. Now that the Light of the world stood in the midst of mankind, John's burning flame would have to be consumed by the reality of that Light.[4] He would simply cease, while the Light of the world increased in importance and purpose. This is the way it was designed to be. This is the way it had to be. John had to regress, so that Jesus could progress in the hearts and minds of people.

As I considered John's example, I began to realize that the tendency of people is to put their confidence in their religious leaders. This is a natural response of those who are struggling to develop their lives in God. The flame of passion may burn brightly

---

[2] Matthew 3:1-3
[3] Matthew 4:14-17
[4] John 1:6-9

in their pastors and teachers, but to the followers or students of that leader, that flame must become dimmer and dimmer in the light of Jesus. These leaders must constantly point to and give way to the leadership of Jesus in the lives of His sheep. Their greatest goal must be to see those whom they have been entrusted with developing a flame of passion for Jesus.

It was at this point that I began to realize that ministry is about Jesus. Ministers of the Gospel may say the right things in regards to effective ministry, but behind the words can be struggles with pride and battles over being personally exalted in the kingdom of God. They may verbally give God the credit for any spiritual successes, while behind closed doors, they are putting a notch in their spiritual belt buckle. It is easy to get caught up with the many means of ministry, and forget the source, authority, and power behind all successful ministries. In fact, if ministers lack integrity, they may be portraying outward humility to hide their arrogance, while actually giving way to prideful exaltation in the sanctuary of their hearts and minds.

As I studied John the Baptist's life, I could see that John understood His place in the kingdom of God. He was simply the voice and not the Way.[5] The voice prepared for the Way, but once the Way began to be revealed, the voice became quieter.

What was my place in God's kingdom? Sadly, God rarely is allowed to define people's place in His kingdom. Leaders, needs, and circumstances often place people in their perspective places. Leaders must avoid defining people's place in the kingdom of God. They can give advice, but they must always encourage God's sheep to seek His face about such important matters to avoid creating an unhealthy dependency towards them.

I had been presented with various needs and responded accordingly. This is appropriate as long as one remains available

---

[5] John 14:6

to change direction if God calls him or her to do so. The needs of others can become dots that take away a servant's focus from God's eternal plan.

I also had to learn not to let circumstances dictate my place in God's kingdom. God will use circumstances to guide people in a certain direction, but open and closed doors will determine their place.[6] The circumstances I am talking about create an urgency to respond. Commitments based on such circumstances often enslave people into unpleasant situations. It becomes a place of burden, rather than growth.

Initially, I understood that my responsibility was to preach the Gospel and make disciples of Jesus. As I grew in my understanding of redemption, I realized the greatest challenge was to teach people to follow Jesus. It is easy to make vulnerable people converts to your way of thinking. But, my whole goal was to cause people to consider, partake, meditate, and fall in love with the Jesus of the Bible.[7] The emphasis had to be the reality of Jesus. This would hopefully develop a love relationship with Him that would cause individuals to follow Him into the abundant life.

As I considered my real responsibilities, I wondered how many times I had made ministry about me by expounding on my own personal causes, rather than Jesus Christ. How many times had I touched His glory by taking credit for His truth and wisdom? How many times had I used Jesus and His Word as a platform for my own self-glorification? I was beginning to get a glimpse into my pride.

Pride is a sin that is downplayed in the light of sins such as adultery and murder. The reality of pride is that it is a hidden sin behind all conflicts and idolatry. It destroys more people and their homes than any other sin. Since pride does not create an obvious offense against others, it is ignored or lightly touched upon. Jesus

---

[6] Revelation 3:6-8
[7] Matthew 28:19-20; Mark 16:15-16; John 10:1-10; 13:34-35: 15:9-27

showed compassion towards the adulteress, ministered to a woman with demons, and supped with the sinners. However, He resisted and rebuked the religious pride of the Pharisees.[8] This is why He made this statement in Luke 18:14, "...for every one that exalteth himself shall be abased; and he that humbleth himself shall be exalted."

Glimpses of my pride made me realize how foolish I had been. Pride sets you up to be made a fool of in your arrogance and self-sufficiency. I marveled at how blinded I was to this sin, and how I must have irritated and pushed against people. I could see its treacherous tendencies and sense its fake humility. If it couldn't be honored, it would be noticed through false debasement.

Regression was the first lesson that addressed the issue of personal pride. I had to cease from being the focal point to others, as well as in my personal life. This pointed to changing my preference. I had to prefer the well-being of others over personal causes and agendas. I had no intention of being these ladies' focal point, but any type of exaltation takes away from the place Jesus must have in a person's life. Such exaltation will cause Him to step on the scene and call for regression in the life of His servants. I don't know if any of these women had put any dependency on me, but God was ensuring the integrity of His work in their lives as well as mine.

This brought me to a dilemma. I could physically back out of these women's lives, but how would I deal with pride reigning from the personal throne of vanity and ego? After all, I sincerely wanted these women to know Jesus for themselves. I wanted them to have a walk with Him that was intimate and life-changing, but my pride was subtle and treacherous.

First, I had to recognize how my pride operated. It is easy to see pride in other people, but it serves as the beam in your own

---

[8] Matthew 9:10-13; John 8:1-21

eye. It deludes and justifies actions. It judges and criticizes, while remaining hypocritical in attitude and conduct. Therefore, how do you subdue pride? Jesus' first instruction to His disciples was to deny self.[9] I realized that pride's domain will diminish through neglect. In other words, you deny yourself the privilege or right to consider or give way to the authority, rule, and delusion of your pride. In order to neglect my pride, I would have to change my focus. My life before God had to be about Jesus. This would not be easy, since a person's tendency is to make everything about self.

To change my focus, I needed to recognize how my pride worked. For me to understand its subtleties, God had to bring me down to my motivation. The Lord gave me the opportunity to minister to another group of people. In fact, I witnessed a revival take place among people who had been involved with perversion, drugs, and alcohol.

God miraculously moved on each individual. There were many conversions due to the Holy Ghost's convicting power, along with some rededication of lives. There was no way that man could take any credit for this miraculous work. I stood back in amazement as God brought these different individuals into my life to disciple. It was in this atmosphere that I learned that conversion is just the beginning.

Discipling is greatly lacking in the Church. Without this step, people are not properly established on a sure foundation. When people are not properly discipled, they erect their own gods and define the Christian life according to fleshly and unrealistic standards. To me, discipling is the real test in any ministry. In the right situation, it is easy to accumulate converts, but discipling takes a commitment that will not only test every aspect of a person's patience, but will expose personal motives.

---

[9] Matthew 7:5; 16:24

Two of the women I was discipling were quite loose with their tongues. They actually reminded me of sailors. One day, I met them in the store. Their language was wallowing in and out of the gutters. I think in one incident, they even embarrassed themselves. I went to the Lord about this situation. Should I teach a lesson on the tongue? I heard the Lord ask me why I would want to see their language change. I could have easily given Him all the scriptural reasoning, but before I could open my mouth, He revealed my real motivation. I wanted their language to change so that I could look good as their teacher.

Once again, it was all about me. The Lord then asked me if I wanted these women to conform to my religious ideas of perfection so that I could look good, or whether I preferred Him to transform them from within so that He could receive the glory. The choice was obvious, but I began to see how self-righteous and deceptive my pride was.

Each time my motive was revealed to me, I could see my pride peeking out from behind the corridors of sincerity. Occasionally, I felt it rising to a place of exaltation in my religious zeal. Although often neglected, it was always waiting to make a grand stand to take credit for the work of God when I was tired, overwhelmed, and not discerning. I began to see how treacherous I was. Needless to say, this was hard on my pride.

To keep regression and my pride in the right spirit, I once again turned to John the Baptist's life. Jesus said of him in Matthew 11:11, "Verily I say unto you, Among them that are born of women there hath not risen a greater than John the Baptist: notwithstanding he that is least in the kingdom of heaven is greater than he." John never did any miracles, but he did something greater by preparing the way for Jesus. He could have been a priest, dressed in religious garb, yet he chose simplicity of truth to expose hearts. In light of the priest, John must have appeared crude in his dress, but in light of God's kingdom he was considered great. He seemed like an insignificant reed in light of the religious system, but in Jesus' eyes, he was a giant among men, for he understood the real disposition of servitude.[10]

Out of servitude comes regression. Regression gives way to something worthy or greater than self. John had simply given way to Jesus. As a result, the King of kings and the Lord of lords honored John.

John's regression finally gave way to death. Most of us know the story about John the Baptist. He held the line of righteousness in regards to Herod's sin. This was a man who never compromised what he knew to be true. He would not soft-pedal sin, nor would he cow down to the power of others. When John's ministry was completed, he was put in jail. Due to his uncompromising stand, he lost his head.[11]

Pride must lose it rights and influences in our lives. It must suffer neglect through self-denial. It must be caged up with diligence, so it cannot run rampant. It must be put in chains to ensure that it will not be in competition with Jesus. It must be cut off at the point of its reign.

Although John's beheading was unjust, as well as gruesome, it reminds us that self must give way to the true head of the Body, Jesus Christ. John gave the ultimate sacrifice, so that Jesus could take His rightful place. This is the legacy of true regression. It will give up all to ensure that He who is all in all becomes a reality to every longing heart.[12]

John is not the only one who regressed in the kingdom of God. Jesus Christ also typified this regression in His own life. He regressed as God in order to become a servant. He regressed in authority in order to become a Man subjected to the will of the Father. He gave way to the cross in order to become a substitute

---

[10] Matthew 20:25-27
[11] Matthew 14:1-13
[12] Ephesians 1:20-23; Colossians 1:18

for each of us. He regressed in physical life in order for us to have eternal life. He ascended to heaven so the Father could send the Comforter, the Holy Ghost.[13]

We see this regression in every servant of God. Abraham ceased to be a citizen of Ur in order to become a sojourner, looking for a city made by God. Joseph became a slave and prisoner in order to become a savior for his family. Moses fled the courts of Pharaoh and became an abominable shepherd so that one day, he would become the leader of Israel. David was exalted as a warrior, only to find himself considered a traitor. He spent years as a fugitive before he became the king of Israel.

Regression is an ongoing process. Over the years, God has asked me to regress at different times. Each time, I can see testing and growth for the parties involved. Sadly, pride is still alive. Although it has lost much influence and power in my life over the years, occasionally I find myself quite tempted to let it sit on the throne of vanity and glory. However, the emptiness that quickly invades my soul makes me realize how foolish it is and what a stench it is to God. Immediately, it is brought down for being an imposter, as it gives way to the true King.

I have realized that this regression will not be complete until this body has been replaced with a new incorruptible body. When the flesh falls to the wayside, my pride will remain with it. What will be left is the consuming reality of Jesus in His unhindered glory.[14] It will be a glorious time for me to realize that my pride is properly in its place, and Jesus is being lifted high above all that deemed itself as important. When He truly reigns, I can rest in the beauty of His grace, redemption, and victory. I can know that all is well with my soul.

---

[13] John 14:25-28; Philippians 2:5-8; 2 Corinthians 5:21
[14] 1 Corinthians 15:50-53; 2 Corinthians 5:6-8

5

STIRRING THE NEST

God was bringing a series of separations in my life. I had no idea how far these separations would go and who or what would be included. Before He could effectively accomplish this feat, He would first have to prepare me to properly accept and endure the separations. This preparation meant stirring my comfort zones.

The comfort zones remind me of an eagle's nest. My understanding is that the eagle designs the foundation of the nest with abrasive objects, while putting some type of soft substance on the top. Needless to say, the nest starts out as a place of comfort for the eaglet. This allows the vulnerable bird to grow in strength. However, there comes a time when this inexperienced bird must leave the nest. It must reach the potential for which it was created. The problem is that it is safe in the nest, while beyond the nest is a frightening reality of heights and uncertainty.

Needless to say, the eaglet does not voluntarily leave the nest to discover its potential. As a result, the parent must stir up the nest by alleviating it of that which is comfortable. The stirring exposes the abrasive substance that will cause the young bird to become uncomfortable, forcing it to spread its wings and risk it all.[1]

---

[1] Deuteronomy 32:11

God had to make my nest uncomfortable. At first, I did not understand the purpose for this stirring. Later, I discovered that it was His way of changing my priorities, values, and perspective. In fact, it was His way of defining life. Surprisingly, I did not understand what constituted life. I had taken my life for granted without ever thinking about the purpose of it or the fading glory of the vanity of my past worldly pursuits and successes. Much of my life had been a form of existence and survival. This attitude towards life served as a prison that prevented me from discovering the beauty and mystery associated with true life.

God wanted me to understand life as a gift that had to be lived out in light of His eternal purpose. Some of the stirring seemed unbearable at times, but I realized it was necessary to prepare me to risk the present life I knew to gain my real life in Christ. The Apostle Paul summarized it best in Philippians 3:7-8, "But what things were gain to me, those I counted loss for Christ. Yea doubtless, and I count all things but loss for the excellency of the knowledge of Christ Jesus my Lord: for whom I have suffered the loss of all things, and do count them but dung, that I may win Christ."

Some of the stirring not only caused me to fall into utter uncertainty, but I found myself walking in darkness concerning the things I did not understand. This darkness is not darkness caused by sin, but darkness created by a lack of understanding. It is in such darkness that one's faith is tested and refined.

My first stirring was when I asked God to take me home if I could not serve Him. He had put leanness in my spirit to consider what was important in the scheme of eternity. This is when I realized that the possessions of the world held no real significant value. Jesus confirmed this in Luke 12:15, "Take heed, and beware of covetousness; for a man's life consisteth not in the abundance of the things which he possesseth."

I took pride that I did not have to heap material possessions upon myself in the name of happiness. This pride blinded me to the fact that I did put stock in these temporary dots of life. In the right circumstances, these dots would subtly take my focus off of the eternal and put it on earthly avenues. It took some rough, challenging years for God to expose the depth of my dependency on the things of the world, but He initially started my process at the point of my declaration of total consecration.

God was causing me to consider what I valued. In my heart, I valued Him and a relationship with Him. He had to establish this important fact in the beginning of my process to counteract the demands of the flesh. As Jesus said, "the spirit is willing, but the flesh is weak." I would learn how true this was when my flesh kicked and threw tantrums over inconveniences. Lack of funds and the severity of challenges often caused these inconveniences. In such times of distress, I had to be reminded of the sincere desire of my heart.[2] This caused my focus to come back to what was important, rather than remain upon what was temporary. Regardless of circumstances, God held my heart and it remained true to Him. However, I had to learn to discipline myself during the testing of my faith and listen to my heart, rather than my spoiled, self-centered flesh.

Another area where God had to challenge me was my vision. My vision was adjusted to serving Him within the church system. I enjoyed being a Sunday School teacher. I felt at home in the comforts of my pew, and relished the fellowship of those close to me. Nevertheless, God began to stir up my nest in the church in order to make me available to do His bidding.

Denominational churches have their place in God's kingdom, but they must not define God's will for a person or replace what constitutes true service to Him. God will lead people to different

---

[2] Matthew 26:41

fellowships for growth, testing, and training purposes, but He also will occasionally lead people away from these fellowships in order to prepare them for His use and glory. To do this, He will allow circumstances to occur that will cause the leadership, or the church itself, to fall off of its idolatrous pedestal. This will produce a discontentment in the soul.

I was happy in my church until a grave sin of the pastor ripped at its seams and threw the congregation into chaos. It caused a tidal wave that left some people devastated. I rode the tidal wave out praying that this devastating situation would bring maturity to the fellowship. My heart was to see a pastor come in who had the maturity to pull the church back together, the meekness to gently lead, and the vision to reach beyond acceptable boundaries, and challenge Jesus' sheep to come higher.

This was not to be. The congregation chose an immature pastor. The inevitable occurred. This young pastor did not have what it would take to pull the church together. In fact, his arrogance not only tore more at the fiber of the congregation, but it set him up to fall. It turned out to be a bad combination.

God used this young pastor to move me on to the Assembly of God. Once again, I was willing to find my place in this body and complement it according to God's leading. It was here that God taught me about His Holy Spirit. It was a glorious time, but it would only last for a season before heresy infiltrated its corridors. Through both of these ordeals, I had to confront the pastors about my concerns. Needless to say, I was not appreciated.

I cannot say that I handled each matter correctly, but I was aware that I was in training. There is a tendency in training to make mistakes, but God never falls off of His throne during such times. Later, I learned that being effective in ministry was more about learning what not to do, rather than what to do. In those initial years of training, I made my share of mistakes, but I also learned valuable lessons.

Looking back, I can see where God was trying to get me past the established church mentality and learn to walk by His Spirit. I had years of this mentality ingrained in me. To me, this was normal Christianity. God had to expose this mentality and root it out. He had to change my focus from what was acceptable to what was considered impossible.

The first thing God had to do was enlarge my vision. One night, I was praying about those in my community. It was a small community, but it was as if in one second, God showed me the pain, loneliness, and sorrow of those in my small town. It was so overwhelming to me that I almost buckled under the burden of it. It was so great it left me at a loss as to how I would wade through the maze. He allowed me to carry the burden for a couple of days before He lifted it. Once He lifted it, He revealed the extent of real ministry.

Such ministry was not needed exclusively in the church or in homes, but in the trenches of people's hearts, minds, and souls. It is the deep, hidden recesses of heavy-ladened souls that are tucked away behind doors of fear, turmoil, and hopelessness. The harvest is ready at all times, but I was not responsible for the whole harvest, just the souls that He would bring my way.

Even though I forgot this lesson a couple of times, it was to be one of the most important lessons I learned. It is easy for over-zealous ministers of the Gospel to take detours in ministry and chase down every rabbit trail they see, but eventually they will suffer from burnout.

The next vision He gave me involved eternity. I had worked as a janitor at the local high school. During the summer, young people helped with the various janitorial duties. There was one girl who had a tendency to use Jesus' name in vain. I let it slide by a couple of times. Finally, after hearing it one too many times, I told her that He had nothing to do with it. My statement not only shocked her, it silenced her. Eventually, my repeated response to her verbiage caused her to change her expression. Surprisingly, we became friends. At different times, I would talk about God to my co-workers. There was no doubt that everyone knew where I stood in my faith, including her.

Summer ended, and I did not see the young girl until later that year. One night when I was cleaning the gym after a basketball game, she came up to me. She was excited to see me, but she also was under the influence of alcohol. I looked at this beautiful young girl and realized that she was miserably lost and did not know how to stop her decline. Her language revealed that she was back to her old ways. She once again used Jesus' name in vain. Again, I reminded her that He had nothing to do with it. It was as though she immediately became sober. She looked at me and apologized, admitting that she knew He was my friend.

It was not until almost two years later that I encountered her on the sidewalk. She was now married and had a child. She was sober, but miserable. We exchanged greetings, but I did not have the time to talk to her because I was on company time. I look back at that time and wonder if I was insensitive, because a year later, I received the shocking news that she had been killed in an accident. I attended her funeral.

Mortality is a harsh reality that carries only one guarantee-- physical death. I pondered the mystery and uncertainty of life. As the pastor was preaching, it struck me that she could be in hell. I silently cried out to God, "Oh, Lord is she in hell?" Suddenly, I received a vision of hell right in my church pew. I watched people walking blindly towards the abyss. As they stepped off the edge of the abyss, the flames reached up and pulled them down into the fires. I heard their screams. The vision went down into the recesses of my being. I realized the awesome responsibility of possessing the Gospel, and the urgency to be available to share it with anyone God brought my way.

God never really gave me a sense as to whether this young woman was in hell. All I know is that if she left this world without Christ, she is now tasting the torment of the fiery judgment of separation. The part I have to struggle with is whether I had missed the opportunity to speak into her life. The broad road to hell is paved with missed opportunities of failure to put roadblocks in front of those who are on this path. In most cases, God's people never receive a vision past their own comfort zones to put such challenges in front of those on the broad road. They never see past their pews, churches, and personal worlds. They fail to receive an eternal vision that will never dull with weariness, complacency, or purpose.

It was at this point that Proverbs 29:18 became alive to me, "Where there is no vision, the people perish..." I wanted this vision of hell to be etched in my memory so I would not forget why I am here. I am not here to live unto myself; rather, I am here to be broken and spilled out for the glory of God. I am not here to sit in comfortable pews as people blindly walk into hell. Rather, I am here to testify of what Christ has done for me on the cross, and what He is presently doing in me so that the light of His Gospel will penetrate through the darkness of men's souls. I have been equipped to share this Gospel with power. I have also been given the eyes to see the despair of lost souls, the ears to hear their cries, the heart to reach out, the hands to minister, and the mouth to proclaim the only good news that is true and life-changing.

This vision of hell changed my way of thinking about my purpose. It started as a small flame, but at different times, it has been fanned into a raging fire that is ready to consume me with an urgency that is hard to describe. I could no longer be content with the idea of my going to heaven when so many are on their way to a Christless eternity.

The Lord eventually took me through various seasons of my spiritual life. Each season involved a stirring up for the purpose of preparation and training. I began to realize that God must have the freedom to move His servants as He will. They must not be set in their way of thinking or doing, because they could easily be left behind and never reach their potential in Christ. I began to hold lightly to the places He brought me to and the people He surrounded me with. My life was not my own. He led and I followed. As a result, I needed to keep myself prepared and available at all times. This meant my body was to serve as a living sacrifice that had to be offered up at any time.[3]

God's training and preparation have proven to be challenging and glorious times for me. He still has to stir up my nest to get my attention, but it is no longer frightening. I just put out my wings of faith and step out of the nest. I have learned that if the wind does not catch hold of my wings, then He will catch me and usher me up into its very currents. The sights from those currents are not only majestic, they are life-changing and eternal.

---

[3] Romans 12:1-2

6

THE CALL

Separation occurs after God has called a person to do His bidding. God calls all believers into the harvest field of humanity. However, how He uses each of us in this harvest field will vary. Although I was going through a separation and spiritual training at various levels of my life, I had a sense of my calling. My initial response to it was to ignore it because it was not something that would be readily accepted by many Christians.

I have always had a certain sense of the gifts that God had entrusted to me. One of the most obvious gifts was the ability to teach His Word. The world grew dim and insignificant when I was preparing for and teaching a Bible Study class. The Lord was always present to impart to me themes or an outline of a study. Then, I would study the Bible to fill in those themes or outlines. It always proved to be a beneficial time of partaking of the Word and enjoying the simplicity, but infinite depths of His truth.

Abilities and callings are not the same. This does not mean that God will not use a person's abilities to carry out their calling. This was one of the lessons I had to come to terms with. I loved teaching, and could see how it could give me access to various opportunities to serve Him, but there was more.

A person's calling can be separate from obvious talents. In fact, real callings can put a person into unknown elements that will cause them to fling themselves on God in utter desperation. Calling has to do with carrying out the Christian commission in both the Church and the harvest field.

Since I never considered myself outside of teaching a Bible Study class, I never thought about what it would mean for me to do God's bidding. I just assumed that He would probably use me in this capacity within the arena of the Church. God had to challenge me in my way of thinking for me to accept my calling.

The first shaking happened when I was sharing with an individual about some spiritual insight I had received about God's Word. This man sat in amazement as he listened to me. After I finished my exhortation, he declared, "You need to be a preacher." This statement shocked me. First of all, this man did not believe in women preachers. Secondly, I had no intention of becoming a preacher. Nevertheless, the statement penetrated my spirit. Like some of the statements made to Mary about her son Jesus, I kept the statement hidden in my heart to ponder at a later date.[1]

The next incident caused me to consider my comfortable attitudes about women in the kingdom of God. The Lord had stirred up my comfortable theological nest. My foundation was Baptist. I appreciated the sound foundation that had been placed underneath me, but I knew there was more. I knew that more had to do with the third Person of the Godhead, the Holy Ghost.

I had been taught that the gifts of the Spirit were done away with. As I studied the Word, I could not help but question this theological stand. After all, the Apostle Paul instructed the Corinthians to covet prophesying and to not forbid tongues. He also told the Thessalonians to not quench the Spirit in one verse, and in the next one, he told them to not despise prophesying.[2]

---

[1] Luke 2:51
[2] 1 Corinthians 14:39; 1 Thessalonians 5:19-20

Obviously, I had a choice to make. Either I would hide behind the familiar interpretations that I had been constantly exposed to out of blind loyalty, or accept by faith what the Word of God says about such issues. As I thought about it, I could not stand before God and claim ignorance because I owned various Bibles. It was my responsibility, and not the responsibility of my spiritual leaders to resolve this matter for myself. In order to give it a fair shake, I had to recognize that my present understanding of this issue might not be anything more than man's traditions or personal interpretation of Scripture.[3]

This is when the Lord led me to an Assembly of God Church in my hometown. These people had personal knowledge of the working of the Holy Ghost. After all, they believed in the gifts of the Spirit. These gifts were His manifestations, and these people had witnessed His moving and work.[4]

I became aware that even though the people at the Assembly of God believed in the gifts, they could not really explain to me how they worked. About this time, new people were coming into the church. They also had questions about the work of the Holy Ghost. I decided that it was not enough to get my feet wet, I had to jump completely into the current. I received permission from the church to teach on the work of the Spirit. I had witnessed the operation of the gifts a couple of times, and I understood the power of the Word. By faith, I believed that God would use the teaching to verify and confirm what I needed to understand about the supernatural work of God's Spirit.

I relied upon God to bring a simple understanding to me. I knew that if the information did not become truth to my spirit, it would not make an impact on those who were seeking answers. Some of the Assembly of God women attended my first class. To

---

[3] Matthew 15:3-9
[4] 1 Corinthians 12:7-10

their amazement, the work of the Spirit was scripturally explained in simplicity, and to the satisfaction of those present.

One day, the Lord impressed on me to approach the pastor about sharing a message He wanted me to give to the Body. I was surprised at such a prospect. Even though I knew the Assembly of God believed in women preachers, I was not fully convinced that I was to preach. I had no problem with women preachers. I assumed that such women had resolved the conflict that raged in some denominations about women being in any kind of leadership position, but I had not resolved the issue for myself.

Obediently, I went to the pastor. Surprisingly, he agreed to turn over the pulpit to me, and a Sunday was scheduled. I did not have any confidence in myself, but I had assurance in my God. Even though I was treading in uncharted territories, I knew that the message He was imparting to me was real. When Sunday came, I was nervous, but as soon as I started to deliver the message, I felt the power of God move upon and through me. It seemed that the people were shocked at my deliverance, but I knew Who the source and authority was behind it.

It was later that the struggle over the issue of women preachers occurred. I knew about the two main Scriptures that were used to squelch women preachers. I could not debate what they said, but I also had an awareness of the complete Word of God. The Word was either inconsistent and the Apostle Paul a male chauvinist, or there were other explanations for these Scriptures outside of the literal, acceptable presentation.

I could no longer ignore the fire that was burning in my spirit. After I had gotten past myself being behind the pulpit, I felt alive. It was as if preaching was natural or an extension of my life in God. I had no qualms in my mind about the One who was behind the power and authority, but also I could no longer shake this feeling that I was being called to preach in some type of capacity.

I appealed to God. "God, if I am meant to preach, You must resolve these issues. After all, your Word is true, and I know there are no inconsistencies. I will accept what you show me. If women are not allowed to preach, then take the fire away from me before it consumes me."

God did not disappoint me in bringing understanding about this subject. The information came in bits and pieces over a five-year period. Each bit of information either reaffirmed what I knew or explained the events or situations behind the Scriptures in question.

The first step towards resolving this was to remind me of my commission. As a Christian, my commission is two-fold: to preach the Gospel and to make disciples of Christ.[5] Preaching means to proclaim something. Discipling points to intense teaching that comes through instruction and example. Therefore, I had to conclude that preaching and teaching are not just allotted to men. According to Matthew and Mark, it is every Christian's responsibility to proclaim the Gospel and disciple people to be followers of Jesus. However, will a person's gender determine the capacity in which they are to carry out this commission?

I was not about to let my gender prevent me from adhering to God's commission. I realized that I could play with words and make it more tolerable to those who could become offended due to my gender. But, did I want to play such games to make the truth agreeable to others? Regardless of my personal struggle, the Word remained clear that I have been commissioned to preach or proclaim the Gospel and to disciple people.

One of the problems people can encounter is the bias of history. Those who are writing history will determine the emphasis and heroes. This was brought out in a movie portraying the influence and impact that women had on the history of Texas. One

---

[5] Matthew 28:18-20; Mark 16:15

woman showed tremendous heroic feats after the events of the Alamo. In the process of her brave leadership, she lost two children. Years later, when the history was presented about that particular episode, her part in the event was missing. A relative of hers commented on her absence from history and quoted her teacher as saying that the reason she was missing in history is because men had written the history books.

Preaching can encompass evangelizing, prophesying, and pastoring. As I studied the lives of women in the Scriptures, I found that history was very unbiased in the Scriptures. Women's influences are clearly reported. For example, Anna, a prophetess, Mary Magdelene, the woman at the well, and even Mary, the mother of Jesus, proclaimed the Gospel. In some cases, these women were the first to proclaim the Gospel to their particular group of people. Philip's daughters prophesied.[6] According to pastor and author George Watkins, history shows that these four women evangelized throughout the known world.[7]

As far as being overseers, Moses' sister, Miriam, and a woman named Hulda were prophetesses. Miriam was named in leadership along with Moses and Aaron. Priests actually sought out Hulda to be informed of the mind of God.

Deborah, the judge and prophetess, and Phoebe were overseers of God's people. Balak sought out Deborah's leadership. Some consider this weakness on his part, but based on the Word, he was considered a man of faith. According to George Watkins, Phoebe was widely traveled and had a legal mind.[8] She argued cases for the churches in the courts of her land, and was an evangelist and superintendent of at least two

---

[6] Matthew 28:1-8; Luke 2:36-38; John 4:28-29; Acts 1:14 refer to 2:4; 21:8-9;
[7] Women in Today's Church, George Watkins, pg. 20
[8] Ibid, pg. 16

churches. The Apostle Paul even instructed those at the Church of Rome to assist her in whatever way she requested.[9]

Obviously, these women affected the lives of men, and it was not just in a subservient position. They were leaders in their own right. Women served alongside the Apostle Paul, and he commended them. One of these individuals was Priscilla. She, along with her husband, risked their lives for Paul as well as for others. Priscilla was the one, along with her husband, who instructed the zealous Apollo. In a couple of Scriptures, her name is used first before her husband's name. This implies that she was the dominant one of this team.[10]

As I thought about Priscilla, I was reminded of how many women died for the sake of the Gospel. According to Wycliffe Bible Translators, the ratio for men and women on the mission field in the 1990s was eight women to one man. Amazingly, women can risk their lives on the mission field, start churches, and teach the Word, but to many, they remain incapable of being considered qualified leaders in the American Church, simply because of their gender.

Regardless of the examples in the Bible, the historical record and examples of women's devotion and work in the present, many hide behind two main Scriptures concerning women in any kind of leadership or teaching positions in the Church. It is clear that women were in leadership and teaching positions in the new Church. How is it that the Apostle Paul could honor and exalt women in Romans, but deny them similar honor in 1 Corinthians 14 and 1 Timothy 2?

As I studied Scripture, I realized that there had to be an explanation that would maintain the integrity of the complete Word of God. Eventually, I found that explanation. As you study the letter to the Corinthians, you will find that there was a debate going

---

[9] Exodus 15:20-21; 2 Kings 22:14-20; Judges 4-5; Micah 6:4; Romans 16:3
[10] Acts 18:18, 19, 24-26; Romans 12:3-4, 6, 12

on concerning the Oral Law or the traditions of the Jews. Sadly, the Corinthians were integrating these traditions into their customs and practices. You can see some of this debate going on in 1 Corinthians 7-11.

The Apostle Paul made a distinction between the Law of Moses and the Oral Law or the traditions of the Jews in 1 Corinthians 9:9-10. In 1 Corinthians 14:34, he mentioned another law, but this law was not of Moses nor was it his law. This is clear when he states that, according to this law, a woman is not permitted to speak. Again, Paul is quoting an outside source, not establishing or reaffirming a law. What law was he quoting? Apparently, he was quoting the Oral Law of the Jews.

By studying the whole chapter, you will see where Paul was contending with the issue of order. Was he actually quoting the law to drive home a point about order? Keep in mind that the main theme of 1 Corinthians 14 was Paul's instruction concerning the gifts of tongues and prophecy due to the abuse that was going on. However, Paul makes it clear that if one has a gift, a song, and message, they must be allowed to share it regardless of gender, but it must be done in an orderly manner.

The Apostle Paul was not the type of man who changed the subject in midstream. I believe he was clearly making a point. For example, consider the verses after 1 Corinthians 14:36-37. You will see that he was still talking about the proper attitude concerning gifts and their usage by the complete Body of Christ.

To consider these two Scriptures on women outside of the debate in this epistle and the theme of 1 Corinthians 14 is to create inconsistency in the Word. In fact, it does not make sense. This is why these two verses have been made a law unto themselves. People who defend their stand on women according to these Scriptures as being limited in what they can do for God, must do so out of context as to the intent of the epistle, the theme of the chapter, and the complete counsel of God.

Of course, for those who hold to this perception on women, they can also cling to 1 Timothy 2. There is no way a person can get around this chapter. After all, it is clear that Paul is addressing women. There is still one problem. Its acceptable presentation or understanding remains inconsistent with the rest of the Word. How could Philip's daughters or Phoebe remain quiet? If it was true, how could Paul quietly sit back and let Priscilla teach Apollo? We cannot forget the single women who chose to serve God. Paul instructed the women who desire to serve God to remain single, so that there would not be any division in loyalties and duties.[11] Therefore, who will try to oversee them in their calling or speak on their behalf?

It is important to test Scripture with Scripture. You do this by making sure that you maintain the intent and integrity of the complete Word of God. If an interpretation of Scripture does seem inconsistent, then put it on the shelf, and ask God to bring the proper understanding of it.

My studies revealed that the issue in this particular chapter in 1 Timothy 2 was political unrest. According to George Watkins' findings, the Romans were cracking down on Christians.[12] Keep in mind that the Jewish women were conservative in their dress and were not allowed to learn or teach. Since Christianity brought freedom to the women, Roman soldiers were looking for change in dress and conduct in order to root out Christians. The Apostle Paul was calling for discretion as a means of protection. However, he maintained that even though women should not be allowed to teach, they must continue to learn to avoid deception.

The information that God brought to me calmed the nagging questions surrounding the controversial Scriptures. However, I still struggled with the idea of preaching. Underneath, I did not feel

---

[11] 1 Corinthians 7:25, 34-35
[12] Women in Today's Church, pgs. 26-27

the freedom to do so. I did not understand whether it was the restraining hand of God or personal bondage.

I made a simple decision. I would choose to trust God to get me where He wanted me to be. I would accept the doors He opened and confront the challenges He brought my way. This helped me take some necessary steps, but God was not about to let me off the hook. I needed to come to terms with these unseen barriers that were causing confusion, in order to walk out my calling. At the time, I had no idea as to the extent these barriers had in my own life and how they would affect my pursuit to find my place in God's kingdom.

7

BARRIERS

People will always encounter barriers in their journey through life. Barriers are not prisons, but they can become dots that will create confusion and chaos as they cause people to take detours in their lives. Barriers are hindrances, and serve as points of personal testing as well as a means of testing others.

These unseen barriers can powerfully determine a person's walk. In fact, they can comprise a maze that will make people feel lost and overwhelmed. These feelings will create hopelessness or frustration because these barriers serve as immovable walls.

Encountering these immovable walls can be the means by which people can justify giving up on life. These walls are unfair, hypocritical, and cruel to those who encounter them. These barriers exist in the hearts and minds of people. Ultimately, they will limit you in what you may experience or encounter. In Christianity, they become hindrances that cause many to throw up their hands at the rhetoric and the hypocrisy of it all, and either run back to the world, and decide to play the game, or live in limbo in their Christian walk.

I have encountered various barriers in my walk with God. Sadly, these barriers are not always established by the world. They can be found within the church system. The first barrier I became aware of was the financial wall. Due to this particular barrier, I was treated as subhuman as a fourth grader. I did not wear the right clothes nor did I have the right associations. This made me aware that barriers will place you outside of what is considered the inner core, and label you according to what is considered acceptable and noteworthy.

The financial barrier followed me into ministry. The status quo in ministry involves extreme appearance. This depends on your place in the kingdom of God. For example, if you're a missionary, you must look the part. Your dress must not only be conservative, but it must not be too elaborate. In other words, your clothes and possessions should look like you came out of the thrift store. On the other hand, if you are to be considered successful, as well as credible and worth supporting, you must look successful. You must dress, act, and talk like a professional. This is nothing more than worldly glamour. Nevertheless, this false light becomes a standard. It matters little to too many people whether you have the goods behind that glamour or whether it is simply show. Appearance is everything, even though it is just a façade or false image.

God somewhat defined my place in His kingdom as being a missionary in America. This type of call means a person must live by faith, putting the individual on a tight budget. Surprisingly, this position placed me in a precarious place. To one group, I had to look like a devoted missionary who understood sacrifice, but to the other group I had to look like a plastic movie star.

The budget I lived on, and the lifestyle I did manage to live put me in the middle of these two extremes. You can probably guess what kind of attitudes I encountered along the way. It seems like you cannot win for losing. One group judges you for having anything of quality, while the other group will either barely tolerate you or mock you if you fail to qualify. I found consolation in knowing that God does not judge by clothing or financial status. In fact, He has chosen the poor of this world to be rich in faith and heirs of His kingdom. Therefore, the Bible calls such judgment sin.[1]

The next barrier that I encountered was my gender. I never asked to be born female. In other words, I had no say over the matter. I learned early in my life that gender determined a person's lot in life before they could ever discover their personal identity. In summary, regardless of personality or abilities, the culture and standards often predetermine a person's place according to gender.

Attitude about the roles of men and woman are a matter of culture and belief, and each person based on gender is somewhat conditioned to fit into this predetermined place. As I began to explore my personal likes and dislikes, I started to resent my lot in life. I observed how everything appears to be directed at the men in our society. I watched how little boys were treated as potential kings and women were conditioned to serve them. It was as though women could not find their identity outside of the man.

This attitude is reinforced as you see foolish games in the relationships between young men and women because of this conditioning. I personally thought such games to be silly and unproductive. I began to discover that I did not have the desire to fall nicely into some type of square or hole as a woman. In fact, in many areas, I did not fit the criteria, nor did I have a desire to. I had no idea how I would discover my identity outside of womanhood, but I concluded that I wanted people to either accept me or reject me on the basis of my person or character. In my mind, this would do away with games and help me establish healthy relationships. However, to possess such an attitude often labels a woman as being rebellious, foolish, a man-hater, or in some religious circles as having a "Jezebel Spirit."

---

[1] James 2:2-9

Sadly, the barrier erected in regards to gender is even more concrete in religion. Clearly, God has established responsibilities in the family based on gender, but not in His kingdom. In His kingdom, there are no distinctions such as male and female. He is not a God of favorites, nor does He see the distinctions by which so many judge others. He sees the heart. And, what society often discards, ignores, and demotes to substandard levels are the very things He exalts in His kingdom.[2] Obviously, the barriers that are established in the religious sector exist because they are often interpreted according to the barriers of culture, rather than the Spirit and truth of God's heart.

For a woman to minister in many religious arenas, she has to prove herself ten times more efficient than her male counterpart. In fact, in some cases, it matters little if a woman has the goods. People will even prefer a man who is a wolf in sheep's clothing to a woman who is of God.

The next barrier I encountered was my education. Most people are judged according to degrees, rather than their knowledge and experience. In Christendom, degrees should never be the determining factor. After all, a person can have all the religious degrees that are available and still not know Jesus. These educated people may have many facts, but still would be considered fools, for they lack faith in Christ. Regardless of what people know on the intellectual level, only the heart can know the revelations of God. These revelations are not imparted by man, but by the Holy Ghost.

Although barriers can cause various levels of distress, my lack of degrees has not caused me as much distress as my lack of abilities. My lack of certain abilities made me vulnerable and put me at the mercy of people. For example, I wish I knew how to fix things such as cars, appliances, sprinklers, etc. This barrier has

---

[2] 1 Samuel 16:7; 1 Corinthians 1:24-29; Galatians 3:28

created some of the greatest hindrances. These hindrances force people to rely on the integrity of man. As most women can testify, they are often viewed as easy targets or weak vessels. I realize some men receive the same labeling, but the natural tendency in our self-serving society is to take advantage of such weaknesses. Ultimately, people who give way to this tendency become predators who have no problem preying on victims.

Another barrier that has caused some difficulties is my marital status. When you combine the fact that I am a woman and divorced, I already have two strikes against me. The other part of this denominator is that I live with my co-laborer and our team is made up of single women. Since I don't date, the usual question I get about my situation is, "Do you hate men?" Needless to say, there are other deviant suspicions behind the questions or so-called "concerns." I have often wondered how many men in a similar position are asked the same questions.

The suspicion that a divorce often stirs up is understandable, but the Church must not allow suspicion to determine attitudes. Suspicion labels and isolates people without fair considerations. Christians must learn to test the spirits, and always be in the place of reconciliation and restoration.[3] Such a place points to healing, which allows a person to be restored in God's kingdom.

Associations can serve as another barrier. You have to know the right people to get anything accomplished, regardless of what you are offering. Most people in high positions will not give anyone the time of day, unless those close to them prepare the way. This is understandable, but it often proves to be unfair. King Solomon put it in this perspective, "There is an evil which I have seen under the sun, as an error which proceedeth from the ruler: Folly is set in great dignity, and the rich sit in low place. I have seen servants

---

[3] 2 Corinthians 5:18-19: 1 John 4:1

upon horses, and princes walking as servants upon the earth" (Ecclesiastes 10:5-7).

You may possess something of value or worth, but if you are not in the right crowd, it may go unnoticed. This can prove to be a hard pill to swallow when you watch charlatans sell poison to the masses in the name of God, religion, country, and Jesus Christ.

I have encountered all of these barriers. What is a person to do? I had to make a decision about each barrier I encountered. Would I allow it to become an excuse to cease from running the race, thereby making it an oppressive dot? Or, would I come to understand that it is simply a barrier? No barrier is too great for God. These barriers allow God the opportunity to show Himself mighty and faithful.

Barriers can become points of character building, spiritual growth, and godly discipline. For example, by not allowing the barrier to be an excuse, character would be established. Each barrier contains vital lessons in regard to life. By learning the lessons, I would be encouraging spiritual growth. I could consider each barrier as a point of oppression or one of godly discipline. Discipline helps people recognize and accept limitations. This not only does away with expectation, but it allows a person to accept barriers.

The challenge of barriers is that you have to wade through the emotions they stir up in you. For example, the financial barriers have caused skepticism in me. The gender barriers produced anger and resentment. The educational hindrance resulted in much frustration towards the lack of mercy and indifference. The barrier caused by my marital status stirred up mocking. The barrier created by a lack of associations resulted in disgust.

The problem with these emotions is that they require some type of response. For example, I found myself trying to adjust to the financial barriers only to be left feeling like a hypocrite. My initial reaction to the gender barrier was knocking the wall down by setting the record straight. I recognized that I was about to make this issue a cause, and all I would come out with was a headache. In regard to education, I accepted the fact that I would never know it all. In the area of abilities, I had to accept my vulnerability and become cognizant of those I did business with. As far as the challenge caused by my divorce, I had to realize that there are people who still test you according to who you are and not by obvious failures. Such people are also open for ministry, instruction, and change. In other words, these people are the sheep.

As far as associates, I learned to see them as open and closed doors that God would put before me. Through the years I have met people from many different walks of life. The one quality I have noticed about the people that represented open doors is that they were open to be used of God. Regardless of their type of influence, God often used them in unusual ways.

It was vital that I learn the spiritual lesson of each barrier. In the area of finances, I had to trust God as my provider. I learned to look to Him to supply what I needed to do His bidding. He has never let me down. Although I may not fit people's criteria as far as being a minister of the Gospel, I am able to put forth a conservative presentation. I do not scream of success in my appearance, but I do display authority in Christ when necessary, which is far more important.

The area of gender has presented me with a couple of vital lessons. Besides realizing that God does not see us according to gender, the cross of Jesus clearly puts me on an even level with everyone else. The next comforting reality is that God sees people as His vessels and instruments. The test in God's kingdom is not based on the type of vessel He uses, but on whether the vessel is speaking forth His truths. For example, He has used an ass, young people, and unbelievers to speak His truths.[4] Regardless of the vessel or instrument, it is up to each person to test the spirit and quality of the message. If something is of God, it is up to the person to receive it.

The second lesson is that God uses vessels to prove the hearts of people. If people truly love God, they will not care if He uses a weak, despised, rejected, or base vessel. They will gladly receive. However, a person who strictly judges based on the type of vessel, is not truly concerned with spiritual matters. Such people are dictating to God the conditions in which they will receive from Him. This is like the vessel telling the potter how it will be used and what it will receive. Such a state of affairs not only speaks of foolishness, but of arrogance. Such people do not love God. The proof is in the fact that they prefer their ways to God's perfect ways. [5]

In the area of education, the Lord has taught me what it means to be a student. The whole world is a classroom. There is no way that everyone can know everything. This is why everyone is at the same level of lack and needs. Granted, some people may know a variety of things I do not know, but I know things others do not know. This has helped me realize that no one is meant to be an island unto him or herself. Such a state exposes the delusion of self-sufficiency.[6] As believers, we all possess different abilities and means, so that we can help one another.

This lesson showed me the necessity and working of the Body of Christ. It takes each of us to work in the vast harvest field of souls. It is sad that people abuse others' vulnerability, which often proves to be their particular test. Failure in such tests proves that the individual lacks integrity. The test for me is that I must be true

---

[4] Numbers 22:28; 2 Kings 5:2-4; Jeremiah 1:6-9; Romans 6:13: 2 Corinthians 4:6-10; 2 Timothy 2:20-22
[5] Proverbs 14:12; Isaiah 55:8-9; Romans 9:18—23; 1 Corinthians 2:14
[6] 2 Corinthians 3:5

to what God has given me, in spite of the abuses. Every day I am tested with my talents or gifts. Will I unmercifully abuse someone who is in need of my talent, or will I see it as an opportunity to become an extension of Jesus in this world?

As far as associates, team members etc., I realize that God wanted me to trust Him in that area as well. Surprisingly, the people who made an impact in my life were not those in high places. They were people who would seem insignificant in the scheme of things, but proved vital as far as God's plan. They were vital because of their humility, openness, faithfulness, and obedience towards the Lord. These are the people who shake heaven with their prayers.

I began to understand that God uses what many people would consider as foolish, base, and despised. As a result, He does things in unexpected ways, showing His power, love, and faithfulness. Over the years, I observed that God always handed us blessings in unexpected packages.

The people we thought would help, did not, while those, whom we never considered in that capacity, stepped up to the plate and often sacrificed. I begin to realize that the sacrifices that came out of need from such people ensure the multiplication of blessings for us. Out of this realization, grew an appreciation for God's faithfulness that He displayed through unlikely people. These people proved to be faithful. Not only did they often give sacrificially, but their sacrifice also allowed God to show Himself in greater ways.

Before I could appreciate my barriers, I had to come to terms with their presence in my life. In fact, God used the barriers to bring forth my calling. Even though I was shying away from preaching, the barriers not only helped me to face my calling, but they also helped define it. Instead of the barriers stopping me, they actually gave me a newfound liberty to examine my life outside of what is so often considered normal and acceptable by the visible Church. This allowed me to venture into unknown territories. The results were incredible.

First, I had to understand the makeup and purpose of barriers. The main purpose of barriers is to control or maintain some type of semblance in society. Barriers are based on what is deemed normal by society. Therefore, everyone has their place. But sadly, they are based on the obvious or surface distinctions.

This brings us to the subject of order. Order is vital to ensure the functioning of any society. The problem with this type of unspoken order is that it is based on prejudices found within cultures and societies. Prejudices are not a product of differences, but of conditioning. Conditioning determines attitudes. Culture, parents, education, and religion are responsible for this conditioning. Attitudes are a reflection of each of our dispositions. Disposition is determined by spirit.

In these prejudices are definitions as to what constitutes acceptability. Therefore, prejudices serve as points of distinction. These prejudices point to the reign of pride, which strictly judges according to personal preferences. In this order, superiority is established. This means that there must be those who are inferior to lord over. These points can be based on financial status, gender, race, or creed.

I did not understand the dynamics of prejudice until I was in the military. My years in the military occurred during a transitional time in our culture. It was right after the Viet Nam conflict. The country was in a state of unrest. It was as if all of the fiber of nation had been torn up, and as a result, nothing made sense.

At this period of time people were, in a way, snatching at straws to bring some kind of meaning or order to the chaos. It was a time of questioning and examining accepted values. It was a period when many Americans found themselves lost in the uncertainty of who we were as a nation. This uncertainty caused fear, disillusionment, and discontentment.

The military was no exception. Women wanted to step outside of conventional roles and tread into areas that had been reserved only for men. This brought to the surface the issue of prejudice. At the time, I did not realize that the prejudice that broke the issue wide open was not really centered on race, although that is what the military focused on, but on gender.

The prejudice that existed towards women had been cleverly hidden behind the idea of the proper place everyone fits into within society. I had been conditioned to believe that as long as women stayed in their place, that all was well. As long as they dressed right, they would not be violated. In this conditioning, I never thought about who or what determined a woman's place. I did not see that women were being made responsible for men's actions. After all, I had been conditioned to accept this prejudice as a matter of proper conduct, rather than an attitude that harbors irresponsibility, fear, and immaturity.

As I stood in the midst of this transition in the Navy, I observed how women took up the challenge to tread in uncharted territories. I also witnessed the reaction of many of the men. They showed anger. I could even sympathize with them, for I was conditioned to do so. However, I could not help but see that behind their anger was fear, and behind their fear was insecurity. Whenever insecurity reigns, there is uncertainty. Uncertainty implies chaos or the loss of order. It was as if men's identity and personal conduct hinged on women being in their right place. For women to step outside of acceptable boundaries meant that they were now at equal standing or in possible competition with men.

Prejudices ultimately produce hypocrisy. This hypocrisy became noticeable. After all, men did not mind competition among themselves, but they resented the idea of women being capable of doing certain jobs that had been off limits to them in the past. I could not help but wonder if they were afraid that women would not only prove to be capable in certain areas, but as worthy opponents to be reckoned with.

I did not understand the face of prejudice until I faced the impact that diversity has on a society. The Navy's way of addressing the uncertainty was to deal with prejudice at the level of race. At the time, I did not realize that the military was trying to deal with prejudice at the most obvious level as a way to address other issues. After all, the prejudice towards gender is considered an acceptable attitude in societies. For example, if prejudice expresses itself in the area of men and women, it is considered a relationship problem, not an attitude inspired by prejudice.

The military developed mandatory seminars. There you had to face your bias. In my book, I did not have any prejudice. After all, I did not dislike or hate anyone based on race, color, or creed. I felt confident that I was all right. Little did I know that everyone harbors some form of prejudice.

As I look back on this educational period of my life, I see that I went into the seminar thinking that I did not have any prejudices, and came out with a revelation of how prejudice operates. I did not like the face of this creature. It was clever and sinister. Over the years, I have come face to face with this creature many times. I have gained some unusual insights about it.

Today, there are some Christians who have taken up the cause of exposing and doing away with prejudice. Sadly, they never get past the surface of prejudice to really deal with it. Prejudice is not a matter of difference, but one of attitude that has been conditioned within the individual. It is not the eyes that distinguish the difference. Rather, it is the heart attitude that establishes one's worth on the basis of gender, race, or belief.

Therefore, it is not enough to complain about prejudice at one level, for it exists at many levels in various ways, using different disguises. In fact, the one who makes prejudice a cause because of personal experiences often harbors like prejudices.

The first realization that prejudices are a matter of conditioning occurred when a black girl revealed her unacceptable conduct towards me. I never realized that I had been conditioned to classify or accredit unacceptable conduct to a person's color or culture. It never dawned on me that the conduct of people had nothing to do with race, culture, or creed, but with the fact that we are all part of the fallen Adamic race.

Unbecoming conduct can be found among all the different groups of people, but prejudice will classify it, making it look as if a person's race, culture, or belief is what determines their attitude or conduct. Granted, race, culture, or beliefs do bring distinction, but prejudice is a heart attitude that often puts diversity into an inferior category. This classification exalts one to a superior position, while labeling all people into general groups based on outward distinctions, financial status, differences, or associations, rather than individual character.

Just because prejudice is often conditioned into our way of thinking does not mean we should condone, ignore, or practice it. For many people to face their prejudices, they must be brought forth. Such prejudice needs some type of breeding ground. There are three main breeding grounds that will bring this creature forth with a vengeance. They are ignorance, fear, and hatred. Sadly, these three sources often walk hand in hand.

The race-based seminars in the Navy revealed the source of my prejudice to be ignorance. I never realized that my conditioning created a prejudice that was based on my ignorance. My conditioning caused me to attach a prejudice for people's behavior to the obvious physical distinctions or differences. I failed to realize that behind the various diversities that often classify people, are individuals with similar likes, dislikes, desires, dreams, and hopes. They live, love, feel, cry, laugh, and die.

I was shocked at my prejudice, but I realized that either I could face my ignorance or become enslaved by its walls. At that point,

91

my ignorance was a dot, but it could become a hideous prison that would rob me of what character I possessed. I had to admit that I did not like how my prejudice made me feel about life in general. I needed to educate myself about my superstition towards people I did not identify with, and remain on guard against it.

Fear is the next breeding ground for prejudice. What people do not understand, they cannot control. What cannot be controlled will produce fear. Most people fear that which is contrary to what they perceive to be normal and acceptable. When something is different, we naturally focus on it. If it acts offensive or contrary to our comfort zones, we explain it away by attaching a justifiable prejudice based on the obvious difference and call it a truth. Needless to say, it is not truth because it is inconsistent. Truth always remains consistent and unchangeable.

Differences are obvious, but they must never become a point of judgment. We must never judge people based on what is obvious, and we must avoid drawing conclusions founded on visible differences. We need to keep in mind that there are various aspects of life that influence people, but a person's real measure must be based on personal character.

We not only fear what we do not understand, but this fear can turn into anger and hatred if we do not keep it in perspective. Eventually, anger gives way to hatred. Hatred is the most visible expression of prejudice. Hatred must have a platform. Parents or negative incidents usually erect this platform. One bad incident can give such platforms life to manifest the ugly face of prejudice. From this point, ignorance blooms into a hatred towards all those who outwardly could be associated with the experience.

However, there is nothing harsher than prejudices hiding behind scriptural rhetoric and a religious cloak. As a woman, I have encountered this prejudice. Some people are simply ignorant about God's ways and accept assumed beliefs or interpretations of others. You can tell such people because they want the truth regardless of how something may have served their purpose.

Others are afraid of anything that might challenge their own comfort zones. These people fail to realize that God will shake every foundation that is not resting on Him. In order to do this, He will run contrary to what is personally acceptable, so that He can be God.

These people can be identified by the struggle that occurs. If they sense it is truth, they will usually put aside their fear and receive it. Afterwards, they have a puzzled look because their prejudice was challenged, instead of reinforced.

The hardest Christians to confront are those who harbor hatred behind Scriptures. These individuals will justify their attitudes with Scriptures that have been taken out of context. These people do not love the truth, because they adamantly insist on their own perverted view and interpretation. Their arrogance shows with a vengeance, as they insist that you must agree with them or they will consider you an "infidel."

I remember encountering this hatred in a man I had respected and supported until he showed his true colors in regards to the issue of women. When I challenged him and his attitude, his response was that of cruelty and hatred. This subject came to the surface when he mainly blamed a man's heresy on the fact that he had sat under a woman's teaching, instead of the fact that the man obviously did not love the truth. I considered such logic utterly ridiculous. No doubt, the man reacted to my disgust for his male-chauvinistic view. We could have vehemently agreed to disagree, but the man clearly revealed darkness, as an unteachable, hateful spirit was revealed.

Later, this man's attitude was exposed to all of his supporters. As this man presented his views on women, he revealed that he went to great lengths to show how he misinterpreted Scriptures to confirm his perverted, prejudicial views on women. Sadly, I am not sure that I will see this man in heaven. The issue is not only his prejudice, but also how he mishandles Scripture to justify his ungodly attitude. If he properly handled Scripture, the Word could reveal the real issues behind his attitude. Obviously, he controls his interpretation of Scripture, rather than allowing the whole counsel and the correct Spirit behind the Word to reveal his true heart condition.

Although I have not always appreciated dealing with prejudice, it has taught me many valuable lessons about myself. It has been a mirror that I have had to come to terms with. I understand why this issue makes many people angry and hateful, but I also know that the truth will set each of us free from such prisons. Once I realized that God could use the barriers of my life to challenge me to look up and reach beyond acceptable boundaries, I began to see how God used these means to reveal His power and faithfulness to move around such obstacles.

Do you have such barriers hindering you? Do not give way to them. Rather, look up and know that your God is greater than all hindrances. Let His truth, love, faithfulness, and reality set you free from such hindrances, as well as change your focus from the obvious dots such barriers create.

8

IDENTITY

One of the greatest challenges facing Christians is something I refer to as the identity crisis. I understand this crisis quite well. I encountered it when I struggled with finding my place in Christ. I became disturbed when I realized that my place in the kingdom of God, in much of the religious sector, was determined strictly by my gender before I could discover my calling. It was not just a simple matter of serving God, but a matter of wading through all kinds of obstacles. Not only did I have to wade through these obstacles, but I had to also discern them. Did God put these obstacles there for my testing or is man behind them? Perhaps Satan is behind them?

To suffer an identity crisis means a person has become lost in the midst of reality. Individuals who are lost do not have any sense of who they are or where they are going. Life loses not only direction, but also purpose and meaning. I found this true in my own life. I started out thinking I knew who I was, but I was surprised that I was already defined by sources that had no personal knowledge of me. I struggled with this unseen standard. Somehow, I had to come to terms with my personal identity, but what does it mean to have identity? In order to understand the identity crisis that I was struggling with, I had to understand what constituted identity. After all, so many people seem to be searching for it. This search was largely due to the fact that identity is not tangible. Knowing the diversity of people, I also knew that personal identity is not generic.

"Identity" means the essential character or personality of something. No one is born with an identity, but every person has the need and potential to establish some type of identity. This personal distinction is formed in a person as they mature. This means that identity will be defined by outside sources.

The truth is, no one can give oneself an identity. Granted, we are all born with certain traits, capacities, and possibilities, but how these traits are channeled will be determined by the identity that is established. In other words, these abilities will be used to express the essence of who we are: righteous or wicked.

This is where I had to consider the different sources that identified me. It required me to examine what actually was presently identifying me, as well as the type of character that was being established in my life. I could see from my past the things that defined me, but so much had changed. I also no longer could assume that I understood my place in Christ. Until my identity was firmly established in the proper way, I would be incapable of finding my place in Christ.

The first awareness I had that I was different was when I discovered my gender. Sexuality is what initially defines each of us. We are separated by gender. From a young age, I was shaped or conditioned to accept my place in society based on my sex. My first awareness of being an adult was that of becoming a wife and mother.

Since I was young and had no real identity, I never realized that this evaluation of my place had nothing to do with my potential as a person, but with what function I could serve in society. In other words, it was about maintaining some type of order in society.

Identity strictly based on gender leaves a person floundering. This is obvious in both men and women. For men, it is called a midlife crisis. They work all of their lives to accomplish something. Then, one day they wake up in their late 40s or early 50s and at this point they realize that they are getting older, gravity is now in full force, and all they have done is work for something that holds no value or substance. This makes them question the meaning or purpose of their life. What have they accomplished? It is from this premise that everything can lose its value to them as they begin to question their purpose and existence.

Women often hit their identity crisis when their children leave home. Most marriages find their common ground at the point of children. When children leave home, couples discover how much they have invested in their own relationship. Many times, there is no point of communication outside of children. Once this common ground is gone, it will throw the marriage relationship into a crisis. This may cause the woman to doubt her womanhood or worth.

Identity that is wrapped up in gender is only surface and operates from points of vanity and ego. In other words, emphasis on sexuality means that a person's role as a man or woman must be honored, rather than their individuality. Women's vanity must be pampered and men's ego must be stroked. Without this adoration, people become discontented or disillusioned.

I have personally watched such an identity crisis. My mother went through one when all the children left home about the same time. She became lost. She had no sense of purpose, and she almost had a complete mental breakdown. Her struggles caused me to rethink my place in this world. I recognized that reality that is strictly based on gender is fragile. I determined that I would not allow my gender to define my roles, place, or lot in life. I knew that there was more to me than my sexuality, but somehow, I would have to discover it in spite of societies that never really seemed to get past this issue to discover the real person.

Parents also establish their children's identity. Children listen and watch their parents in action. The most indelible impressions that are left on children come by way of example, not instruction. These examples will be interpreted by children and acted out in their lives. Therefore, hypocrisy at any level causes confusion and disrespect in the minds of children.

Parents often raise children to bring honor to themselves. This is a form of identity, but in God's sight, it is nothing more than idolatry. When children are raised for the sole purpose of parroting their parents, this will cause them to become lost. This is one of the reasons some children hit rebellion. They not only oppose being a replica of their parents, but they resent it.

Parents must guide, not dictate or condition their children along the way. They must instill integrity through example, while their children's minds and hearts are still impressionable. Integrity will help their children realize their potential without betraying themselves.

Another source that defines us is culture. Culture actually determines values. It expresses itself in lifestyles. Personally, I was proud of the American culture. America has been a rich country that lacked nothing. This had its advantages. A person could actually work hard and get ahead.

In the Navy, I began to realize that what established America as great was also her biggest weakness. Abundance can make for a spoiled people who lose sight of sacrifice. Eventually, such people will sell their soul to maintain their outlandish lifestyle. This caused me to realize that every society has it strengths as well as its weaknesses. The strengths of a country often harbor prejudices and hypocrisies, while its weaknesses can serve as an expression of its paganism.

As I studied the American culture, I was saddened to realize that Christianity had become a subculture within America. In other words, American Christians took Christian principles and instituted them into the American lifestyle. As a result, much of the Church embraced the prejudices, hypocrisies, and paganism of America. The results have been devastating.

I began to realize that Christianity as I knew it according to my culture was far from the Scriptural mark of distinction and excellence. This became more evident as I studied the pilgrim Church in the first two centuries. I have no doubt that those like the Apostle John would mourn the arrogance and paganism that is being displayed in much of the visible Church in America. The biggest tragedy is that it is all being done in the name of Jesus.

I greatly struggled with this. How could I make sure that I came to terms with real Christianity? Somehow, I had to come to terms with the Christian life in spite of the culture. Like Daniel in Babylon, I had to remain distinct from it influences. This would prove to be a tall order.

The world defines us. As I looked back on my life, I began to realize that much of how I perceived life was based on Hollywood. Romance, success, happiness, and love were defined by nothing more than images on a screen. These images were made to seem real. After all, they gave me a certain feeling and expectation. They defined how something would make me feel if only the right situation were in place. It gave me hope that I could truly live happily ever after.

Sadly, people prefer this immature reality. It serves their purpose, but it is not realistic. It is just an impression that has no substance behind it. It is an illusion that mocks you. It is an image that demands worship, but it leaves you empty and discontent. It is nothing more than vainglory that will cause one's life to become useless in the scheme of things. Yet, people pursue it, only to be robbed and left destitute. I had to recognize the vanity of the world. I can happily say today that I become repulsed at many of these images. They are not only unrealistic; they are becoming ridiculous and foolish to me.

Religion defines us. It can serve as our conscience, but much of religion is just an outward cloak that allows many to hide their filthy rags behind the religious façade. For example, it hides insensitivity, compromise, wickedness, and sin. Today, much of religion has become professional entertainment instead of a high calling. It is all outward conformity, rather than inward transformation. It is about worldly kingdoms, rather than an unseen kingdom made up of believers of Jesus Christ.

Early in my Christian life, the difference between Christianity and religion was defined. I have never forgotten the diverse difference between these two arenas. However, this has not kept me from falling into religious traps. I equated a church building with serving God, rather than being available to people. I have defended leaders, rather than standing for truth and holding the line of righteousness. I took up causes, instead of maintaining the only cause set forth in Scripture: Jesus Christ and Him crucified.[1]

It was also brought to my attention that we look to sources to define our life for us. Anytime someone or something defines life for you, the source will influence the way you look at yourself. In fact, these sources will determine how you feel about yourself. I had to also consider these influences in order to come to terms with my present identity. This enabled me to be open for a new identity.

The first source we usually look to, to evaluate life and our part in it, is self. This involves introspection. The problem is that self holds no answers. The more you look within, the more you become lost. You discover that there is no point of truth or contrast when you look to self. You have to examine what you think, as well as take your emotional pulse about how you feel, but there is no standard by which to compare such conclusions or feelings.

---

[1] 1 Corinthians 2:2

Regardless of how right they seem, how do you know your conclusions or feelings are right?

After hitting one wall after the other, I realized that I had to look outside of self if I was going to get perspective. Where would I look? Could I look to people? I had tried this source. I kept learning the same lesson: People will fail you. After all, how can lost man give you identity? And, if you do manage to encounter someone who possesses identity, there is no way they can give you an identity that is complimentary to your particular personality.

Perhaps I could look to jobs or organizations to give me identity. To look to such sources, simply means that I am looking for a platform that will make me "a somebody," regardless of who I am. This would make my life a matter of performance rather than character. I had previously performed a lot in my life, and now I wanted character.

As I considered all of these influences and possibilities, I began to see how people become confused about life and their place in the scheme of things. I could see the obstacles before me, and the maze that never seemed to lead anywhere but to dead ends. Just who am I? Who or what will help me discover my potential without stripping me of the very qualities that would be used to bring meaning to my life? My examination proved to me that I could not look within nor could I look around to discover my true identity. That only left me with one direction, upward.

The simple truth is that there is no identity outside of Jesus. If a person looked any other place for purpose, meaning, and life, they would find themselves in a maze, lost in the endless emptiness of it all. Nothing really does make sense outside of the life that Jesus is offering those who come to Him.

This reality was not some great revelation, but a simple truth. After a person comes to the end of self, worldly relationships, the world, and activities, one discovers the failure of these sources to give any identity or direction. The life that such things define has no purpose. The identity they offer is elusive. The hope they offer is temporary. Is it any wonder that a person can become lost in the emptiness of it all?

I finally realized that I had to look outside of myself, above man, beyond this present age, and exceed all personal activities and expectations to find the life that I so desired. I needed to find my identity or place in Christ. As Jesus said, He is my life, and as the Bible expounds, my identity can only be realized when I become identified with Jesus Christ in His death, burial, and resurrection.[2]

For years, I had enjoyed the reality of Jesus' cross. His death on the cross was about me. It was the means by which I could discover real life. I had bowed down before it, seeking forgiveness, reconciliation, and restoration from Him. However, the cross is much more. It is a place of identification. When people embrace the cross, the essence of their life ceases to be about them, and it becomes about the consuming reality of Jesus.

It is easy as believers to talk about how our lives are hid in Christ. We can quote Galatians 2:20, that we no longer live, but it is Christ who lives in us by faith. We may be excited about being seated in high places with Jesus. But it just proves that our lives are no longer about us. Instead, they must become about identification and communion with Jesus.[3]

Jesus alone is the One who gives His people their identity. He alone is the One who determines my identity. He is my wisdom, righteousness, sanctification, and redemption.[4] It is His life that must be expressed in me and through me. The way this life is expressed in me will not be based on my gender or according to my culture. It will not be a matter of religion or personal attempts. The way this life will be expressed in me will come down to my

---

[2] Romans 6:3-5
[3] Ephesians 2:6
[4] 1 Corinthians 1:30

choices, personality, and character. His life in me will clearly define my personality and establish my character.

I realized that looking to any source for my identity other than Jesus would either create prisons that limit me or dots that would take me on detours. Personally, I was tired of all the past influences that had tried to define me as a person and the type of life I was to pursue or live.

As I considered the fact that Jesus knew everything about me, I knew without a doubt that I could trust Him with my complete life. I could trust Him not to abuse me, dehumanize me, or try to make me into something I was not. On the other hand, He would use my traits to define my personality according to the way He made me. I didn't have to struggle to try to please Him, nor did He want me to perform for Him. This brought tremendous liberty to my spirit. After all, He is trustworthy.

Do you know who you are in Christ? Are you looking elsewhere for your identity or life? If you are, you will find yourself lost in the ridiculousness of it all. You may not realize the state of your spiritual condition at this point, but down the line, emptiness will mock you, disillusionment will rob you, vanity will consume you, and hopelessness will overtake you.

9

POSITION IN CHRIST

It is easy to say there is no identity outside of Jesus. You can sound intelligent by advocating that you will not allow gender to define you. You can sound spiritual by talking about the simplicity of your life in Jesus, to avoid the complication caused by so many outside influences. The reality is that it is not easy to find your identity in Christ because you have to crawl over so many issues. You may struggle against your gender, culture, and religion defining you in the many arenas of life, but that is how one functions within societies, and that is how one's importance and sense of worth are initially established.

Obviously, people must get past those things that define them in order to come to terms with who they are in Christ. They must get past worldly identity to establish their life on an eternal plane with God. They must foremost establish a relationship with God before they can make sense out of their lives, as well as find meaning and purpose.

Outside of God, life holds no lasting meaning. In fact, life is senseless unless people make it count for something. I had to question myself as to what kind of legacy I wanted to leave, especially since everyone leaves some kind of initial impression. Many want to leave a legacy of money, success, or prestige. I could be spiritual and noble by declaring that I wanted to leave a spiritual legacy behind. However, what does such boasting speak of—my goodness or God's glory? To come to terms with legacy, I had to first find my place in Christ. Before I could find my place in Christ, I had to become established in a more intimate relationship with God.

To come to terms with my legacy in a relationship with God, I had to understand what it meant to really have my life in Christ. The Apostle Paul declared that my life is hid in Christ, and that I am seated in high places with Him.[1] It is not enough to have knowledge of something, a person must have a "knowing." Such "knowing" points to actual experience where a person knows what it means personally to have their life hid in Christ. True spiritual searches begin with Jesus, but they must end with Him being lifted up in glory.

Jesus possesses the real identity that can bring a person to realize their purpose. The puzzling question is how He will be able to bring forth a person's identity? The answer is found in the fact that His saints have been positionally placed in Him.

Ravi Zacharias maintains that position is the vantage point from which people can view life because of Jesus. The Bible is full of what it means to have a place or position in Christ. In fact, the consistent word that points to this position is the word "in". This word is used to describe what it means to **be in Jesus**, and what it means for **Jesus to be in us**. Amazingly, few ever consider or take note of what it means to be in Christ. They assume because they have said some prayer or go to some church that all is well. Such assumption is not only incorrect, but it is also dangerous.

Everybody is in some type of position. Whether it is the low position of living on the streets or the high position of leadership, people hold some type of position in their homes, family, society,

---

[1] Ephesians 2:6: Colossians 3:3

105

and the kingdom of God. It is from this point that they will make conclusions about life.

Today, there is much promotion of self. The problem with this promotion is that when self serves as the vantage point, there is no point of real identity. These people become lost as they try to find some purpose to life by looking within.

For example, self is only the expression of the "old man." This does not constitute identity, but the essence of fierce individuality or independence. The old man strives to become different outside of conventional roles that are often defined by culture. In fact, culture basically tries to civilize or discipline the old man. Any time culture influences the old man, individuality becomes an expression of the vanity and fluff of the world.

In order to be defined, our personality must be brought forth. Personality is the truest expression of who we are. It is also the basis by which God will bring forth our potential. The problem with personality is that it remains lost in the midst of activities, the cares of the world, and rebellion, unless it is regenerated.

The potential of our personality is to reflect Jesus. This is what God formed man to do in the first place. Adam was to reflect the image of his Creator, but marred his potential to do so when he rebelled. Due to the fallen condition that we inherit from the first man, we all fall short of reflecting this glory in a lost world.[2]

As the second man or the second Adam, Jesus brought this purpose out as He served as the visible reflection of the Father's glory. Jesus' identification with the Father not only defined His personality, but also resulted in His death on the cross. Likewise, Christians are to reflect Christ through their personalities.[3]

Personality established in Christ through the working of the Holy Ghost is done so through discipline, godly position, and exercise (obedience). Discipline is vital in every Christian's life.

---

[2] Genesis 1:26-27: Romans 3:23
[3] John 14:9; 1 Corinthians 15:45-49; 2 Corinthians 3:18

Such discipline entails self-denial to the ways of the old man. This is where the pride of the self-life is denied its right to its demands in order to give way to that which is worthy of all consideration, Jesus Christ.[4]

Godly positions find their sole origins in the redemptive work of Jesus. They stand because of grace and withstand because of God's Word and power. These positions find the essence of life through death. This life serves as the identifying mark in every Christian. In fact, there are three identifying marks.

The first mark is the mark of death to the self-life. The mark of death identifies us with the cross of Jesus. Such a mark implies that I am no longer at the foot of the cross, but now I have embraced the cross to become identified with Jesus in His death, burial, and resurrection.[5]

The second mark is that of a new life, the life of Jesus in us. I am no longer living according to the old man. I walk to a different drum beat. My disposition is not the same, my attitude has been greatly adjusted, and I am becoming a reflection of the One I now follow and serve.[6]

This brings us to the third mark, the reflection of Jesus. The new life I am displaying is His life. The disposition belongs to Him. I am walking according to a cross that limits and guides my steps. Clearly, it is no longer I who live, but Christ who lives in me and through me by faith.

The Apostle Paul tells us in 1 Timothy 4:7-8, "But refuse profane and old wives' fables, and exercise thyself rather unto godliness. For bodily exercise profiteth little: but godliness is profitable unto all things, having promise of the life that now is and of that which is to come." The present disciplined life of Christ in me will cause me to exercise unto godliness. "Godliness" means

---

[4] Matthew 16:24-26
[5] Romans 6:1-6; Galatians 2:20: Ephesians 2:8-10
[6] Romans 6:4-5; Colossians 3:5-17

I am righteous in my ways because all I am and do finds its source in God. My conduct is a display of what is godly and acceptable before God.

The life of identification with Jesus' death, burial, and resurrection brings forth my personality. This is where self ceases to be, and where Jesus becomes the way, the truth, and the life. As I give way to the working of His Spirit, the real potential and purpose of my personality will come forth as I begin to reflect Jesus Christ.

Today, people are serving as some form of legacy. The impression that is left will be determined by the influences that each person exposes self to. If individuals are reflecting rebellion, they are operating according to self or individuality. If self appears to be civilized, but not regenerated, then it will be reflecting the world. If Christ is present, then His glory will be shining forth in a magnificent way.

Position in Christ defines personality. Once personality is brought out, a person is able to express that personality through gender. As you consider the pattern to identity, you will see how *position* comes first, followed by *personality*. The last part of this pattern is *gender*.

As I began to understand this pattern, I was a little shocked. All the struggles I encountered could have ceased if only I had understood my position in Christ. He initially strips people of everything that identifies them to the old life, so that He can bring forth their personality. Once He is able to establish their position in Him, they will be able to view life from His perspective. Obviously, such a perspective is quite different from the viewpoints of the old man and the world. It is so liberating to discover the depths in God and the potential of your personality as you become more and more defined by the life of Jesus in you.

The more I realized this, the more I became appreciative of not only how God made me, but my womanhood. It was no longer a terrible burden to bear, but a point of discipline that ensured order. As a result, I could even appreciate His order in the family. For example, womanhood expresses Jesus in godly submission in the family, while husbands express Jesus through their manhood with godly love. Therefore, gender is not the point of identification, but a means of determining how the different aspects of Jesus' character will be expressed in a particular situation.

Obviously, expressing Jesus in submission in the family does not determine a woman's personality, but defines the type of discipline that must be evident for a woman's personality to reflect Jesus. Likewise, manhood does not determine worth or position, but should serve as a means for men to reflect the sacrificial love of Christ to their families and in the world. Both of these positions in marriage personally honor those in their respective gender, and do not encourage superiority, but brings an equality of oneness of agreement through the humility of submission and love.

As Oswald Chambers pointed out, the differences in the responsibilities of husbands and wives do not promote superiority or slavery in this relationship. Whether this relationship is presented in light of submission or obedience, love will always produce equality.[7] If only God's people would get a vision of this truth. It would alleviate prejudices and wrong teachings, and bring agreement and order in His kingdom.

By understanding how position works in the family, I could now explore what my position would be in His kingdom. Since I am not married, I am free to serve God without attachments, demands, or hindrances from the world. My focus could be undivided and complete. My sole responsibility would be to serve God.[8] The question is, how is personality established through position to ensure an undivided life before God? It begins with disposition.

---

[7] Shade of His Hand; © 1991 by Oswald Chambers Publications Association Limited; pg. 126
[8] 1 Corinthians 7:22-23, 32-35

The Apostle Paul gives us insight into the necessary disposition that would establish a person's position through the example of Jesus. "But made himself of no reputation, and took upon him the form of a servant, and was made in the likeness of man" (Philippians 2:7). There is only one position that will establish a godly personality—that of servitude.

Jesus confirmed this in Matthew 20:27. His disciples were upset because John and James' mother asked that Jesus give her sons special preference in His kingdom. Jesus explained to His disciples that in His kingdom those who would be regarded as chief would have to be a servant of all. This was contrary to the disciples' way of thinking. To them, leadership implied ruling or reigning, not becoming a servant. However, real leadership in God's kingdom is contrary to the world's evaluation of leadership. In God's kingdom, it comes down to having a right disposition.

Even though we are all servants, developing a disposition of servitude is one of the greatest struggles. The disposition of servitude is totally contrary to arrogant, self-sufficient man who desires to be served rather than serve. Servitude speaks of humility and meekness. Neither of these qualities come naturally. Jesus had to take on a lesser state in order to display true meekness, while He learned obedience through suffering.[9]

For people to take on a different state, they have to become spiritual, cringing beggars in the kingdom of God. Jesus established this fact in Matthew 5:3 when He stated that, "Blessed are the poor in spirit; for theirs is the kingdom of heaven." "Poor" in this Scripture means cringing beggar.[10] This state implies that a person recognizes their true spiritual condition. As a result, their perspective changes.

Jesus took on the form of a servant, but He walked this servitude out as man. He allowed Himself to be fashioned as a

---

[9] Matthew 11:29: Hebrews 5:8
[10] Strong's Exhaustive Concordance # 4434

man. In essence, He submitted everything about His life to the Father. This made Him a vessel in the Father's hands. It was the Father who decided His purpose on earth. Jesus carried a life-changing message. He became the living example of what is righteous, and finally, He allowed Himself to be offered up as a sacrifice in line with the Father's will.

The Word of God tells us that man is nothing more than a clay vessel. We will serve as vessels of honor or dishonor in the hands of God. Many people take pride in the fact that God once used them. The fact that God will use us, in spite of the type of vessel we appear to be, means little. The key is, what kind of vessel are we before God? Perhaps we have been refined in the fire as gold because of our faith, silver due to realizing His redemption in greater ways, or precious stones as He places us in His Body for His glory. Maybe our works will melt in the fire because there is no real substance to endure such adversity. We may get into heaven, but there will be no works to cast before God's feet as crowns for His glory.[11]

The potter forms vessels for a particular purpose. The status and appearance of these vessels have little significance as long as they are shaped for the job that they have been designated for. These vessels may be unusual, unassuming, or insignificant, but once the potter takes them in hand, they become necessary, important, and beneficial to others.

For the vessel to be used in honorable ways, it must be submitted to the Potter's hands. It must accept the lengthy process to prepare it to be a vessel of honor. It must face the fires of adversity and rejection. It must become of no importance, to be made insignificant according to the world's perspective. It must be willing to lose its contents on a daily basis, as the life of Jesus is poured out in others for His glory and honor.

---

[11] Romans 9:20-22; 1 Corinthians 3:11-15; 2 Corinthians 4:7; 2 Timothy 2:19-21

Finally, I realized that I was to be His instrument. As a servant, I am to do His bidding. As a vessel, I am to carry that which must be poured out daily into others. But, as an instrument, I must be ready to be used at all times. Perhaps, I will be an instrument that will sing praises unto God for others to hear of His majesty. Maybe, at another time, I will be an instrument that will challenge hearts, contend for lost souls, encourage struggling souls, or edify the members of Jesus' body. Perhaps, the Lord wants me to sit at His feet and simply enjoy Him. The Apostle Paul put it this way in Romans 6:13: "Neither yield ye your members as instruments of unrighteousness unto sin: but yield yourselves unto God, as those that are alive from the dead, and your members as instruments of righteousness unto God."

As a servant, I must obey. As a vessel, I am to give way to the Great Potter, but as an instrument, I must yield. This implies total abandonment to the will of God. In essence, as a servant of the King of kings and the Lord of lords, I must serve as an empty vessel and a righteous instrument. In God, I have no status other than that I belong to Him and am available to do whatever He bids me to do. I do not question, debate, or use logic with Him, for He is the Master and Potter, and will utilize my life according to His heart, purpose, and plan.

As I considered my Christian life, I could see how I complicated my life in God because I failed to see the simplicity of His life, will, and call. This complication created spiritual prisons and dots. These prisons and dots had clouded my position in God with the interpretation of man, the philosophies of the world, and the influences of the culture. However, when Jesus became real, His simplicity became a key that began to set me free from the bondage.

The final part of this puzzle is that I realized that it matters little how others may respond to me. God uses His different vessels to test the hearts of others. The issue in God's kingdom is not the type of vessel He uses. Rather, what matters is if the vessel is speaking forth His truths. If God is using the vessel to challenge, test, and instruct, it is up to His people to humble themselves and receive from that vessel, regardless of the vessel's outward status. To fail to discern if something is of God in this matter not only stipulates an arrogant heart, but judgmentalism that will eventually expose and become a point of judgment towards the individual's heart.

It has been a glorious freedom. I have been able to accept my position in Christ without all the debates and doubts since it often goes against the normal way of doing things. It has allowed me to enjoy the Father as a child, walk with Jesus as a friend, and allow the Holy Ghost to be a constant, abiding companion.

What about you? Do you have such liberty or has your life been complicated? Do you know your place in Christ or are you being defined by every other source? Know that your spiritual search can only come to an end when you find your place in Jesus.

Let Jesus' words serve as an inspiration to you,

Let not your heart be troubled: ye believe in God, believe also in me. In my Father's house are many mansions: if it were not so, I would have told you. I go to prepare a place for you. And if I go and prepare a place for you, I will come again, and receive you unto myself; that where I am, there ye may be also (John 14:1-3).

10

COMING BACK TO CENTER

One of the hardest struggles in my spiritual walk has been to maintain balance. The natural tendencies of the old man are to go into extremes with everything that feels good or appears to work. Perhaps this is why the Apostle Paul instructed believers to do all things in moderation.[1]

In my initial years as a Christian, I had become extremely judgmental and legalistic about what I considered to be acceptable. Each new extreme brought me to the end of myself to reveal hypocrisy and arrogance. During a vulnerable time of growth and struggle, God began to reveal how my relationship with Him affected my disposition, attitudes, and conduct.

During the last couple of years of my marriage, my world began to gradually spin out of control. Eventually, nothing made sense. It was during that time in my life that I learned to cling to God. This was important because everything was being called into question. My Christianity was being assaulted, my reality was often mocked, my struggles were used against me, my sanity was questioned, and my reputation was being offered up. I couldn't trust anything about my reality except God.

There were times that I had to choose to believe and trust God's character even though I saw hopelessness in front of me

---

[1] Philippians 4:5

and my feelings were going in every direction. Even though my world was caving in, the immovable Rock of Ages remained sure and strong. In spite of the darkness that surrounded me, I chose to believe that God was near. Without realizing it, the reality of God was taking root in me in greater measure. God was going deeper to bring me higher. At times, I felt like I stood at the very edge of the abyss. Fear would grip me, but I would look up to sense that God was gently guiding me on the narrow path. At other times, I sensed His presence, while in uncertain times He seemed distant and unaware. However, I would choose to believe that He was still very much involved in my life.

Although the occasion of my divorce was a frightening time for me, it was also a time of growth and preparation. God had to go deeper with me in order to reveal what needed to be the center of my life. For most of us, we would quickly shrug such a challenge off because as Christians we can quickly answer the question. God must be the center of every believer's life.

However, passing the test in the kingdom of God is not a matter of answering the question right. Passing the test actually hinges on whether a truth becomes a reality. Otherwise, it remains a simple assumption that has no life or power behind it.

Before one of God's truths can take on dimension, it must become revelation to a person's heart. The only way a truth of God can become revelation is for the Holy Spirit to reveal it to our spirit. Once a revelation is unveiled, a person must walk it out in practical ways to make it a personal reality. Reality implies that one has experienced the humbling impact of this truth in a way that changed how they now perceive God. As a person's perception of God enlarges, spiritual growth takes place.

I knew God needed to be the center of my life, but what does that mean in practical terms? It was not enough to understand it. After all, understanding something does not make it a reality. In fact, intellectual understanding can create its own reality, making the individual indifferent to actual reality around them. A good example of this is when people test themselves according to what they know about God, rather than by their fruits. Fruits are what constitute the actual reality in regards to a person's spiritual condition.

Eventually, the Holy Ghost imparted revelation into my spirit in regards to God being the center of my life. He used the small book of Haggai. God made this statement through His prophet Haggai, "Now therefore thus saith the LORD of hosts; Consider your ways" (Haggai 1:5). He not only said this once, but twice.[2] "Consider" in this text means coming back to center.[3]

The children of Israel had been in captivity in Babylon for 70 years. The prophet Jeremiah had prophesied this because they had not allowed the land to rest during the Sabbath year for 490 years. This meant they failed to let the land rest every seventh year. As a result, God caused Israel to go into captivity to allow the land to rest for every Sabbath year that it was overtaxed by the disobedient children of Israel.[4]

After seventy years, some of the children of Israel came back to Jerusalem. This city, along with the temple that God had put His name on, laid in total ruin. For years, the temple had represented the presence of God in the midst of Israel. It had served as the center of all religious activity for the children of Israel. Although God had lifted His presence from the temple due to idolatry and wickedness, the temple still represented His name. When some of the children of Israel returned to Jerusalem, they not only had the task of rebuilding the city, but the temple.

The first course of action for the children of Israel upon their return to Jerusalem should have been to reestablish the representation of God in the Promised Land. This would have

---

[2] Haggai 1:7
[3] Strong's Exhaustive Concordance, # 3820
[4] 2 Chronicles 36:21; Jeremiah 25:11-12: 29:20; 34:13-22: Daniel 9:2

116

been the means of reestablishing the center of their life to ensure God's blessing. Sadly, other than the foundation, the temple was put off. The center of their lives remained missing from their activities.

When the center is missing, there is no point of stability and testing. Granted, people's activities might start from the point of necessity, such as houses and crops, but eventually these activities will change emphasis. In the case of the children of Israel, this emphasis graduated from necessity of establishing their basic needs and escalated into the pursuing and securing of abundance.

As I studied Haggai, I realized that one's center is determined by one's priorities. Obviously, God was not the priority of Israel. This is a grave tragedy. The children of Israel not only came back to reestablish their presence in the land, but also the representation of Jehovah God in their midst. After all, Jehovah God is the one who gave them life, identity, and distinction. It was Jehovah God who designated and secured the land for them. It was Jehovah God who blessed them. Yet, He was missing from their activities. No doubt, they religiously tacked Him on to their lives, but His visible presence was missing.

It is easy to be condemning towards the children of Israel, but how guilty are Christians for not ensuring that the center of their lives is God and not personal pursuits, agendas, and activities? In our religious zeal we can tack Him on to our activities like Israel. We can convince ourselves that He is in His rightful place, when in reality, He is missing. Obviously, God's absence will be blatant, but there are always the excuses as to why God's temple lies in ruin, as we establish our physical lives.[5]

The children of Israel stated that it was not the right time to build the Lord's house. My question is, when will it be the right

---

[5] Haggai 1:2; Matthew 22:2-13

time to build God's house? In the case of Christians, when is the right time for each of us to establish our life in God? After all, as believers, we all serve as His individual temples.[6] As a result, when will be the right time to make sure God is the center of our decisions, goals, and activities?

What were the children of Israel waiting for before they would finally ensure that God's representation was in their midst? Were they trying to build a home? According to Haggai, they were dwelling in paneled houses, while His house lay in ruin. Were they preparing the land for crops? According to the prophet, they not only had the land prepared, but they had sown much.[7] Therefore, what was their excuse? Everything was in order as far as their physical needs, but the center of their well-being was still missing. Obviously, they were spiritually vulnerable.

God was not their main priority; therefore, His house could be put off to another day. How many people are playing Russian roulette with their souls, as they put God off in regards to their salvation? How many Christians are living on the abyss of ruin, as they put off establishing God as the center of all of their lives and activities?

The Holy Ghost was reaching through years of history into my heart with the challenge of Haggai. "Consider your ways, Rayola. Consider your priorities, disposition, goals, and direction. Where is God in your priorities? Is everything in your life tested, adjusted, and lined up to His character? In other words, are your ways, God's ways?"

When you study the children of Israel, they erred in their hearts. This error occurred when they failed to first enter the Promised Land because they were ignorant of God's ways. Ignorance of God's ways simply means that you do not know God. As a result, the children of Israel walked in unbelief before God,

---

[6] Haggai 1:2; 1 Corinthians 3:16; 6:19
[7] Haggai 1:4, 6

as they walked according to their ways. I began to understand that I am in "a way," but am I in the "way of Christ?" If I am in the way of Christ, He will always lead me back in faith to the character and Person of God.[8]

The counselor of my soul began to reveal my priorities.[9] I was surprised at how selfish, self-centered, and self-serving they were. I did much for the purpose of receiving personal glory. I would strive to get recognition, and I often did only that which served my purpose. As the Holy Ghost stripped me of each layer of self, I had to face the harsh fact that God was not always the center of my activities. I failed to go to Him about some decisions. I never considered Him in my outside activities. I rarely regarded Him in light of my pursuits. Although God was the center of my world at times, He was crowded out by activities that I presently deemed important.

The children of Israel had failed to erect God's house, and now they were paying the consequences. Haggai gives us this insight in Haggai 1:6, "Ye have sown much, and bring in little; ye eat, but ye have not enough; ye drink, but ye are not filled with drink; ye clothe you, but there is none warm; and he that earneth wages earneth wages to put it into a bag with holes." The children of Israel were living for themselves. They had sown in abundance, but they were now reaping leanness from their activities. This must have been defeating, but what did they expect? God was missing.

Through the years, I have encountered many people who have sown much in personal pursuits as they played the harlot with the world. They also chased after the illusive carrot of personal happiness and success, only to reap leanness, defilement, and hopelessness of soul. Instead of realizing that they were reaping fruits according to the flesh and not the Spirit, they become angry

---

[8] John 14:6: Hebrews 3:20, 12-13, 18-19
[9] John 16:7-13

at God. How could God allow this poverty, sin, and consequences to overtake them? However, the reality was that God was missing. If He were present and leading the person, they would have been in "a different way," investing in their life in a righteous manner, while experiencing the abiding protection and blessing of God.[10]

God sent a physical drought to reveal a spiritual drought that existed in the children of Israel's spiritual life. Heaven kept its dew back, just as the children of Israel reserved the right to determine when God's house would be built. The earth kept back her fruit, just as the people of Israel decided that other things were more important than God.[11]

This drought not only affected the land, but the mountains, corn, wine, and oil. The situation was dismal. The land kept back the fruits, the mountains failed to yield living water, the corn lacked nourishment, the wine had no ability to bring joy to the heart, and the oil could not anoint.

As you consider this scenario, you can see how a spiritual drought affects God's people. Our lives become unproductive in His harvest field. There is no living water to revive or refresh. The things we partake of have no lasting substance to spiritually maintain us. The wine that brings joy is missing because salvation seems far from us. The anointing is absent; therefore, there is no power or authority.

As I considered my life, I could see where I suffered such spiritual droughts. I had taken detours away from the center, only to encounter insufferable prisons. I had chased after many illusive carrots, only to end up with vanity. These prisons and dots caused me to realize that only God makes sense. However, is He truly my center? Do I love Him with all of my heart? Do I desire Him to be my all in all? Do I live to worship Him with every breath? Is He

---

[10] Galatians 7-8; James 4:4
[11] Haggai 1:9-11

truly the center of my life, where every way that I walk in will automatically lead me back to Him as being the director of it?

In this examination of my life, I could see His faithfulness to use the droughts in my life to bring me back to Him to revive me. As Jesus said in John 7:37, "If any man thirst, let him come unto me, and drink."

The Holy Ghost used the book of Haggai to establish a simple reality. God must be at the center of all that I do to ensure balance in my life. If I begin to operate in the extreme, it is because I have gotten out of the way of Jesus. God's instruction to Israel to remedy the drought was simple, "Go up to the mountain, and bring wood, and build the house; and I will take pleasure in it, and I will be glorified, saith the LORD" (Haggai 1:8).

In order to come back to the way of God, we must accept Jesus' invitation to come higher. We must get beyond ourselves to reach higher to receive His perspective. We need to bring our lives to God and offer them up freely, so that He can be established in our midst. This will allow Him to take pleasure in us, as He is glorified by His presence and reality in our lives.

When was the last time you considered your ways before God? What would they declare about you? Would you find extremes operating in your life because God is not in His rightful place, or would you find balance, because He is the center of your life in every possible way?

11

THE WALK

What is Christianity? My initial introduction to Christianity was going to church, reading the Bible, and praying. However, I realized that I simply sat in my pew in church to receive from God's servants, but there was no evidence of outward commitment or devotion.

As I read the Bible, I sat at His table, so the Holy Spirit imparted in me the truths of God. Prayer required some effort on my part, but it was about seeking God's face in order to discover His heart. Although these things are very important in their own right, each aspect benefited my personal spiritual survival and growth. I came to the realization that all of these activities were about me and not God.

Although my initial goal in being involved in these activities was to discover what God wanted me to know, none of them really benefited Him. As I studied aspects about the Christian life, I began to realize that the purpose for my life on earth was to bring glory to God.[1] It dawned on me that most of my Christian existence had never gotten past the self-serving stage in order to really bring glory to the One who deserved honor. It also occurred to me that most of my struggles, spiritual leanness, and stagnation were due to this self-centered emphasis.

---

[1] Matthew 5:16

Obviously, I had to get beyond my religious comfort zones if I was to ever discover the depths of God. What would this entail? It would mean coming to terms with what I valued. What I valued would determine my dependency. To expose my value system and to understand how if affected me, I would have to consider not only Jesus' words, but also His examples. The Apostle John put it in this perspective in 1 John 2:6, "He that saith he abideth in him ought himself also so to walk, even as he walked."

As I considered my Christianity, much of it had simply been head knowledge. This knowledge had fed my pride, but it had not enlarged my soul or changed my heart.[2] As I studied the concept of 1 John 2:6, I realized that God's truths had never become reality to my heart because I had never walked them out.

Christianity is not a passive life, but an active life. This life does not consist of only plush pews, chairs for the audience, and elaborate sound and light systems, but it is full of obstacles that must be overcome. There are trenches that must be explored for the purpose of locating wounded soldiers and crossing valleys of humiliation that will leave you uncertain. The key about each of these areas is that it requires you to first walk out your life in God before you can encounter and walk through such challenging arenas.

At this point, I realized that I was walking on a path towards a destination. I was aware of the broad road that leads to destruction. Sadly, people walk this path without realizing that they are moving towards an eternal destination. On the other hand, it appears that some Christians are not aware that they are on a path or in the way of something either. They give the impression that they are riding an unseen mode of transportation that is automatically taking them to heaven. They do not seem to realize

---

[2] 1 Corinthians 8:1-2

that Christianity is a daily walk that involves self-denial, picking up the cross, and following Jesus.[3]

Jesus left believers two examples—that of servitude and suffering. It is easy to talk about being a servant, but hard to practice the lifestyle. To be a servant, one must develop a right disposition. As believers, we can talk about going all the way for Christ, but our claims are often based on inexperience. The Christian walk is a hard walk. Those who walk it out will suffer opposition and persecution.[4] Ultimately, it will test character and devotion. Acts 14:22 summarizes this walk, "Confirming the souls of the disciples, and exhorting them to continue in the faith, and that we must through much tribulation enter into the kingdom of God."

"Confirm" means to reestablish, strengthen, and support.[5] Christians must avoid making assumptions about souls. They must be active in assuring that souls are clearly established in God's kingdom. They must exhort God's people to continue in the real faith, and that the only way to enter into the kingdom of God is through much tribulation. Obviously, the Christian walk is not a cakewalk. It involves intense struggle and travail.[6]

For believers, the way is Christ and the narrow entrance begins with His cross and redemption. Past this straight entrance is the narrow path that leads to worship and communion with God. It is on this path that salvation is worked in lives, as followers are transformed within. This transformation allows God to work salvation through their lives, as they become His vessels. Once this salvation is manifested in His followers' lives through love, service, and sacrifice, God will be glorified.

---

[3] Matthew 7:13-14; Luke 9:23
[4] John 13:12-15; 15:18-20; 2 Timothy 3:12; 1 Peter 2:21
[5] Strong's Exhaustive Concordance
[6] Luke 13:24

The secret a person must discover is that not only are people in a way, but they are walking their life out according to the dictates and boundaries of the path they are on. What path was I on? It is easy for each of us as believers to take so much for granted. I could assume that I was walking in the narrow way of Christ, but what if I was deluding myself? I had to come to terms with the Christian walk. This involved studying the life of Jesus. Where did Jesus tread? Where did the way lead Him? Where did the boundaries of this path ultimately direct His steps?

I followed Jesus' life from obscurity to baptism. From there, He was led into the wilderness where He was tempted, but He overcame. From that point, His ministry began. At first, He was popular as people benefitted from His miracles and stood in awe of His simple, but profound teachings. There was something fresh, true, and real about Jesus. Most were willing to follow Him to discover His secret. However, there was no secret to His success. He knew the Father. He lived a life in subjection to the Father's will. He never strayed from the path that was set before Him. As He drew closer and closer to His final destination of the cross, He became more determined to be offered up on the altar.[7]

We can romanticize about Jesus' life, but there was no glamour in it. Granted, there was power that inspired, teachings that astounded, and examples that drew people, but most of Jesus' life was spent in obscurity.

Obscurity implies drudgery and is devoid of personal honor or exaltation. "Obscurity" means that you are hidden away. What was happening in Jesus' life during that obscurity? Obviously, as Man, Jesus was getting to know His Father in an intimate way. He was being prepared to walk this path, as His life brightly shined for a short season, and then, He would be offered up for man's benefit and God's glory.

---

[7] Matthew 7:29; 4:1-14; Luke 9:51

It is noble to declare that we want to serve God, but are we willing to pay the price in obscurity to know God? The irony in all of this is that most people's perception of the Christian walk is breezing over the obscurity part to ministry. The truth is that one must walk through the formidable shadows of obscurity before they can walk in the light and exaltation of God's authority, power, and glory.

A minister introduced me to that glorious aspect of walking in the light of God's glory during a meeting at my local church. I was impressed with his testimonies about God's constant intervention when he was in the harvest field in Russia before the Iron Curtain came down. However, something else struck me about this saint—He knew God in a way that few know Him. In fact, I had never met an individual who knew God like this man did. I was impressed with the miracles he described, but I was especially awed by this man's relationship with God.

It was obvious in this saint's mannerism, attitude, and authority that he knew how to get a hold of the Lord. I wanted what this man had. I realized that God had to go deeper with me in order for me to speak with the same type of authority. That night, I committed my total life to God. Although I was married and saw no real way to experience this life, I could not settle for being a pew warmer, a nominal Christian, or someone who was content doing good deeds. I wanted more of God, and I knew that only He could make a way for me.

At the time, I did not realize that what I would be embarking upon was something known as the walk of faith. The Apostle Paul tells us that we are to walk by faith and not by sight.[8] There have been many times when I automatically quoted that Scripture to people, who were in utter darkness about their life in God. As I meditated on it, I realized that we all walk by sight without knowing

---

it. For example, we walk according to our understanding, feelings, standards, and ideas. We walk according to what we already know or perceive, but faith is beyond such fleshly calculations.

Faith is when you walk according to the character of God and the truths of His Word. At this point, you are not walking according to what you perceive as reality. Rather, you are trusting God's evaluation about a matter. It is not making intellectual assumptions about matters, but praying about everything to gain His perspective. This is how one becomes totally dependent on God. Some matters may seem simple enough, but by applying the ways of God in a situation, you add the element of eternity. There is something about the eternal perspective that will clearly change earthly approaches and understanding. In fact, you begin to recognize that you really are limited in your perception and calculations about all matters.

There was something else that I was keenly aware of about this desire. God had put it in my heart not to settle for less. I could not feel noble or declare spirituality because I wanted more of God. It was His doing. Now, I had to submit myself to Him by faith for Him to open the way for me to experience this life.

Eventually, the door opened for me to embark on this life. The first lesson I had to learn was that I had no faith. God had to give me a measure of faith to even take the next step. As I took the next step, He was able to meet me in my walk to endow me with more faith. However, I noted that He only gave me enough faith to take the next step.

These steps taught me some very important truths about faith. As Christians, we talk about justification and righteousness due to faith, but how many of us really understand the implication of faith in these areas? Justification means that we will be accepted just as we are when we come to the cross of Jesus by faith. It is here our search for forgiveness and initial salvation ends.

However, righteousness is different from justification. Justification is obtained when a person believes in their heart what Jesus did on the cross. However, righteousness must be imputed to a person.[9] This occurs when a person by faith counts all that God says as true and responds in obedience. As a Christian takes a step of obedient faith in confidence, God is able to count it as righteousness. Since it is considered righteousness, God is able to meet and honor the person in their life.

I did believe God's Word was true, but it was limited as to the affect it had on my life. The only way to enlarge its impact was for my faith to be tried by fire.[10] These fires came soon enough. To my surprise, much of what I believed had little dimension to it. I recognized that many of God's truths and principles were not reality to me, but just a matter of mental exaltation of concepts and facts.

The initial fiery trials of my faith proved to be unnerving and humbling as I failed the test each time. I was shocked to find out how shallow I was in this area. In reality, I still did not know the character of God in the way I needed to. I had prided myself on the concept of faith, but when tested, much of my actual walk was devoid of it.

One of my favorite Scriptures in the Bible is Galatians 2:20, "I am crucified with Christ: nevertheless I live; yet not I, but Christ liveth in me: and the life which I now live in the flesh I live by the faith of the Son of God, who loved me, and gave himself for me." I have often talked about how Christians must cease to live according to their old way of doing, but it is easy to overlook what it means to walk out the new life. It comes down to walking out this life according to the faith a believer must choose to have in the Son of God.

---

[9] Romans 4:22-23
[10] 1 Peter 1:6-9

Christianity has largely been demoted to terms, concepts, and ideas, but it is so much more. It is a walk and a way of living. It is an expression of the life of Jesus. The more a person is dead to self, the greater the reality of Jesus. However, this reality must be walked out in faith or confidence that His words, examples, and instructions are true and are of vital importance for our life. This walk is about apprehending the ultimate prize. It is about possessing the true treasure of heaven, Jesus Christ.

When I started my faith walk, I had no idea how little I really knew God. I had a lot of head knowledge about God and some life-changing encounters with Him, but I had not experienced Him in my walk. I had been self-sufficient and independent in my life; therefore, I never realized my need to learn total dependency on Him for all of my needs.

I marvel at how patient God was when I first started out on this new adventure. There are many times when I acted like a spoiled-rotten American in my times of testing. It took three years for God to get me past the initial stage of me, myself, and I to experience His incredible character. It was then that I learned that faith is about letting God be God in your life. In fact, real faith is about what God wants to accomplish in you in order for Him to be glorified in the circumstances.[11]

It was not until years later that I understood that the display of faith on my part allowed God to show me His incredible faithfulness. So many times I was faithless, but He was faithful to show the commitment He had towards me. It was His abiding faithfulness that allowed my faith to mature in my Christian life. This maturity not only developed a greater testimony in me of His unchangeable character and ways, but it also brought me higher in my understanding of Him.

---

[11] For more insight on the author's walk of faith, see her book, *In Search of Real Faith* in Volume 2 of her foundational series.

It has been a challenging walk, but I would not exchange it. I really do like my life in Christ. It has meaning and purpose. I have witnessed miracles and partaken of His promises. The greatest advantage of this life is that I do know God. He has become my abiding confidence that never moves from that which is right and acceptable.

Through the years, the Apostle Paul's words in 2 Timothy 2:11-13 began to summarize my understanding about what I have learned through this growth, "It is a faithful saying: For if we be dead with him, we shall also live with him: If we suffer, we shall also reign with him: If we deny him, he also will deny us: If we believe not, yet he abideth faithful: he cannot deny himself."

12

CHARACTER

The faith walk was a trying experience. It would reveal my heart and attitudes. My heart was sincere towards God, but my attitudes illuminated that there were inconsistencies in my Christian life. As I struggled with the different challenges the faith walk produced, I began to recognize it was exposing the caliber of my character. In many situations the challenges actually revealed that I was a hypocrite.

Oswald Chambers stated that character determines the revelation of God.[1] I had some revelation in the past, but I was aware that God wanted me to have a deeper sense of who He is. Sadly, you rarely hear about character, yet it determines the quality and strength of your life.

In my senior year of high school, I had been awarded the "I Dare You" award. It was a challenging book about character. I had always perceived myself as being of good character. Although some of my actions called my conclusions into judgment, I felt that I had tried to be honest when confronting life. I didn't realize that character entails more than honesty or even moral conduct. For example, spiritual character could be described in one word—integrity.

---

[1] Daily Thought for Disciples; © 1990 by Oswald Chambers Publications
Association, August 4 devotion

Character is not something we are born with. It must be formed in us. It would be nice to think that God forms the character. But this is not correct. He often sends the circumstances that can produce character, but it is actually developed as an individual makes right decisions.

Right decisions go against the natural scheme of things. They challenge the grain of a person's fallen condition. In other words, they challenge the preferences of darkness. They shake a person's way of seeing, thinking, and doing. And, whenever character is formed, it is often in the midst of chaos. Nothing makes sense as the person's life before God is being tested. Regardless of the circumstances, will the individual choose to do right or will they give in to the preference of escaping reality by making excuses or running away from the challenge?

This was the first indication that character is a choice. Character will choose to do right, establishing integrity. Integrity was accredited to King David in 1 Kings 9,

> And it thou wilt walk before me as David thy father walked, in the integrity of heart, and in uprightness, to do according to all that I have commanded thee, and wilt keep my statutes and judgments: Then I will establish the throne of thy kingdom upon Israel for ever (I Kings 9:4-5a).

Integrity is associated with the heart. As I studied the word "integrity," I found that it points to perfection.[2] "Perfection" means mature or complete but points to the fact that everything is done out of a pure heart. Spiritual maturity or completion is developed or realized when a person is doing the will of God.

My secular dictionary defined integrity as soundness, incorruptibility, a state of being complete, or undivided.[3] I began to see that my heart may have been pure before God, but it was

---

[2] Strong's Exhaustive Concordance; #8537
[3] Webster's New Collegiate Dictionary

not sound or complete. This caused the inconsistencies in my Christian life.

What did it mean for my heart to be sound or undivided? As I considered my life, I realized that I had played games with people to get my way. The Lord had already revealed the treachery of my games. But I never realized the extent of such treachery. In my mind, I had played the game to keep the peace. To me, this reasoning seemed quite noble. After all, I was coming into subjection to what I considered to be unreasonable demands from others, for the sake of peace.

It dawned on me that this nobility was not my true motivation. My motive was nothing more than selfishness. I hated confrontation, and avoidance of it was my way of becoming a suffering martyr, while trying to maintain my so-called dignity and control. Although my goal was to keep the "sleeping beast" at bay, I had simply prolonged many of the problems that had plagued my life. These problems turned into tidal waves. To survive each tidal wave, I was eventually forced to face each one. Sadly, my games not only prolonged the inevitable, but they allowed each tidal wave to gain momentum. By the time these waves landed, they left devastation in their wake.

The Lord was impressing upon me that I needed to face my problems and learn the lessons of life to keep them from becoming unresolved issues. If I faced each problem head on, I would actually take the power out of their influence to take root and bring destruction. If I learned the lessons, I would never feel that my detours in life were a complete waste. These measures would keep these unresolved issues from developing into tidal waves of frustration, anger, and depression.

I had learned to face most of my challenges up front. I knew that games were treacherous, making people unstable in their motives and actions. I was also aware that such games were also foolish for they are always based on fantasy and unrealistic expectations. But I had not come to terms with the underlying motives of these games.

Each right decision uncovered another aspect of my games. To reveal this final aspect of them, the Lord used another game player to show the real insidious side of how they impact the lives of others. This individual had appeared to be a sweet, committed Christian. We had admired her and relied on her wisdom to speak into our lives. Eventually I began to notice that there were inconsistencies in her life. These inconsistencies did not have to do with personality or manners. This person actually displayed a pleasant personality and impeccable manners.

The problem with her inconsistencies is that they set off my spiritual alarms. Outwardly, she was a picture of what many would consider as being exemplary Christianity. As I stood back to discern, I received mixed messages. This means that even though something appears proper, there can be a wrong spirit. A wrong spirit will cause confusion.

Confusion in this sense will automatically make you doubt your own conclusions to a matter. You will find yourself examining your motive to make sure you are not jealous or just being judgmental about your concerns. You also must consider whether Satan is trying to cause division through lies and false accusations.

I often went back to the drawing board to try to map the events or situations to see if there was a problem in the person's life or with my own attitude. Each time, I concluded there was something amiss in her life. The more I was involved with her, the more I became irritated. The irritation became so great, I closed down to ignore how it was affecting me. Even in this state, I felt like I was being pushed.

Finally, one day I decided I had had enough. Confrontation is a quick way to expose everything that has been operating in darkness. Interestingly, this woman played her hand. I have to admit that I was surprised to see what was behind her. She had a great deal of self-righteous pride which made her the judge of all who failed to live up to her example of Christianity. She had a religious spirit that was deluding her about her level of spirituality and her maturity. Since she saw herself as superior, she had not only been judging me, but others. She felt she had insightful wisdom into our problems and failures in our spiritual lives.

As I thought about her, I could see where she had an outward compliance, but inwardly, she was arrogant. She thought herself to be superior to those who did not exhibit her calmness and sweetness. Her superiority reeked with incredible arrogance. Suddenly, I realized that she was trying to draw people to her, rather than to Jesus. I also began to see how she subtly played the Holy Ghost in people's lives. Obviously, she either had to come out as the exalted Savior or as the victim who silently suffered in her fake nobility.

As I considered all of these factors, the last curtain parted to reveal the underlying motives of the games people play—that of control and manipulation. I never realized that I had played games to control my world and manipulate people. Even though I prided myself in being as honest as I could, I still tried to control my reality by the type of emphasis I put on words. My twist of reality helped me to avoid dealing in reality about myself.

At first, I was shocked to discover this harsh truth. Until Jesus got a hold of me, everything had been about me. Although I thought myself to be quite noble in my motives, I was self-serving. Being self-serving made me dishonorable and untrustworthy.

Even though the Bible tells us there is no good thing in us, we have a hard time believing it. We choose to believe our reasoning that will always put the blame elsewhere. We agree with our logic that justifies and whitewashes our selfishness. We want to believe that we are noble, so we delude ourselves to our self-serving motives.

It is only when we truly agree with God's evaluation about the selfish disposition within each of us that integrity can take place. Up until that time, there is a great battle with truth. The truth is, there is "no good thing in us."[4] The reality is that every day our thoughts and motives will confirm this harsh reality.

The tragedy is few will turn around and face such indicators. Most continue to delude themselves about their so-called "goodness," as well as their wretched state. For example, some people wear their wretchedness as a badge of courage or honor. Consider how noble they are in being honest. This type of nobility becomes a point of personal goodness. As long as there is a concept or appearance of personal goodness, a person can maintain their dignity. However, there is no dignity in sin, delusion, treachery, or game playing. Therefore, as an individual maintains any concept of personal goodness or dignity, they will walk in darkness, ignorance, delusion, and rebellion.

The Lord faithfully showed me my wretchedness. I was appalled at my motives, repulsed by my way of thinking, and disgusted with my way of being. There was no way around it. I was in trouble unless I agreed with God's evaluation and repented of my wicked, fleshly ways.

Once I agreed with God about His conclusion of my spiritual condition, integrity started to be established in my heart. I recognized that it was not enough to be honest about things or sincere towards God. I had to have integrity to make my heart sound, my character consistent, and my ways sure before God.

To have integrity required me to come to terms with the characteristics of integrity. I have met people who perceived that they had integrity. Yet, they very much lacked it by how they handled the challenges of life.

---

[4] Romans 3:10; 7:18

The first characteristic of integrity is that it is teachable. It neglects pride to ensure humility. It denies self in order to give way to submission to what is right. It is willing to be wrong in order to be made right.

The second characteristic of integrity is truth. It insists on possessing truth. In order to accomplish this, it must regard personal conclusions as vain. It must hold opinions lightly until they can be established as truth in the right spirit. Integrity faces reality with clarity and honesty. It does not ignore problems, hide from challenges, or operate in darkness to maintain control. It displays godly wisdom that is founded upon the fear of the Lord.

Sobriety is the third quality of integrity. Sobriety implies wisdom. Wisdom considers everything from God's perspective, while applying it to matters of life in practical ways. It regards all fantasy as foolishness and immaturity. It avoids extremes as it maintains balance. Sobriety cannot be easily moved, nor will it compromise that which is holy and pleasing to God. It always calls the individual to be vigilant in their way of thinking, being, and doing.[5]

The final quality is righteousness. Integrity will result in upright conduct. It is morally responsible and spiritually accountable. It will strive to come into perfection or maturity in God. It will walk in confidence before Him. Ultimately, it will be recognized and honored by God. Psalm 7:8 says, "The LORD shall judge the people: judge me, O LORD, according to my righteousness, and according to mine integrity that is in me."

As I considered my life, I could see how God put it within my heart to be a person of integrity. It is true that I had to purpose in my heart to not play games with others.[6] I had to honestly face reality and make the right decisions to have integrity formed in me. However, God still put it in my heart to desire Him over my way of

---

[5] 1 Peter 5:8
[6] Daniel 1:8

living. He still puts it within my heart to pursue Him, no matter what obstacles I encounter. He also is the one who puts in my heart the need to look to Him regardless of the circumstances.

Developing character was not always easy. There are many times I could have complied in order to play games to get my purpose served. It is sad that most people prefer that you play the game. By playing the game, it puts you on equal footing with them in their compromise. It often feeds their ego, while benefiting you in some way. Everyone appears to win, while people take their respective places in the scheme of things. Sadly, no one wins because truth is missing. Without truth, people are walking in delusion towards destruction.

Character was also developed in me when I had to redo the same projects over and over until I felt I was giving my best to God. I cannot tell you how many times I wanted to throw up my hands. Everything I was involved with required me to go beyond limitations, push past excuses, and persevere until something was as right as I could get it. For example, the Discipleship Course was typed four times before we were comfortable with it. I redid the workbook for the seminars at least four times. I had to wait 18 years before seeing completion of my first book. Then, I still had to rewrite it.

I cannot tell you how many projects I had to redo and how long I had to wait to see them completed. Each time I managed to gain a few feet, I was knocked back at least ten feet. Every accomplishment involved intense battles. Instead of enjoying them, I simply thanked God for His faithfulness through the long periods of development and travail. Through this character building, I learned that eternal accomplishments are always purified in the fires of waiting, affliction, and tribulation.

Not only did I learn patience, but after much struggle how to wait in quietness and confidence before God. After all, it was His business. Like King David and the cup of water from the

Bethlehem well that was sacrificially obtained in the fierce battle, each accomplishment was offered up to God for His glory and use.[7] The intensity of each accomplishment made me realize that it had to be offered back to God, for He is the only one who is worthy of such sacrifices and glory.

As I considered how character was forged in me, I began to realize that it was the work of sanctification. The Holy Ghost had to put fire to every aspect of my character to work godly integrity in me. I began to recognize that the character that was being worked in me actually belonged to the character of Jesus. As His character was worked in me, godliness became a natural response. Today, I do not have to think about what is right. Now I know. Doing right is no longer a big self-serving debate, but in many arenas, it has become a natural response.

Through all of this, it has occurred to me that character has given me the freedom to discover my life in Jesus. It has become an avenue where my personality has been refined. I do not have to put on any show or try to maintain consistency in my claims and thoughts.

Through all of my struggles, the refinement of my character has proven to be a glorious, rewarding time for me. How about you? Do you possess the character of Jesus or the twisted character of the old man? Do you have the freedom to be all that God wants you to be or are you contending with bondage in your life? Do you have the strength of Christ or the false sufficiency of the old man? It is vital that godly character be established in you, so that you can stand in the times of grave testing and withstand adversity.

---

[7] 1 Chronicles 11:17-19

13

PROGRESSION

Christianity is an incredible journey. However, you never spiritually arrive until you come face to face with the Lord. As I considered this journey, I never felt I made much progression. I always felt that whatever steps forward I had accomplished, I was pushed back at least ten steps. The road has never been smooth, rather it has been tedious and muddy. The rivers have rarely been calm. Most of the time, they have been raging white water, always leading to falls of destruction. The seas have been rough, plagued by contrary winds and tropical storms.

Through these many obstacles, I have learned valuable lessons. Each lesson has enlarged my understanding of God and my capabilities to receive from Him. However, for most of this journey, it seems that I have been stuck in mud, fighting against the currents, struggling against contrary winds, and barely surviving storms. Although I knew these obstacles were refining my faith and developing character, I wondered how much was being accomplished for God. My desire to serve Him and make a difference in His kingdom was sincere. Granted, I always had to climb over my pride and crucify my flesh to ensure that I would not touch His glory, but the desire was pure.

At times, I would struggle with my place in His kingdom. I knew my life was hidden in Christ. I had experienced death to self, to know greater depths of His life. I understood the value of suffering as a means to learn the secret behind identification and the strength behind obedience. I had witnessed His miracles and His abiding faithfulness.[1] He had given me incredible gifts that were often wasted or used up by those who have no regard for the things of God. However, I wanted to do something for Him in a special way that revealed my devotion. I wanted to please Him in some way, but my hands were tied, preventing me from offering up the sacrifices I thought would honor Him. My inward struggle was in regards to why God allowed my hands to be tied, since He could see my heart and knew my desires.

I remember my initial attitude when I officially started this journey. I had such high hopes, enthusiasm, and romantic notions about where my walk of faith would lead me. I started out with the world's idea of success. It was based on numbers and recognition. My logic was all quite noble. I wanted to affect many lives for His kingdom. Eventually, my hopes were knocked down to stubble and my romantic notions gave way to the harsh realities of life. My enthusiasm ebbed away as I faced each new challenge.

My struggle brought me back to the same point. Regardless of what I thought or desired towards God, I had to trust Him with my life. I had to wait on Him, while occupying. Occupying is nothing more than being faithful with what you are being entrusted with on a daily basis.[2] As a result, I continued to plod through each day, wondering if God would ever open the gate so that I could run the course that I had envisioned was before me.

Amazingly, I could vaguely see this course in the distance. I could not really see the terrain, but I knew it led to my final destination. Like most travelers, I wanted to be on my way. I wanted to see the terrain get miles behind me, and be on my way to my destination.

---

[1] Colossians 3:3; 2 Timothy 2:11-13; Hebrews 5:8
[2] Job 13:15; Isaiah 40:29-31; Luke 16:10-12; 19:13

As I was meditating on my life in God, I suddenly realized that I had made much progress. Although I had not recognized it in the past, my plodding through each day was taking steps down this road towards my destination. These steps seemed like the pace of a snail, but I was actually making some progress. I had been so focused on being set free to run the race set before me, that I was unaware that I was on course, and that the spiritual terrain of my life was constantly changing.

Although I wanted to do great things for God, I had failed to realize that the measure of my life in Him came down to how much I would allow Him to do in me. My purpose on earth was not to do great things for God, because such a goal was still self-serving. Rather, my purpose on earth was to learn to love and worship Him.[3] He wanted me to come to a place of rest in Him where I would enjoy Him in intimate fellowship. In order to bring me to this point, He had to get self out of the way with all of my high hopes and romantic notions.

To bring this into focus, He had to remind me of some of my requests. "Lord, if I cannot serve You, take me home." "Lord, I want to know You in greater ways." "Lord, please do not let me touch your glory." "Lord, have Your way." "Lord, I do want to possess You as my true treasure." As I was reminded about these requests, along with others, I realized they were about discovering Him in the midst of this demanding world. These requests showed me that I did not want to accept religion or nominal Christianity. They revealed that, like Paul, I wanted to be apprehended by Jesus and to apprehend Him.[4] It was at this time that I humbly recognized that the Spirit of God had put these desires there so God could honor them in my life.

As I meditated on these simple requests, I began to see what God valued. When we consider the cross of Jesus, we know God

[3] Mark 12:29-31; John 4:22-24
[4] Philippians 3:12-14

values souls. When we think about our commission, we recognize that God is after souls.[5] When we look at the harvest field of humanity, we cannot help but remember Jesus' words after He looked upon the multitudes who represented the lost, scattered sheep of God, "The harvest truly is plenteous, but the labourers are few; Pray ye therefore the Lord of the harvest, that he will send forth labourers into his harvest" (Matthew 9:37-38).

The heart of God is souls. To focus on His heart is the means to get a person past self, so they can consider the possibilities of His work and kingdom in the lives of others. However, what many of us believers of God forget is that our soul is included in that work. The Apostle Paul brings this out in 1 Corinthians 3:9, "For we are labourers together with God: ye are God's husbandry, ye are God's building."

Christians are both God's field and building. Obviously, He wants to cultivate our lives and establish us in His work. Although I read Scriptures that talked about God doing a good and lasting work in me, I had kept most of my life in Him external. In other words, I always made my service to Him as being about the other guy.[6] Needless to say, this philosophy made me quite noble in my dedication, but it was not what God wanted. He was interested in the internal, meaning, my life, heart, and mind. He was first interested in doing a work in me.

John 14:6 was brought to remembrance. Jesus had summarized His ministry in this Scripture, "I am the way, the truth, and the life: no man cometh unto the Father, but by me." Jesus was not the way to fulfill some ministry. He was not serving as the truth concerning service. The life that He promised was not filled with worldly success or recognition. Rather, Jesus was and is the way to a relationship. He serves as the truth about this

---

[5] John 3:16: Mark 16:15-16
[6] 1 Corinthians 12:6; Ephesians 1:11; Philippians 1:6; 2:13

relationship. And, out of this relationship will come true, lasting life. Jesus is the way to the Father.

At this point, I recognized that the Christian commission was to get me outside of self, so that God could begin the real work in me. Since God is God, He has the world at His disposal. He utilized circumstances to direct my steps. He employed adversity to expose my character. He used obscurity to fine-tune my spiritual hearing and to bring restoration to my soul. As I considered the means He used to make me pliable in His hands, I could see where each one had formed my cross.

I had discovered the value of self-denial and death, but I had to come to terms with the blessed discipline the cross brought to my life. For years, I had thought my hands were tied from doing what God wanted me to do. I wrestled with Him many times over this issue. Eventually, He revealed that my hands were tied, but it was to the cross. The cross was His way of disciplining my walk. It kept me from getting ahead of Him. It held me in step with Him, and it disciplined my unmanageable character and earthly vision as I constantly wrestled with it to remain faithful to Him. It forced me to trust Him in practical ways, and to give way to His perfect ways.

This cross allowed God to do the work in my life. He was able to change the terrain of my heart. He used it to transform my way of thinking to embrace the mind of Jesus. He disciplined my walk so that I could follow Jesus down this path of life into a relationship with the Living God.

I had not always enjoyed the discipline of the cross. At times, I was frustrated with the limitations it placed upon me. I resented the weakness it exposed in me. I struggled against its harshness, as it brought me to the brink of collapse and destruction. I used to silently rage against it when it caused me to experience the dark night of my soul.

Now that I look back at these times, I realize that it was the work of God. In my limitations, He taught me to lean and rely upon Him. In my weakness, His grace was made real to me. In the midst of harshness, His faithfulness was manifested. In the dark night of my soul, He went deeper in my life to illuminate greater measures of His character and work. [7]

It was humbling to recognize that my progression in the Kingdom of God had nothing to do with my work in His harvest field, but His work in my life. God had to do work in me before He could work through me. This is confirmed by Jesus' own life. He spent 30 years in obscurity before He worked in the harvest field. Then, His earthly ministry lasted only three years. If the Son of God was hidden away for years before His ministry started, why should mere man be impatient with his process?[8]

I realized that God had to make me pliable in His hands before I could work in His harvest field. As I submitted to His work in me, an incredible transformation took place. My cross became a yoke. This yoke did not belong to me, but to Jesus.[9] It was then that it dawned on me that the cross disciplined me, so that I could walk in step with Jesus under His yoke. It was this yoke that would guide my steps in His harvest field.

Jesus commanded His disciples to deny self, take up their cross, and follow Him.[10] The purpose of following Jesus is not only to discover the life He has for each of us, but to be prepared to take up His yoke, to learn of Him and become co-laborers with Him in the great harvest field of humanity.

Through my journey, I have learned one consistent truth, it is and must be God's work. He is the One who saves and changes people. It is His work that is eternal. It is His presence that people

---

[7] Proverbs 3:4-7; 2 Corinthians 3:5; 4:7-15; 12:8-11; Hebrews 13:5
[8] James 1:2-4
[9] Matthew 11:28-39
[10] Matthew 16:24

must sense, His glory that people must experience, and His plan that people must see. It is His truth that makes a difference, and His life in us that serves as the light in this dark world. Ultimately, Jesus must be lifted up in our lives so that people will be drawn to the eternal, the impossible, and the majestic.[11]

As I compared my limited vision, temporary attempts, and fickle vainglory, I began to understand why God had to take me through the process. Even though we Christians talk about the simple truths of God, much of what we do, believe, and think comes back to personal agendas and priorities. These aspects have nothing to do with God's heart or will, but about our perception of how we are going to carry out our religious notions. Such attempts prove to be futile.

These attempts will remain devoid of power until we experience the revolution they are meant to create in our personal lives. Everything becomes a substitute in our lives until we understand that only God is real and lasting. We can glory in our knowledge about God, but until He ceases to become a fact and becomes a living reality, He will never be glorified in our lives. Until we realize that the life we live in Christ is not about personal accomplishments, but about God having His way in us, we will strive for the earthly, instead of the eternal. When it is all said and done, the Apostle Paul's words will become a reality, "That no flesh should glory in his presence...He that glorieth, let him glory in the Lord" (1 Corinthians 1:29, 31b).

The road has been difficult, but well worth it. I have become weary, only to be refreshed by His presence. I have become discouraged, only to find hope in His faithfulness. I have become overwhelmed, only to find His peace. I have become uncertain, only to experience His grace. I realize that through it all, God has

---

[11] Matthew 5:13-16; John 12:32

answered all of my heart cries. What is most important is that I have gained Jesus Christ. He is so very precious to me.

Obviously, I complicated the progress in my spiritual life. As I decrease, Jesus increases in me. Therefore, spiritual progression is simple: the life of Jesus being worked in me. It is refreshing—His life filling me. It is glorious—His life being manifested in me. Progression is all about Jesus becoming a consuming reality in and through me.

Where are you in your spiritual journey? Is God making headway in you as you decrease in importance and regress in conceit? Is Jesus' life being worked in you as you deny self and give way to the sanctifying work of the Spirit? Is Jesus' character being forged in you as you carry the cross? Is your cross now His yoke as you serve as His co-laborer in the great harvest field of humanity? Jesus' life in you is the secret to destroying all prisons and subduing all dots, allowing you to soar in the glorious liberty of His Spirit.

14

RUNNING THE RACE

A young friend of mine summarized Christianity by saying, "It is not a destination, but a journey." There are some in the Christian realm who act as if their initial encounter with Jesus at the cross implies that they have arrived. This is erroneous. The initial experience of salvation means that the individual has turned around from their present course to begin a journey of discovery and growth in God's kingdom.

As I think about my spiritual journey, I become overwhelmed with the feeling that there is no way to describe what I have experienced, and what I presently possess because of this incredible journey. The road has been long and ongoing, but rewarding. The battles have made me weary, but through it all, I have discovered aspects of God's character that have forever changed my limited perception of Him.

At times, I have become enslaved to the prison bars as the different enemies of my soul have tried to take me captive, only to be given a way out of the trap by the abiding presence of God. I have become aware of how easy it is to become hindered by my frailties and the depravity of my being, only to discover the keys of Jesus' truth. Sometimes I have become afraid of the entangling tentacles of the old man, only to realize that God's mercy is a heartfelt cry away. Other times, I become aware of my tendency to be stopped by the many dots that loom before me. I have become discouraged by how easy it is for me to be led astray. It has been at such times that God has been faithful to remind me that it is Jesus' grace abounding in my life that will keep me in the way.[1]

Facing the harsh reality of the wickedness behind my natural tendencies could cause me to fall into the prison of despair if it were not for His immovable joy in my soul. The reality is that my foolishness sets me up to fall into the traps of my pride, while those insignificant dots cause me to shake my head at the ridiculousness of all of it.

I am constantly reminded of how wretched I am. It all seems so hopeless until I look heavenward and remember that it is not about me, but Christ in me. It is His work, His redemption, and His life that lifts me above my hopeless plight to soar on the wind of His Spirit. It is from this heavenly perspective that my spirit is once again revived, my soul refreshed, and my faith enlarged to embrace the eternal and the impossible.[2]

The Christian life is about Jesus. It is about discovering Him in His glory. In order to discover Jesus, one must be apprehended by Him and to apprehend or possess Him. It is the revelation of the Person of Jesus that causes Christianity to cease from being a belief system or a religious activity and become life itself.[3]

When Jesus became my source of life, I started to walk this life out in faith.[4] The walk of faith took me into some incredible places with God. It challenged my perception, enlarged my vision, and brought me into deep places with Him so that He could bring me higher. Along the way, I had to travel through valleys of humiliation where I tasted failure. At times, I found myself abiding on plateaus where I had to learn to wait on God. I had to cross rushing rivers

---

[1] John 14:6; Romans 5:20-21
[2] Matthew 19:26; Luke 21:28; Romans 7:18-25;
[3] Ephesians 1:17-23; Philippians 3:12-13
[4] 2 Corinthians 5:7

of doubts, endure the wildernesses of testing, and the contrary winds of unpleasant circumstances. The mountains always have led me to exciting pinnacles, but they would quickly descend into the enemies' territory where confusion abounded, despair dogged my heels, and the apparent ridiculousness of the battle all mocked me.

The victory of this challenging journey is that I have become a seasoned soldier who has endured hardships. In the battles, I have learned that the world holds no value or importance. I have indeed become dead to it, as it has become crucified to me.[5]

This journey has prepared me to take on the final challenge of my Christian life—to run the race. If you had asked me at the different stages of my spiritual journey if I understood that everything in my Christian life was to prepare me to run the race, I would have questioned you. After all, in the initial stages of my Christian life, I was enthusiastic about this new adventure. In my mind, I was already running the race, but it was zeal without knowledge.[6] Granted, my attempts were in my personal strength, and they brought me to a weary state of despair and defeat, but I felt I was nobly running the race.

My next stage was sitting at Jesus' table. It was a time of learning of Him, which did not involve any race. The next level was my walk of faith. This was when character was being established in me as the flesh battled to stay alive. In the next stage, I was being trained as a soldier. This required me to learn how to march in God's kingdom and wait upon His commands with the readiness to respond. I now realize that each stage was enlarging my endurance as a means of preparing me to run the race.

The Apostle Paul talked about running this race to receive the prize in 1 Corinthians 9:24-27. He also pointed out that in order

---

[5] Galatians 6:14; 2 Timothy 2:3-4
[6] Romans 10:2-3; 1 Corinthians 9:24-27; Hebrews 12:1

to run this race, he had to keep his body in subjection to ensure that he would not be a castaway.

The author in Hebrews 12:1 also talked about running the race, "...let us lay aside every weight, and the sin which doth so easily beset us, and let us run with patience the race that is set before us." This Scripture tells us what we must do to run this race. We must put off any weight or sin that would hinder or entangle us, and with patience or endurance run the race that is set before us.

The author of Hebrews 12:2 also gives insight as to the goal or prize each Christian needs to possess at the end of their race, "Looking unto Jesus the author and finisher of our faith; who for the joy that was set before him endured the cross, despising the shame, and is set down at the right hand of the throne of God."

Jesus is the prize. He is the One who will ensure each of our finishes. He is our example of enduring the hardships of this race. Although He appeared to suffer the shame of defeat, today He declares victory as He sits on the right hand of the throne of God.

In 2 Timothy 4:7, the Apostle Paul declared that he had finished the course. He identified the course before him as his own personal course. In other words, each person has a different course to run. Therefore, it is unfair to make the Christian journey generic. It is also unfair to test other Christians' walk according to your own personal experiences.

In 2 Timothy 4, Paul was aware that he was in the last stage of his course. He was coming to the end of his earthly journey. He was willing to be used for God's glory as long as he was needed on earth, but he also was homesick for heaven.[7]

As you watch Paul run the race in Acts and throughout his epistles, you can see how focused he was. He only had one cause that he distinctively expressed in 1 Corinthians 2:2, "For I determined not to know any thing among you, save Jesus Christ,

---

[7] 2 Corinthians 5:6-8

and him crucified." He kept his vision clear and his life simple with this one consuming goal. As he ran this race, he became more of a stranger to the world that had long lost its grip on him. He had one purpose and that was to finish the course and gain the prize of eternity.

Interestingly, when Paul realized that he was coming to the finish line, he offered himself up on the altar of the world. He made this statement in 2 Timothy 4:6, "For I am now ready to be offered, and the time of my departure is at hand." This is incredible. The Apostle Paul offered himself up at the finish line. In the end, he became a sacrifice. Is this true for all those who run the course set before them? I believe the answer is yes.

Each runner in God's kingdom is running towards death in order to gain life. Each weight they throw off and each sin they leave behind will free them to run towards their demise. The more they are enlarged in their endurance, the more intense their race becomes, and the harder they must run.

Due to Paul's commitment to finish the course, he was able to make this declaration in 2 Timothy 4:7, "I have fought a good fight, I have finished my course, I have kept the faith." Paul gives us a summary of this Christian walk. He had to fight in order to finish the course. At the end of his faith, he was standing firmly on the immovable Rock of Jesus Christ.

Since Paul was finishing the course, he made this statement in 2 Timothy 4:8, "Henceforth there is laid up for me a crown of righteousness, which the Lord, the righteous judge, shall give me at that day: and not to me only, but unto all them also that love his appearing." Paul knew a crown of righteousness was awaiting him upon his glorious homecoming.

As I look back on my own journey, I can see how Jesus became more precious to me. As a result, I could never settle for being a spectator in His kingdom. I wanted to experience Him in every way. I could not settle for just knowing Jesus as my Savior.

He had to become more. I had to discover His heart. That is when my greatest desire was to become His faithful servant who is available to do His bidding.

I was content with the position of a servant. I found Jesus to be a fair, loving, and committed Lord. However, He called me higher. One day, a woman was ministering to me. She told me that I desired Jesus to call me His faithful servant, but He wanted to call me friend. The idea of my precious Lord wanting me to be His friend was overwhelming and humbling to me.

In this journey, Jesus not only became my friend, but His place in my life took on other positions. After discovering Him as a friend, I found Him to be a faithful husband who never betrayed my love for Him or let me down when I needed Him the most. From the realm of husband, He became my Father who truly gave me identity and purpose. Finally, He became the lover of my Soul who wanted to walk into the gardens of my heart in an intimate fellowship.

Each stage of revelation has made the reality of God real to me in a more personal way. Each place of growth caused the world to look less attractive and made me more homesick for the One who guards my very being.

Today, I am running the race. I feel time is winding down and that there is not much time left to complete the course set before me. Everything in me is running this race. I ask God for time, strength, and wisdom to finish the course before me. I so much want to do right by Him and for Him because of my past prisons and dots. I failed Him many times in my first years as a Christian, but I do not want to fail Him the last few steps of the course. There are times when I fear that I will give up before I reach the end because the flesh is weak. I cry out for mercy and ask for a greater measure of His grace and faith. I know that I will need each of these aspects to finish this course.

Sometimes, I shake my head at the seemingly impossible task before me. However, I remind myself that it is not my strength that will bring me to the end of this race, but His. It is not my work, but His work. He is the One who holds times, events, and each day in His hands. My responsibility is to keep running the race until I can offer all up to Him of what remains of my life.

As I run this race, I become more homesick. I am not homesick for heaven due to the fact this world is becoming more frightening. I am homesick for Jesus. Each day, He becomes more real and more precious to me. As a result, He is becoming my most desired possession. He is the only One who makes sense in my life. He is truly my hope and desire. I just want to experience His unhindered glory and hear Him welcome me home for good. It will be at that moment that I will know that I have truly finished the course, and now I can cling to my prize for eternity.

Will a crown of righteousness be awaiting me? To be honest with you, I am not concerned with rewards. I have actually wondered if this crown of righteousness is not Jesus Himself. If He is the crown that awaits me, then I want to receive Him in all of His glory. However, if it is a reward, there is only one thing I could do with it—cast it down at the feet of Jesus like those in Revelation 4:10. After all, all rewards that will be given to the saints are a product of Jesus' redemption and the abiding work of the Holy Spirit.

There is one more thing I would do after I cast my reward at Jesus' feet. I would fall at His feet in adoration and worship. I would thank Him for saving such a sinner as me, while I wash His feet with tears of joy. After all, I am finally home with the One who Loved me so.

What about you? Are you running the race or sitting around waiting to realize your Christian life when you die, or when Jesus comes for His Church? The truth is, Christians must find their place in Christ in this present time so they can embrace and enjoy Him with gladness in their hearts for the ages to come.

SO
YOU WANT TO
BE IN
MINISTRY

Book Two

INTRODUCTION

In Christendom, it seems the greatest pursuit for countless people is to be part of a ministry. Through years of observation, four distinct attitudes towards ministry have become apparent.

New or young zealous Christians who often seek out ministry for the frills and self-serving gratification represent the first group. They are often inspired by misguided loyalties and fleshly immaturity that is marked with inexperience and romantic notions about serving God.

The next group is comprised of those who are the "wannabes". They want to be a "somebody" in the kingdom of God. These people usually have high opinions of their spiritual abilities. They are motivated by self-righteous pride that reeks of morbid spiritualism. They have a tendency to make Christianity appear unrealistic and ridiculous.

The third group is comprised of those individuals who have recognized their calling and even set out to serve God. However, like all serious servants of God, they were met with resistance and adversity, causing them to become disillusioned and skeptical to the Christian faith and practice. These people usually abandon their calling.

The fourth group is comprised of the servants of God who have matured in spite of the adversity. Sobriety has replaced all romantic notions; godly discipline has overcome foolish zeal, and self-confidence has given way to humility. These people have stepped outside of the normal boundaries of what is often considered "acceptable ministry" and found the course God has designed especially for them. They have gone against the current of popular religion to come to terms with their calling and vision. They have managed to overcome all disillusionment with real faith, chosen to love God in the face of great disappointment, and have clung to Him in the midst of overwhelming obstacles and great loss.

This book takes a person on an incredible journey that will not easily fade within the recesses of the mind. It is the uncompromised truth about real ministry. It is honest about misconceptions, blunt about human frailties, and candid about the overwhelming obstacles that those who pursue their calling face. It exposes attitudes that hinder God's kingdom, strips away excuses that justify the nominal, and expounds on priceless lessons that every servant of God will learn in the course of godly service.

This book will help the person who truly desires to count the cost to serve God. It gives a reality check to the immature and inspires the weary servant to not faint, but cling harder to the immovable Rock. It will challenge those who are disillusioned due to adversity and the hypocrisy that abounds. It will inspire the weary to run the race, knowing their prize is Someone who will never leave nor forsake them. It will encourage the struggling servant to keep their eyes heavenward.

My prayer is, once a person reads this book, they will cease to consider ministry in a casual, unrealistic light. The reason for such a prayer is that ministry is not about a worldly profession, a good cause, or the latest fad. It is not a matter of doing good deeds or receiving some eternal recognition or brownie points. Godly ministry is about knowing, loving, and ministering the Person of Jesus Christ to a lost and hurting world. It is about stepping outside of man's comfortable religious boundaries to discover one's identity and eternal treasures that can only be found in

Jesus. It is about a relationship with God Almighty that transcends all worldly pursuits, religious goals, and personal agendas. It is about going against what is considered to be normal to discover the eternal. It is not about doing business as usual in the religious setting of a subculture known as "church" or as "Christianity"; rather, it is about doing business with God in order to gain His perspective. It is about becoming the salt of truth to challenge deception, and the light of the love of God to silence complacency and expose hatred in the great harvest field of humanity. It is not about doing for God, but about being a person that God has the freedom to work in and through. It is not about greatness, but about becoming a simple, clay vessel that is made fit by the Holy Spirit for the Master's use in the midst of fiery trials.

My prayer is that every servant learns the secret of serving God, and in so doing, will be enabled to change the face of every mission field in the world, beginning within the home, then reaching out to the Church, community, nation, and world.

1

IN THE BOAT

For thou hadst cast me into the deep,
in the midst of the seas; and the floods
compassed me about: all thy billows
and thy waves passed over me.
(Jonah 2:3)

Jeannette stood in the transmission shop and braced for the bad news. "You need a new transmission. It will cost you $900." We didn't have $900, but we had a credit card with a limit of $2700. This repair bill would almost max it out, but what could we do? We needed a vehicle.

A photograph on the wall caught Jeannette's attention. It was a rather famous picture of a boat encountering an incredible wave somewhere off of the coast of Washington. From all appearances, it looked as if the wave would win. After all, the boat hit head-on into the wave's gripping jaws. Obviously, the wave had an unseen power behind it that could not only take the boat hostage, but also bring it down into a watery grave.

This boat was frozen in time—its destiny known only by those who knew the story. Jeannette found herself relating to the boat. Spiritually, she felt herself in the powerful grip of some unseen force that was tossing her around like a cork on the ocean.

Like the boat, she felt frozen in time. It was as though she was stuck in some kind of dimension that seemed unreal, but held her captive in a tormenting and relentless way. This force had no right to destroy her, but it took great pleasure in keeping her uncertain about her life and future. She suffered the torment of being robbed of everything she had had for the past five years. The force was determined to keep her life up in the air, leaving her uncertain about where she would finally end up.

I had met Jeannette two years prior. She was part of a ministry team as well as a professional artist. She had been invited to give her testimony to the women's Bible Study I attended. Her sense of humor about her challenging life definitely won my attention and respect. I knew she had something that was special. I wanted to not only discover her secret, but also, if possible, have her as my friend.

A series of events did allow a friendship to grow between us. While this friendship was growing, my personal life was falling apart. I was married to a man who did not share in my love for Christ. He claimed to be a Christian, but as time went on, I discovered the fruits of his life were quite carnal.

I had told him in our courting days that I had failed my Lord in the past, and it was my desire to serve Him. He seemed to be in agreement with my goal, but later, I learned that his concept of serving God was totally opposite of mine. It was a hard reality, and I discovered too late that we were unequally yoked. I did not realize at the time that the real meaning behind being "evenly yoked" goes beyond acceptable definitions that are often advocated in the Church. Even though we both laid claim to Christ's salvation, we were not likeminded in our Christian goals.[1]

I remember reading in Oswald Chambers' famous devotional book, *My Utmost For His Highest,* that if you are a committed Christian, it will cost those around you who simply want to play a game. I had decided to serve God no matter what my husband's

---

[1] 2 Corinthians 6:14; Philippians 2:2-3

spiritual level of commitment or growth was. Eventually, a stone wall began to be erected between us.

I want to stipulate at this point, I did not preach or even talk to my husband about my life in Christ. I simply tried to live it. I taught women's Bible Studies, and even discipled young adults without sharing any details with him. However, as I ministered to these people, the wall between us was reinforced by mistrust, frustration, and anger. I concluded that something would eventually have to give.

At the time, all I knew was that I could not let go of my life in Christ. I had fought for this life, and Jesus had become more and more precious to me even in light of my worldly marriage. In the midst of all the silent battles, challenges, and uncertainties, Jesus was still the only one who really made sense.

Something did finally give—my marriage fell apart. The devastation it wrought in both of our lives was incredible, but the blame for its demise would rest on both of our shoulders. There are always things you could do differently in any relationship. My biggest mistake was marrying him in the first place. In spite of my mistake, I was not about to compromise my life in Christ to keep a carnal marriage together. From all appearances, my husband's ego could not accept coming in second to my relationship with Jesus.

I could speculate about my husband's choices, but the only thing I can tell you is that the decisions that were being made by both of us brought a greater separation between us. The fruits coming out of our lives during the death of our marriage and since could possibly serve as a gauge as to who was trying to be upright in the situation. However, only the great Judge, Jesus Christ, will truly sort out all unrepentant sins and attitudes in the end.

The end of my marriage set me free to follow Jesus in total abandonment. His leading led me to embark on a new adventure with Jeannette. I felt I was to help Jeannette and her partner in ministry. I simply saw myself as a "gopher". I was there to help lift the burdens of these two women until Jesus told me differently. I had no visions or preconceived notions as to what I would be doing. I was ready to go with the flow and learn about front-line ministry.

This new adventure had led me to the transmission shop with Jeannette. I was about to learn my first lesson about true ministry. It is a rough road full of potholes and obstacles. I stood with Jeannette, looking at the picture of this boat that was suspended in time. Jeannette turned to me and said, "This is where we are right now. We are encountering a big wave that could devastate us."

I looked at her and said, "If we are like this boat in the picture, I wonder what happened to it."

She said, "I know. It actually survived."

I remembered exclaiming under my breath, "Thank God!"

This was my first introduction to the adversity that we were about to face on the ocean of life. We would encounter many more storms and gigantic waves that would bring us close to destruction.

God often showed us our pending storms or challenges by using symbolic boats. The first time He showed me what was about to come upon us was early in our adventure. He gave me a vision of Jeannette and me being thrown into a small rowboat without oars.

This was confirmed when Jeannette and I started Gentle Shepherd Ministries in a time of grave adversity. It was obvious that this small boat was on a fast-moving river. The rapids were quickly taking us towards a spiritual Niagara Falls. I knew we were going to survive, but barely.

Another time, the Lord showed us that we were going down a river channel in a little bigger boat. The river was calm, but we were about to encounter some locks, or a different level in our

Christian ministry. We found this to be true when we moved from Idaho to Washington State. It was relatively smooth sailing, but we found ourselves at a different level that presented unfamiliar challenges to us.

In another incident, God showed Jeannette that we were on a luxury liner in port. It was a beautiful ship indeed, but it never went far away from the pier; therefore, it was useless. God was challenging us to be ready to leave our comfortable lifestyle, and face the real ocean where we could embark on the unknown and encounter the deadly storms. This happened when the ministry started to close down for us in Washington.

The last time I saw us aboard a vessel, we were on a 54-foot yacht in the midst of a hurricane. I knew that we were about to meet the same fate as the Titanic. We were going into the watery grave. The Lord graciously reminded me that this was not just any grave, but a prepared grave. He was preparing this grave for us like He had prepared the fish to serve as Jonah's watery grave. We would be swallowed up, but not destroyed. We would feel everything close in around us, but it would not crush us. We would be in limbo, but our prayers would reach the throne room of God. We would be in obscurity, but not forgotten. We would die, only to be raised up into resurrection power and with a new life.

As I meditated on all of our spiritual "sea" adventures, I could not help but remember Jesus' disciples. They had real life sea adventures that taught me two valuable lessons. These lessons not only encouraged me, but they helped me to look beyond the waves and storms of life.

The first account is found in Matthew 8. Jesus was in the boat fast asleep, while a great storm raged. His disciples were panicked as the waves overwhelmed the boat. Let's face it, in times of life's great storms, we often feel God is asleep. However, Psalm 121:3 assures us that God never slumbers.

During this storm, it appeared as if Jesus was unaware of their plight, while He was sleeping. However, Jesus was aware. He knew trouble was on every side, yet they weren't in any real distress. He knew they were perplexed, but not in despair. He knew they were being cast down, but not destroyed. Jesus knew. After all, He is God in the flesh.[2]

Here, we see unbelief in action. These men were focusing on the storm. They were aware that Jesus was in the boat, but they still did not believe He was aware of their plight.

The important lesson I latched onto in this situation is that the Lord is always in the boat with us in the storms of life. He may not be saying anything, but He is aware. Even though He can rebuke the wind at any time, He wants to see if we will simply trust Him to stand up at the right time.

Recently, I heard another take on this. Instead of looking at the waves, they could have laid as close to Jesus as they could and rested in the fact that nothing would happen to them without it first touching their Lord. Clearly, this is what it means to rest in the midst of the storm, knowing that we are part of the Body and nothing can happen without the knowledge of God and affecting Him first.

In the second incident, Jesus had been on the mountain praying. The disciples were out on the sea when a contrary wind came upon them. Note, it was not a major storm, but a contrary wind that hindered their progress.[3]

The disciples were struggling to bring the boat under control in order to reach the other side of the shore. Jesus came to them walking on the water, but they failed to recognize Him. He had to call out to them to not be afraid.

The second lesson I had to learn was that in the midst of our struggles, Jesus will come to us. The problem is, we can miss Him

---

[2] 2 Corinthians 4:8-9
[3] Matthew 14:23-33, Mark 6:46-52

because of erroneous preconceived notions about how He will come. In fact, we can go right by Him because of fear or because our eyes are on the struggles, rather than on Him.

I also had to note that the disciples' hearts had become hardened. They had forgotten in a short time that this very Jesus had miraculously fed 5,000 people. If He could feed 5,000 people, He certainly could walk on water.

We Christians have a tendency to forget how Jesus died to save us, was buried, and rose three days later in resurrection power and glory. How soon we forget that He so loved us and is full of grace to meet us with blessing and possesses mercy that will show compassion and forgiveness. How we forget that He is longsuffering and does everything for our benefit until we can humbly come to Him in repentance. No wonder Peter always wanted to bring people to the remembrance of the preciousness of Jesus. Because the disciples looked at their struggles, instead of believing in Jesus, their hearts became hardened. Take heed friend, this is true for you and me too. Every time we operate in unbelief, our hearts will become less sensitive to Jesus and His presence in our midst.[4]

Consider that once Jesus stepped into the boat, all became calm. Jesus took the reins the minute He stepped into the boat. He brought control and order to the elements and peace to His disciples.

When we are in the midst of problems, we often feel that our lives are out of control. What we fail to realize is that our lives will always be out of control until the One who controls the elements around us steps onto the boat of our lives and speaks.

The contrary winds and storms we have faced have been many, but Jesus is faithful. He has been present in every storm, and stepped on the scene at the right time in every struggle. He

---

[4] Hebrews 3:18-19; 2 Peter 1:8-13

has never left us nor forsaken us. And through it all, His power has calmed the storms and His glorious love has overshadowed every struggle. In fact, He has brought us into a spiritual ark of safety.[5]

As a result, I have never regretted this journey through the sea of humanity on the ocean of life. Through it all, I have gained Christ.[6]

---

[5] Colossians 3:3; Hebrews 13:5
[6] Philippians 3:7-8

2

IN THE CURRENT

We are troubled on every side
yet not distressed.
(2 Corinthians 4:8a)

The pastor looked at Jeannette and pronounced the judgment, "God is bringing His hand down on this ministry." He brought his hand down on his desk as a judge would a gavel. Jeannette knew the judgment was final as the sound reverberated in her soul and penetrated every area of her heart, shattering it into various pieces.

We had overcome the transmission obstacle and traveled from the state of Washington to Bullhead City, Arizona to help her partner with some meetings. We had no idea that it would mark a bitter end to a five-year ordeal. Jeannette had given up all of her possessions for the ministry she and her partner had established. She had sacrificed home, security, worldly goods, friends, time, and energy. Now, it was over, leaving her devastated and financially bankrupt.[1]

Jeannette had known that her relationship with her partner was coming to an end, but she had fought against it, ignored it, and even denied it. A couple of weeks before the pastor's

---

[1] Jeannette recounted much of her version of this ordeal in the third book of the 7th volume, *Rose of Light, Thorn of Darkness*.

proclamation, the Lord began to rip out the roots that bound them. The tearing had been so deep that Jeannette had mourned. She recognized that it meant death to a relationship. The pastor's statement was the final nail in the coffin.

Endless questions began to go across the screen of her mind. Did this death mean personal failure or serve as a release to embrace a new life and a new ministry? And finally, what really went wrong?

Jeannette recounted the events. It was just over a year before that her partner had come to her in tears. She shared how the Lord had given her Luke 13:6-9, the parable about the fig tree that had not produced any fruit after three years.

They had been in ministry for three years, and in those few years, there had not been any visible fruit. The Lord was now showing Jeannette's partner that they had another year, and if there was no fruit, He was going to consider their ministry useless and cast it aside.

For a year they had tried various means to reach people, but with no obvious success. In such times as these, one must consider what fruit God is talking about. Is it souls or is it spiritual growth and revelation on the part of those involved? Or, is it both?

In Jeannette's heart, she realized that God kept His word. Their ministry was being deemed as useless, and now was being cast aside. God was bringing a sword down through everything, and from the looks of it, nothing would remain standing.

Meanwhile, I was standing on the sidelines, watching everything come apart at the seams. I had been aware that something terrible was amiss in their ministry. I had even fought for it in prayer and tried to be a mediator. I suddenly realized that my attempts were in vain, and we were all now in a powerful, unseen current.

This current was gaining momentum. It was as though a dam had broken, and the water was rushing down a mountainside.

Nothing was sacred in its path. It was ripping up everything and challenging every obstacle in front of it. It was carving a new route and changing the terrain. At the time, I did not realize that this current was bringing forth the birth of the ministry that Jeannette and I were about to establish in the midst of the chaos and ruin.

Everything had been torn up in my life, and now it was happening to Jeannette. The things we had clung to or valued were giving way to this unstoppable flow. It was obvious that nothing of man would be left standing.

This water was separating and cleansing. It was testing every one of us to reveal hearts. This current was God, and He was on the move, preparing a new route for Jeannette and me to travel.

This route would bring an assortment of debris from our past into our path, to test and change our lives in a powerful way. This path would prove to be hard and straight, as it was designed to build character and produce righteousness. It was steep to establish endurance and unpredictable to cause us to look to our Shepherd and learn to lean on His rod, the Word of God.

Even though Jeannette was aware that the final nail was put in the coffin of the ministry she had been a part of, it had not yet been buried. The hole had not been officially dug, and the pallbearers had not been chosen. The death certificate had not yet been filed, nor the funeral planned and the obituary published.

It was quite obvious that God had brought Jeannette and me to Arizona where this ministry started in order to bury it. I now could see that God was doing all the funeral arrangements.

When I had started this new adventure, I had no idea that it was to witness a violent death of a ministry that I had supported. I never suspected that I was to be one of the pallbearers that would help carry it to its final resting place. I have to admit, there were some warnings, but I felt that God would somehow step on the scene and salvage it. I had grown to love and respect both women, but as Anne of Green Gables would declare, it was with Jeannette that I found a "kindred spirit."

As Jeannette walked into her travel trailer, I could see her brokenness. As she shared the pastor's verdict, I could see a mixture of emotions flooding her soul over the death of the relationship and ministry. Her eyes were wide as the reality set in. Death in any area of our life creates a variety of emotions from shock to sorrow, and then finally anger. Death makes us feel helpless and vulnerable because it is out of our control. It brings us to crossroads where we will have to choose whether we will face it head on, or if we will close down to avoid feeling the full impact. Will we choose to hold onto God for comfort or blame Him for the pain?

I was already aware that Jeannette had been through a great deal. The Lord had given her a vision about what it would cost her to truly follow Him before she ever went into full-time ministry. He showed her nailed to a cross that stood in a circular area that had been devastated by a great fire. The impact and extent of this charred area could not be measured. It seemed that there were no boundaries to its destruction and desolation.

It appeared that Jeannette was nailed to the cross without any hope. She saw no end to her dying out process. This image began to mock her as she realized that over the four years of being in ministry with this individual, her finances had been ravished. She had gone from a new house, furnished to the hilt, to share residency with various critters in an old farmhouse, furnished with old yard sale articles. The new stove and refrigerator she had enjoyed in her previous life had succumbed to a refrigerator that had been new in the 1950's. She cooked on a borrowed two-burner hotplate. As she considered her losses, warnings from family and friends began to torment her mind. People had told her this soft-spoken woman was after her money, and once it was gone, she would be left in the lurch.

All these warnings seemed to be coming true. If these people were correct, Jeannette had been played for a fool, and now she would have to graciously eat crow. I sensed her turmoil. Jeannette had proved to be both an obedient servant of God and a true friend to me. The Lord had shown her before my marriage came down what was going to happen to me. In fact, He showed her four things which all came true. A couple of them involved my husband's ungodly intentions towards me, and the consequences around them. He also revealed that a pastor and a friend would turn on me.

The Lord had instructed Jeannette to go through this furnace of affliction with me. She had been obedient. Now, it was time for me to reciprocate. I needed to go with her through the death and burial of a relationship and a ministry.

Neither one of us realized how long nor how far this funeral procession would take us. The route we would follow would be long and hard, but trying to bury this ministry would cause the greatest ordeal. Instead of being able to close the gaping hole with a backhoe, it would be filled with one handful of dirt at a time.

This burying process would be extended even more so because the handfuls of dirt would often turn into mud as people took sides as to whose fault it was for the breakdown of this ministry. Instead of refraining from taking sides because emotions were raw and perspectives confined to personal, biased opinions and feelings, the mud was often flung as accusations and speculations turned into slander.

By the time it was over with, the stench from the destruction became intolerable in the nostrils of close associates. It was as though the different parties involved had to maintain some kind of dignity in the midst of this funeral. However, the purpose of death is that life will cease to exist as we know it. For example, reputations had to go, rights had to die, and a ministry had to be buried. After all, God ordained this death. Such an ordination requires an individual to be gracious in death, submissive to the grave, and acceptant of the final results.

In this type of situation, it is hard to be gracious. It is hard not to allow raw emotions to determine perspective, pride to take personal offense, and fear to resort to fleshly means. We want to point fingers at others, dodge personal blame, and become justified victims who have the right to respond in an ungodly manner.

Problems of course, always arise when people insist on holding onto their insidious reputations, their arrogant rights, and their sacred cows (ministry). Such an environment will always prolong such a process, causing more hurts. This is what happened in the burial of this ministry. It would be prolonged, causing greater devastation because people would not graciously recognize God's final verdict.

During this time, many people would be tested, and whether they passed the test would hinge on their integrity or willingness to guard their heart, repent of wrong doings, and submit to the will of God. Only the courts of heaven will reveal who ultimately passed the test. Nevertheless, God was on the move. Not only did He ordain the demise of this ministry, but He also ensured its final resting place.

As I considered the situation, I became more aware that we were in a current that we were unable to control. Granted, man may be able to extend the process, but he cannot stop it when God is on the move. God will have the last say by fulfilling His plan. Therefore, all a person can do in such a situation is hold on for dear life and trust God to work out the details.

3

FULL SPEED AHEAD

Save me, O God; for the waters are come in
unto my soul. I sink in deep mire, where there
is no standing: I am come into deep waters,
where the floods overflow me.
(Psalm 69:1 & 2)

"Jeannette, you better pray," I said as I watched the needle on the truck's dashboard begin to climb, indicating the engine was once again overheating. We were pulling the 25-foot trailer out of Bullhead City, Arizona on our way to Phoenix to finalize the death of the ministry she had been involved with for the past five years. This death had already left devastation in its wake.

Jeannette was fighting hard to keep her emotions together and her sanity in place. The incidents at Bullhead City seemed like a nightmare. Even though everything the pastor had declared concerning the ministry was coming true, Jeannette was hoping it was just a bad dream. If only she could wake up, it would be all right.

It was not a bad dream, but a harsh reality. Jeannette's partner had actually shunned her at Bullhead City, while trying to lure me to her side. It was obvious that people were already taking sides or being forced to take sides because of the games and speculations going on.

Jeannette had initially suffered shock from her partner's indifference to her. They had been close friends for at least seven years. She had given it all to the ministry, but that didn't seem to bear any consideration as to how the burial of this ministry was to be carried out.

Instead of being carried out in a godly manner, it became a sick game of cat and mouse. It became obvious to us that we had to collect our thoughts and begin to recognize that a terrible game of chess was going on. If we did not recognize this fact, we would end up in the cold, holding nothing.

We were on our way to Scottsdale to meet with the other officers of the demised ministry. We sensed that we might be walking into a possible lion's den, and Jeannette was not sure she could survive it.

It was hard to believe that we had traveled from Idaho via Seattle, Washington, pulling a trailer to Phoenix, just to put the final nails in the coffin of a ministry. It was impossible to know when we first started out how violent and ungodly this death would be.

Our goal was to be Christ-like about the whole matter and play fair. However, the cat was now out of the bag and survival would come to the forefront. In our naiveté and innocence, we had no clue that the cat had no intention of playing fair. It had become a matter of survival to Jeannette's partner, and now the rules were embracing the world's motto, "Every man for himself."

It is in times such as these that you realize what John 2:24-25 means, "But Jesus did not commit himself unto them, because he knew all men, and needed not that any should testify of man: for he knew what was in man." (Emphasis added.)

Jesus knew that at the door of every man lies treachery. And, it is in such struggles that you will find out how much this treachery reigns in an individual's heart. Unrestricted treachery always gives way to personal rights. It is spiteful, and will sacrifice those who are trying to be upright.

It is amazing how many Christians will give in to treachery to survive. They justify all ungodly actions. They resort to going the way of the world, which takes advantage of, as well as mocks Christian virtues such as meekness and submission.

Jeannette and I had no idea of the treachery that awaited us. We would not only be walking into the lion's den; we would actually be walking right into the mouths of the hungry lions.

I want to state something right now. I do not begrudge what the participants did. Rather, I quite understand it. I understand it because God has shown me my treachery. We would all like to think that we would be Christ-like in every situation, but the truth is, we are not. To proclaim that we respond in a Christian way all of the time would make us hypocrites, and to believe it, would reveal delusion.

If you were to ask us if we handled each of the challenges we encountered in a pleasing way, we would say "no." Emotions were high, the issues confused, and the accusations many. However, what we tried to do was keep our hearts right before God. We knew that we were being tested. And, regardless of what was going on, we needed to guard our hearts against anger giving way to a root of bitterness or turning into hate and unforgiveness.

Jeannette's partner had completed the meetings at the church in Bullhead City where the pastor had pronounced the judgment. Now, we were on our way to face the lions in their own den. The truck engine had already overheated while climbing out of Bullhead City. Praise the Lord, it blew its top right at the only turn-off on that particular stretch of highway.

We had helplessly watched the radiator spew out water and antifreeze as cars flew by. We were both wondering, what's next? After all, we were just two women pulling a 25-foot trailer on our way to be officially offered up to the lions.

At first, I had been excited about starting this new adventure. I knew this marked the beginning of my faith walk, and I anxiously welcomed the new challenge. I knew to walk by genuine faith meant that I would see God move on my behalf. As I considered our present situation, I reminded God that this would be a good time for Him to move.

We waited for the radiator to cool down. We knew all we could do was trust God, and go full speed ahead. We started our ascent once again. I kept one eye on the gauge and the other one on the winding road. I began to eye the needle as it inched upwards towards the red area. That is when I asked Jeannette to pray. As Jeannette prayed, I watched the needle slowly move in the opposite direction.

I was excited. To me, it was the first of many miracles I would actually witness on my new walk. God would constantly prove true and faithful to His promises.[1] However, the excitement died down when we stopped at a gas station to find out what the source of our mechanical problem was. To our dismay, our repair bill came to almost $200.

We managed to get past one obstacle, but we were still heading towards troubled waters. My prayer was for God to somehow deliver us from what appeared to be the inevitable. Little did I know that God would work deliverance, but it would not be from the trouble facing us, but He would deliver us through it.

***

"Why don't you ask me? After all, I did the financial books for the ministry." I couldn't believe the fiasco I was witnessing. I had been doing the books for the ministry Jeannette was a part of for well

---

[1] You can read about Rayola's faith walk in her book, *In Search of Real Faith*, in Volume 2 of her foundational series.

over a year. I could tell when I first met them that neither Jeannette nor her partner understood bookkeeping. However, as I watched Jeannette's partner discuss the financial books with the Vice-President of the ministry, I could tell that she knew absolutely nothing about the financial workings of it.

The Vice-President gave me a stern look to shut up. At least he looked at me, whereas before the presiding officers had not acknowledged that I even existed. Jeannette and I had been treated as if we were invisible since our arrival at the Vice-President's home. They had us park the trailer in their dog run, which was understandable. However, it symbolized the prelude and introduction to the hospitality we were about to receive. I could tell they were not interested in hearing from me. They would rather operate in darkness than submit to any explanation on my part.

Previously, as a bookkeeper for a businessman, I had learned how to juggle finances from different accounts. I never realized this innocent practice would come back to haunt me. Unbeknown to me, in ministry, all designated funds must specifically go to what they are donated for. Friends of Jeannette had given us the money to pay for the transmission repairs. I had paid over half of the bill, but had kept the rest aside for other financial demands, such as the trip to Arizona.

This was an improper procedure according to the laws governing non-profit organizations. I apologized for my ignorance and oversight concerning this matter, but I realized the officers of the ministry were cleverly using it to discredit my credibility.

I suspected that I was being led as a sheep to the slaughter, and I would have to go quietly because the truth would never get further than that room. Obviously, these people had made up their minds, and even though the truth would have thrown questionable light on the honesty and motive of Jeannette's partner, it would remain buried.

The truth is, Jeannette's partner had put financial strain on the ministry by asking for $300 before Christmas. Of course, no one was allowed to ask her about how she used the donated funds.

Another important fact is that the transmission repair was on Jeannette's credit card. Jeannette was the one liable for the repair, and not the ministry or her partner. At the time, my parents were donating to the ministry, and I knew their donation would eventually cover the remaining repair bill.

However, none of these facts were allowed to come out. The officers were not interested in any explanations. They were looking for excuses and a scapegoat. The truth would only cloud the issue or maybe cause some type of inconvenient conviction on their part.

Jeannette's partner asked for her resignation as secretary of the ministry. I helped Jeannette write out a resignation that would officially voice her disapproval of the conduct of her partner. This is when I began to see how much influence Jeannette's partner had over her. When Jeannette came back from meeting with her over her resignation, I found out that she wrote another one, watering it down. I couldn't believe this woman was not being held accountable for her lying and conniving actions. She wanted to keep her insidious reputation, while sacrificing Jeannette. It was shocking to me.

As time went by, the vice was being squeezed tighter around us. The dog run actually became a retreat for us. It separated us from the other side of the camp. But, when we found out that we were locked out of the house and kept from using the bathroom, we realized how far advanced the battle had become.

Jeannette and I found ourselves spending a lot of time at a Denny's Restaurant where restrooms were available. It was there that we tried to wade through our emotions and confusion. Over coffee and tea, we started to brainstorm the ministry God was putting together. We even occasionally found lonely individuals to minister to.

It was obvious that we were not welcome at the Vice-President's home. The tolerance he and his wife showed towards us was barely sociable, but we felt compelled to stay because the issues were not resolved. From all appearances, Jeannette's partner was a coward at best, always ducking the issues and hiding behind the Vice-President and his wife. She criticized us for coming to Arizona, yet she was making moves to discredit Jeannette and get her off the ministry without facing her.

Jeannette questioned her, and asked her non-committal partner how they could resolve these matters if she was a thousand miles away. It was becoming apparent that they were going in different directions, but there were laws governing both Christendom and society that had to be upheld. In fact, they were a means of protection and required such a situation to be resolved in a responsible and mature manner.

It was during this time that Jeannette's former co-laborer began to display paranoia. We could see that she was operating in confusion, speculation, and vain imaginations. Mistrust became a big byproduct. Since all mail was being sent to the Vice-President's house, these people were taking it upon themselves to open the mail, regardless of whom it was addressed to. They were looking for "money" for the ministry. This practice continued for months afterwards. Later, we learned that they had actually held back Jeannette's personal mail for months, until her former partner gave them the go-ahead to send it to her.

I watched this woman's illogical reasoning take over. It was clear that all she cared about was getting all she could no matter what devices she used. From all appearances, this person would not be happy until she succeeded. I felt a stand had to be made or she would leave Jeannette totally high and dry.

Jeannette had invested everything she had into the ministry. Basically, she financed it. She had worked four jobs in Phoenix to keep them afloat, while this woman "evangelist" was enjoying a life of luxury in order to write a book about her life. The few financial supporters they had were Jeannette's friends, and a handful of people who sent monthly payments for paintings they had purchased from her. After the dust settled, we estimated that Jeannette had at least donated over $60,000.00 to the ministry over a four-year period, compared to a little over $100 her partner had put in. This was a conservative figure on Jeannette's part.

The final confrontation happened in a restaurant over their Post Office box. This woman's ministry was originally out of Arizona. It was apparent that Idaho would not be her home, but it would be for Jeannette and me. She had been badgering Jeannette to let her have the Post Office box. I listened as this woman ran Jeannette around about this issue. I could see that she was trying to wear her down even more.

After hearing this woman avoid all accountability and justify every one of her insidious actions, I had had enough. I looked at Jeannette, and I firmly told her to quit arguing with her because she was going to justify every one of her ungodly actions.

Jeannette's ex-partner had given the impression that she was full of love and compassion. I watched as a darkness came over her countenance. She had just run into a wall of accountability, and due to her overrated opinion of herself she became thoroughly insulted. I could tell that I had hit her oversized pride, revealing anything but love and compassion. Intense anger seethed to the surface, unmasking a hypocritical veneer.

I had respected this woman, but now I was repulsed at her actions. I even began to wonder if she was even saved. She claimed that she had a real encounter with Jesus, but the fruits that came out during this testing proved to be far from the fruit of the Spirit. Integrity was definitely lacking, and control (witchcraft), treachery, conniving, and cruelty manifested.

We did manage to finish our breakfast in silence. I had decided to leave these two women, but I knew I had stopped this woman dead in her tracks from taking the territory in question.

I went out to the pickup to wait for Jeannette. The Lord gave me a vision of what this woman wanted to do to me. I can tell you that it confirmed my suspicion regarding her present conduct. She was in a survival mode. Whether right or wrong, she was going to come out on top no matter what she had to do. After all, she was the "evangelist," and it was "her ministry", even though Jeannette had started it with her and supported it. Therefore, she felt that she had every right to protect "her ministry" and secure every asset she could regardless of how ungodly the means.

Later, Jeannette verified what I had seen in the spirit. Apparently, this woman told Jeannette that I didn't know how lucky I was. In other words, I was fortunate she was letting me live.

The glimpse I had into this woman was shocking. Her capacity for anger and revenge were great. What even stunned me more was her ability to excuse it away. Such anger would cause me to examine myself, but it didn't her. It was as though she was totally deluded about herself. It became obvious that godliness did not serve as her real boundaries. As a result of her delusion and unwillingness to be called to scriptural accountability, she became a dangerous foe. In fact, we were about to taste the incredible lengths she would go to wreak revenge on our lives in order to have the last say.

4

IN PORT

We are perplexed, but not in despair; ...
(2 Corinthians 4:8b)

"I can't take anymore. I can't go back into that house. I just can't."
I could tell Jeannette was at the breaking point. Tears flowed from
her eyes, and her body shook as she sat on the bed of the travel
trailer. Jeannette's former partner had left her calling card once
again. She had flown to Idaho while we were still in Arizona, and
ransacked the house we all shared in Fenn, a small rural area in
central Idaho. She had taken numerous articles, some which
actually belonged to me. Obviously, there was nothing sacred
where she was concerned. It had become war, and all was
considered fair game regardless of whether it was Christian or not.

Apparently, she had brought a couple of witnesses to verify
what she took. It was nothing but a sham because neither of her
witnesses had a clue as to what really belonged to the parties
involved. No one could have fairly represented either of our
interests.

Jeannette felt violated. It was as though she had been raped
because all of her rights had been unfairly taken away. She was
not allowed the decency to have a say about anything, including
what happened in her own home. Nothing had remained pure.

I struggled to maintain a Christian attitude. This woman who
claimed to be compassionate and godly had miserably failed to

186

display these virtues in this situation. It was quite clear that she had submitted to her lower disposition. She now appeared to be nothing more than a self-centered, deluded person who was only interested in watching out for herself and her so-called "ministry." I wondered if she could see the havoc she was causing, if she would actually cease from her activities that were characteristic of a snake in the grass. Or, were her actions actually identifying her real identity that may have been cleverly hidden behind a religious masquerade? Meanwhile, she had succeeded in violating everything Jeannette had valued.

It had been a long trip for us. It was late and we were spiritually, mentally, and physically exhausted from all the battles we had already fought in Arizona. I realized that our war was far from over. We would now have to fight other battles if we were going to get some of our possessions back.

Through our ordeal in Arizona, I could see where the Lord had been gracious to us. He had confirmed our ministry and encouraged us by some victories along the way. Two pastors, including the one in Bullhead City, had allowed us to minister in their churches. God gave us favor and the people were blessed.

However, the cloud had remained over our heads because nothing had been truly resolved between Jeannette and her partner. Her partner had become illusive, and people seemed to cover for her when Jeannette inquired about her location.

At one point, Jeannette suspected that she was up to no good, and had probably returned to Idaho to secure all the things she thought were due her since she was the "great evangelist" and the president of her "ministry." I had tried to logic such an idea away, but the evidence confirmed that Jeannette's inner sense had proven to be right.

On top of coming home to a ransacked house, we were also greeted with an inch-thick layer of black topsoil, quietly resting on our floors and furniture. Apparently, there had been a 104-mph windstorm in March while we were ministering in Arizona. This topsoil had found its way into the house after Jeannette's former partner had not properly secured a door, after descending like a vulture on the place in February.

I could tell that Jeannette was on the brink of an emotional breakdown. I was not sure I could convince her to get up and face the devastation. However, I knew if we were going to spend the night in the house, we had to first clean it.

I kept thinking about a disturbing dream that Jeannette's mother had about her before she left Seattle years before with this woman. She saw Jeannette in an asylum dressed in a dirty grown. She was not in her right mind, and there was a rat scurrying around that seemed to cause her insanity. This rat would come out of its hole at different times and torment Jeannette. Finally, Jeannette's mother watched a man stomp on the rat and kill it. At that time, she dreamed that Jeannette gained back her mental faculties.

The interpretation of the dream was being revealed. It appeared as if Jeannette's partner was the rat. I had observed her playing mind-games with Jeannette that produced great confusion and condemnation for her. The man who stomped on the rat was the minister who pronounced the judgment on their ministry in Bullhead City. Although her partner was still tormenting her, advances had been made by Jeannette that indicated victory would come in due time, that is, if we only held on.

I sat beside Jeannette and began to pray for her and reason with her. As I encouraged her in the Lord, I could see that she made a determination to get up and face the devastation head on. The rat would not win.

***

Even though we had worked until 3 a.m. cleaning the house, Jeannette and I were up early to begin our surprise plan of attack. We both knew that the articles that had been taken were being stored in a house two-and-a-half miles away from us.

The individual who was storing the articles had sided with Jeannette's partner before the battle had even surfaced. We both suspected that she was probably the main mastermind behind the procedure and method of securing all of the articles from the house. She did not expect us; therefore, she was unprepared to face us.

I am not sure this individual had any idea about the consequences of her involvement, but when we walked up to the door and confronted her, she actually encountered incredible fallout from the war that had been raging intensely for four months. She, of course, stood gallantly in defense of her friend, but Jeannette had her guns ready. She advised her to get her former partner on the phone or there would be major trouble. The lady wisely responded because she could tell neither one of us were in the mood to put up with any nonsense.

Jeannette became quite a trooper. She went after her cowardly former partner with the tenacity of someone who had the right weapons and knew how to hit the target in the right place. Meanwhile, I was left with her former partner's committed friend. I had greatly respected this woman and valued her friendship in the past, but I knew our friendship would be a casualty. It had already been greatly wounded by what appeared to be her underhanded involvement in the many affairs that had surrounded the ministry. Jeannette had suspected that both of them had made plans together to somehow put her on the shelf in the area of ministry activities.

My conversation with this now "former" friend started out in casual tones, but before it was over, I had hit my limit. I not only became loud, but obnoxious. I had had enough of the baloney, the games, and the lies. I had watched maneuvers go on in the name of ministry that no real responsible Christian would want to be associated with, let alone deeply involved with. I had watched treachery at its best, and I was in no mood to listen to someone defend or justify such actions.

I ended up telling this woman what I thought of her wonderful "godly" friend, and what I thought of the way they handled the situation. The woman kept her calm, but she also knew that I was like an angry, unpredictable tiger that had to be handled carefully.

We did manage to walk out with a few articles, minus one fickle friendship. As I walked away, I basically told myself, "Well Rayola, you blew it big time because you lost it."

Even though we managed to get some of our articles back at that time (minus a computer Jeannette bought), throughout the rest of the year we had to wonder if it was all worth it. As we looked back, we realized that God caused both Jeannette and I to sell or give everything away that was connected to our former partners (or lives) within a three-year period. It was as though God used the ignorance, pride, fear, and greed of others to do some necessary cleansing in our lives.

When you realize this, you must wonder if it is worth losing friendships and reputations over a few worthless articles. On the other hand, was the battle over material things or something greater? I realize the battle was not over a few material things, but over something that was unseen and hard to explain. It was over principles that will not allow you to play dead when such an enemy is advancing. It is over souls that you care about enough to fight back, in hopes of bringing a level of truth and responsibility to them. In such battles, fickle friends will be exposed and reputations will be sacrificed, but the enemy will be put on notice that the territorial lines are being drawn.

Was it worth it? All I can tell you is that the enemy stopped the advance on that particular front and resorted to other means of taking pot shots at us. To this day, I don't know if I would do things differently, but I do know that I learned some valuable lessons about deliverance.

As Solomon said in Ecclesiastes 3:8, there is a time for war. When you are in war, you have to learn when to fight and when to stand still and watch God fight. But no matter what the strategy you develop, you must keep in mind that it is always God's battle and victory.

It is hard to know when to fight. Sometimes, God asks you to stand against evil, but sometimes He asks you to turn the other cheek. I have learned that when a person is required to fight, it is to test them as well as a means to build character. However, when God does the fighting, it allows His soldiers to see His character. Through it all, it is God who delivers.

God may deliver people from something, but in most instances, He will deliver a person through something. We have experienced both types of deliverance, but in the most unpleasant situations, God delivered us through the attacks and storms.

The greatest lesson you learn is that God is faithful. You may not feel His presence in the dark night of the soul. You may even be tempted to question His motivations concerning the trials you encounter, but He is perfect and He will never let you down. As Lamentations 3:22-23 declares, "It is of the LORD'S mercies that we are not consumed, because his compassions fail not. They are new every morning: great is thy faithfulness."

5

IN DRY-DOCK

*…we went through all that great
and terrible wilderness…
(Deuteronomy 1:19b)*

"Rayola, I must be your solution not one of your options." I realized that I had made the world my solution and God my option. Out of love and commitment, God was setting the record straight. I had to totally rely on Him.

I was starting to get a real taste of what it meant to walk by faith and not by sight. My romantic notions about the faith walk were quickly falling to the wayside. This walk was not a picnic. In fact, it was becoming an unpleasant nightmare.

Jeannette and I had finally found ourselves on the shores of Idaho. I was not sure if I secretly desired the fast-moving current over what appeared to be my first official wilderness experience. In the current, I felt alive because there was a constant struggle to survive. However, in the wilderness, I felt as if I was in spiritual dry-dock.

I was reminded of my Navy days when I had been a helmsman on a utility boat in the San Diego Harbor. The crew of my small boat was elated when we found out we were going to be put in dry-dock for much needed maintenance. However, to our surprise, dry-dock proved to be a great drudgery. We had to get underneath the boat, and sand and strip off all of the old paint and primer, along with the ocean's residue in the California heat. Even though it didn't last long, it memorably proved to be tedious, hot, hard, smelly, and dirty work. I remember silently wishing for the breeze of the ocean once again.

The wilderness that Jeannette and I found ourselves in proved to be my spiritual dry-dock experience. Everything came to a halt for us. One minute, we had been in a battle for our very survival, the next, we were faced with great drudgery.

Admittedly, we did have a few skirmishes in the wilderness. Some of them were with Jeannette's former partner. This woman came to Idaho and actually gave the appearance of a big shark always lurking around, ready for the opportunity to attack and conquer as soon as she smelled blood or noted any weakness on our part.

We later learned that she did find ways to attack. She went after our reputations. This woman had the clever ability of planting slanderous seeds in the minds of people. She never came right out and falsely accused, but through innuendoes, she hit the mark she was aiming at. She would reinforce it by giving the impression that she was only hurt and concerned about us. Her clever ways threw suspicion on us, and prevented people from seeing her questionable motivations. She managed to send some well-aimed torpedoes our way, especially at me. In a way, it was both ironic and humorous.

When God was bringing the sword down between Jeannette and her partner, the woman told people that she had to let Jeannette go because she was praying Psalm 35 on those who had been attacking their ministry. Of course, this means that Jeannette was asking God to simply confuse their enemies. Once again, this woman was trying to give the impression that she was so compassionate that she was above such tactics. She also accused Jeannette of having a wrong spirit. It was obvious that the list of charges against Jeannette were soundly in place in her mind, allowing her to justify ungodly attitudes and actions.

When the dust settled, word got back to me that she was now accusing me of breaking up the ministry she had with Jeannette. According to the story, I was forced on her, and she did not think I was ready for ministry. She implied that I had some major problems that would discredit the reputation of her "wonderful ministry."

Meanwhile, Jeannette was still trying to struggle through the fallout of the battle that raged in Arizona and engulfed our home in Idaho. Jeannette was trying to keep her sanity. Because of feeling totally violated by her former partner's actions, she found herself gripped in the jaws of fear. She was afraid to leave the house. It actually held her in bondage and tormented her.

I watched her wrestle with this fear every time we left the house. She knew that God had not given her a spirit of fear, but a spirit of power, love, and a sound mind.[1] She struggled with unbelief that told her that God did not care for her. She hung onto His love, and with everything in her she maintained that part of her mind or soul that had not been shattered. Because of her determination to cling to God, in time, the spirit of fear did lose its grip on her.

It was during this period that God began to train me in confronting the real enemy. Ephesians 6:12 tells us, "For we wrestle not against flesh and blood, but against principalities, against powers, against the rulers of the darkness of this world, against spiritual wickedness in high places."

I was quite aware of who was behind Jeannette's former partner's actions. She had become a willing vessel of Satan because of her pride, greed, and fear. The tragedy is that many Christians avail themselves to Satan. As a result, Satan never has

---

[1] 2 Timothy 1:7

to look far to find a willing instrument to do his dirty work of slander and sowing discord among the brethren.[2]

However, in my spiritual wilderness, I would actually meet the enemy face-to-face. Before Jeannette had taken up residency in the house in Idaho, a New Ager had lived in it. One day, the New Ager was talking to Jeannette. In a quiet voice, she asked Jeannette if she had encountered a presence in the bedroom upstairs. Jeannette immediately knew what she was talking about. She admitted to the woman that she was aware of the presence of an unseen entity.

The New Ager told her that she didn't mind it because the entity seemed friendly enough. Jeannette quickly stopped her logic by declaring that it was not friendly but demonic, and she could be assured that this demonic influence was devoid of any good intentions.

The bedroom upstairs became my sleeping quarters. One afternoon, I was upstairs taking a nap. I found myself falling into some kind of mystic fog. As the fog began to clear, I started to encounter evil images. These images turned into a nightmare that began to shake me out of my restless sleep. As I came out of the nightmarish world, I sensed something evil and foreboding standing in the doorway of the bedroom.

Coldness descended on the room like a giant claw. It began to grip me with a stifling intensity. I sensed a great deal of fear invading every area of the bedroom. I knew that I was encountering a demonic influence. I began to pray and rebuke its presence.

Suddenly, the coldness left the room, leaving me to wonder if I was dreaming. I pinched myself and shook my head. I knew the situation was not a dream or a figment of my imagination. It definitely had been a means by which Satan left his calling card.

---

[2] Proverbs 6:16-19

It was not unusual for us to have confrontations with Satan in the house. It appeared as if the ruler of darkness had some kind of claim on our home. The house was located out on the open prairie. It was in line with a New Age convent and not far from where a witch coven met in darkness and offered sacrifices. The area was also rich in Indian folklore, battles, and rituals. All of these combinations seemed to lay claim to our home.

Satan's claim on our home was more evident after we had been away from the house for a period of time. I can remember one incident when we came home after a ministry trip. Jeannette had gone into the house before me. Within seconds, she came running out of the house. Her eyes were big. I asked her what was wrong. She told me she had encountered one of Satan's cohorts in the kitchen. She described his large size. This evil entity had said to her, "You are not welcome here."

The Holy Spirit at that moment stood up in Jeannette. She started to rebuke the demonic influence in the name of Jesus, and it fled. From that time on, we would enter our house ready for battle if we had been away for any length of time. I was starting to realize that Satan may have claims on certain territories, but through Christ, we had the authority to take back our personal home.

In another incident, we were spending the winter in our home instead of traveling to Washington and Arizona for ministry. We knew our house had little resistance to the wind. There were many cracks in the house and the windows were not properly sealed. As a result, the wind always found its way into our living quarters, at times making our living conditions very unpleasant.

We were hampered even more by our heating challenges. We had a small wood stove. Some friends had located some wood for us, but it turned out to be both green and wet. Unfortunately, this type of wood gives off very little heat and will clog the chimney.

As a consequence, we sometimes had more smoke in our living area than was getting through the chimney.

One cold arctic night, the wind began to howl. We could feel it blowing through the crevices of the windows, especially in Jeannette's bedroom. In order to feel any heat, we had to practically sit on top of the wood stove. Jeannette and I decided to put some plastic on the inside of her bedroom window. We found duct tape and taped up the plastic. To our surprise, the wind was so powerful that it quickly inflated the plastic, pushing out the curtains.

I looked at the inflated plastic and the obese curtains and told Jeannette that it was the first time I ever witnessed pregnant curtains. Just as I got the statement out of my mouth, the duct tape gave way to the pressure of the wind and let go of the wall. We simply watched the plastic deflating like a balloon.

We both knew we had to be resourceful. We had found a big cardboard box that had the word, "refrigerator" on it. Jeannette used cardboard to ship her paintings. Since the box was used to ship a refrigerator, we both noted that the cardboard box with the large "refrigerator" lettering was more than appropriate for the situation.

We cut the cardboard up and put it in the window. Once we had the cardboard up, we put the plastic over it and again taped it to the wall. We just knew our "plan B" would solve the problem. To my surprise, the wind managed to get around the cardboard as well. Once again, our plastic was inflated and our curtains displayed a large middle section. It was a lovely sight as we watched our trusty duct tape give way to the powerful wind and once again pull away from the wall.

By this time, Jeannette had had enough. Her frustration boiled out in a verbal tirade. I sized up the situation and did the only thing I could do, run for cover. I went upstairs and began to play some praise music and pray. What happened is an event Jeannette and I often speak about when we are in the midst of trying situations.

Jeannette was in the bathroom. Her emotions were going in every direction because of the battle that seemed to be raging in the elements. By this time, the wind had escalated, and was sounding like a locomotive. As the wind slammed against the house, howling and fiercely roaring, she reminded God that we were just two handmaidens, not superwomen.

All of a sudden, an inner strength rose up in Jeannette and she found herself making this declaration, "Satan, I don't care how much you come against us, I am going to serve the Lord no matter what." As soon as she got the last word out of her mouth, the wind immediately stopped.

The abrupt silence caught my attention. I rushed into the kitchen, shouting, "The wind has stopped!"

Jeannette came out of the bathroom, her eyes wide with excitement. She said, "Rayola, you would not believe what happened." She then proceeded to tell me the story.

I did not realize it at the time, but all the encounters with Satan were just a prelude to greater and more intense battles with him over the souls of people and the survival of the ministry. I also had no idea that the battles with Satan that we were having in Idaho would pale in comparison with the wrestling matches I would have with the enemies of my own soul, as well as my flesh and pride.

I knew the wilderness was a place where God would take His people, such as Israel, to prove or test them.[3] It was a harsh place where those of the fallen race of humanity saw their frailty, forcing them to totally rely on God or perish. This unmerciful place was where the flesh insisted on murmuring because there were no conveniences, and pride would cry foul play because as the soul

---

[3] Deuteronomy 8:1-8

had to submit to uncontrollable circumstances and trust the intervention of an unseen God.

I never realized that spiritual wildernesses show a person just how fallible and they truly are. This wilderness showed me that I was full of pride and very fleshly. I had to come face-to-face with the fact that I was not some super-spiritual Christian.

Initially, I failed every test of faith I encountered those first few years. My flesh hated each test and would throw a terrible tantrum. My pride resented a God who would not bow down to its every whim and make things pleasant for its selfish demands. And, through it all, I found out that I had no faith. It was God's faithfulness that brought me through each test. He never failed me, even though I constantly fell short of His righteousness.

Time and time again, God would come through for us in the most unusual ways. I remember the day we desperately needed money for rent. I was at my wit's end. In my frustration, I loudly told God what I thought about the whole miserable situation. He patiently waited for me to vent my frustration. He began to gently chide me, and instructed me to ask Him for what I needed. "Lord, I need money for rent." At that moment, I knew my prayer was answered. I went to the Post Office and found two checks in our box for the exact amount of our rent. One of the checks was from someone we didn't even know.

There was the time when we had no money for food or gas. Like always, when you walk by faith, there is no visible ship on the horizon to ensure you that you will be saved from your plight. Jeannette and I went to the Post Office in dismay, only to rejoice as we found a letter waiting for us from a friend who sent us $40.

In another incident, a friend was led by the Lord to sell her jewelry and give us the money. We were quite shocked and secretly wondered what was up. The next morning, Jeannette received word that her grandmother in the state of Washington had passed away. We then knew why God had moved upon our friend to sell her jewelry at that particular time. She was used by God to provide a way for us to go to the funeral. God is faithful.

There was another situation when we needed money to fulfill ministry obligations. Again, there was nothing on the horizon and it appeared to be hopeless. We went to the mailbox and discovered a donation from acquaintances that would cover all expenses.

The thing we had abundance of in our wilderness experience was food. Our precious friend in Washington would send us boxes of canned food and supplies that lasted us over seven years. In fact, we ended up giving some of it away to other people who were in similar circumstances. Although meat is a luxury for many people, our freezer was always full of deer, elk, and beef.

One time, our landlord came over bearing packages of quality beef that they had cleaned out of their freezer to make room for the fresher beef. Since it was homegrown, it was devoid of preservatives and tasted as if it had been prepared for a king.

Walking by faith puts you on the cutting edge. Since you cannot see anything on the horizon, you must trust in God. This causes a lot of struggles, as you strive to get past your spoiled flesh and obstinate pride to trust in something you cannot see. It is quite draining as you learn to become conservative with every penny because you don't know where the next few dollars will come from. It forces you to become wise stewards, and to learn the difference between needs and desires. It is amazing to discover that you do not need 90 percent of what you thought you needed to get by.

Another thing that quickly changes is a person's concept of ministry. Effective ministers of the Gospel are not naturally born, but they are supernaturally made in rough places. As the Lord showed us once, He had to actually carve us out of granite rock. It was no small task, but God knows how to properly use the chisel.

God kept us in this wilderness for three years. The process was quite extreme and there were times that I didn't think I would survive the incredible ordeal. I am quite aware that I did leave many non-essential things in the wilderness, but what I came out with was invaluable.

God had done an exceptional job in my life. He knew how much pressure He needed to put on me to get the desired result. At the time, I had no idea that He was trying to prepare me for the next level of my walk. This preparation was necessary to ensure my very survival.

Looking back, I can see why God put us in spiritual dry-dock. He wanted to salvage Jeannette, and train, test, and prepare me. He showed me how full of self I was, and began the process of stripping me down to nothing, so I could survive my next set of challenges waiting at the next port. Although I was not aware of it at the time, He actually established me on the Immovable Rock of Ages, which enabled me to stand and endure the future storms. I also realized that through it all, God had become my solution.

Praise the Lord for His love, commitment, and faithfulness.

6

IN NEW WATERS

And when the ship was caught, and
could not bear up into the wind, we
let her drive.
(Acts 27:15)

"Lord, if you want us over here, then someone must offer us a house rent-free." This was the fleece Jeannette put before the Lord regarding moving to Seattle, Washington.

We had been on the backside of the wilderness in Idaho for three years. We had greatly struggled financially. It seemed as if we were always on the edge of the abyss, waiting for destruction. Even though we rented the old two-story farmhouse for $100 a month, we lived in a depressed area. The house was uninhabitable in the wintertime, and as a result, we spent two out of the three winters ministering elsewhere. It also appeared to be a fire hazard, especially when the 20 amps would blow, producing sparks and smoke in the fuse box.

Our regular needs such as food, electricity, and insurance overtaxed whatever meager cash flow was left over. The financial struggle forced us to use our imagination. We had some yard sales and sold the pickup and travel trailer to obtain some much-needed cash. Jeannette did oil paint workshops and sold her professional art for practically nothing. She even bartered, by exchanging her famous apple pies for maintenance services such as yard care. We painted windows for the holidays and yellow ribbons during Desert Storm to simply survive in this barren place.

In the spiritual realm, we often found ourselves not only contending with Satan, but with the leadership of different churches in the surrounding communities. On one occasion, we found ourselves confronting a minister's wife who was offering to unsuspecting Christians, *A Course in Miracles*, which is considered the New Age Bible. When Jeannette heard about it, she wrote a letter to the editor warning Christians of this erroneous heresy. The editor titled the editorial, *"Warning to Christians."* It actually submarined the course, and for months afterwards, Christians came up to thank Jeannette for her warning.

We also confronted this same minister's wife with the help of a pastor and his wife on the first night she was to teach the first course of miracles. I will never forget how she sat in a yoga position. I asked her if she had ever really received Jesus as her Lord and Savior. I will never forget her answer, "Yes I did, but it was not enough." *(Prayer: God protect your people from hireling shepherds.)*

The most reaction we received from this woman was when Jeannette began to share her testimony about her short involvement in some New Age beliefs through books she had read. The lady came straight out of her yoga position and was ready to attack Jeannette. Her reaction caused the rest of us to quickly rise up to stand between them.

There was another incident with a church that allowed a visiting evangelist to come in who preached doctrine akin to Mormonism to a gullible congregation. I remember feeling like I was ready to lose my dinner on the church's carpet. My face turned a pale shade of green. Jeannette, who was doing spiritual warfare in prayer, noticed my physical repulsion at the whole situation.

The evangelist knew we were not buying his heresy. He told the congregation that Satan was coming against him, and that if they clapped loud enough, he (us) would flee from their midst. The people worked themselves into a frenzy as they clapped loudly, stomped their feet, and declared victory. The pastor's wife ran around shaking people's heads as she wailed in a high-pitched voice. At the time, I remember thinking I was in some kind of insane asylum.

We held our ground and continued to pray in the spirit. After about ten minutes of total mayhem, he could tell that we were not budging. Everything started to subside. He began to preach his lies as he pranced back and forth in front of the congregation. About this time, we made plans to exit the place. We decided we would go out the back door the next time his back was to us. On cue, we carried out our plan with incredible swiftness.

The next day, one of Jeannette's friends from that church called and asked us why we left. Jeannette explained that the so-called "minister" was preaching lies, which was not readily received by her friend. Later, we heard we were being called witches because we had left the meeting. Apparently, they believed they had managed to drive Satan out after all. We just shook our heads. No wonder God's people are referred to as sheep going to the slaughter. At times, I have to admit you wonder if there are any sane and discerning Christians left.

God eventually vindicated us. This heretic went to a neighboring community and managed to steal sheep from two different congregations and started his own New Age cult. The speculations were now completely silenced. *(Prayer: Oh, Lord give your people discernment.)*

In another incident, we were involved with a pastor who promised us future riches if we stuck by him. Although the real draw towards this man is that we thought he was a godly man. However, one day the Lord opened our eyes to the fact that this man wanted to establish his own personal cult. God chastised us for ignoring this man's real goals. He showed us that this pastor was using and abusing His sheep for his personal exaltation. After three days of chastisement, we were ready to face the pastor over his lack of love for God's people. Needless to say, our relationship with him quickly went by the wayside. *(Prayer: Oh God, heal your wounded sheep.)*

I remember one time we went to another pastor and warned him that some of his sheep were exposing themselves to blatant error. We asked him what he was going to do about it. He stared at us fearfully and asked us, "What happens when you die?" Jeannette and I just looked at each other wondering if this man was joking or if he was serious. By the look on his face, we could tell he was absolutely serious. *(Prayer: Oh God, have mercy on your innocent sheep and ignorant shepherds.)*

In another situation, we found out the people of the church we were associated with was considering the husband of the woman whom we confronted over teaching from the book, *"A Course in Miracles,"* for their vacant pastor's position. Jeannette called one of the board members and informed her of our encounter with this man's wife. She then began to advise the board member as to what questions to ask this man such as, "Do you believe the Bible is the infallible Word of God?" After the scheduled meeting, Jeannette contacted the board member to find out if the board had hired him. She admitted they rejected his appointment when they found out he believed homosexuality was not an abomination to God. *(Prayer: Oh God, give your people a hatred for sin.)*

In another confrontation with a minister, I told him he needed to quit feeding his congregation pabulum and start giving them some meat to chew on. After all, it was time for them to grow up as Hebrews 5:12-14 exhorts. He told me they couldn't handle meat. I told him he needed to quit worrying about whether God's sheep could handle the truth. His responsibility was to preach the truth and edify the local body. Once the truth is upheld, it is up to the Holy Spirit to impart the truth in people's spirits, bringing forth maturity. *(Prayer: Oh God give your people a desire for the meat of the Word and a love for the uncompromised truth.)*

Besides battling Satan and contending with church leadership, we strove to be faithful with our different gifts and talents in order to bring glory to God. Jeannette wrote a book, and we both wrote numerous Bible Studies. All of this was done on two electric typewriters. We worked with a youth group at a church and developed a New Age Seminar to inform churches of the wicked intrusion that was finding its way into the Christian's belief system. We also went to Washington and Arizona a couple of winters to do evangelistic work and help other ministries. It was while we were in Washington in our third year of ministry that the doors appeared to be opening wide for us.

It began with us speaking at a Full Gospel Businessmen's Luncheon. There we met a woman by the name of Elaine Johnson who was impressed with what she heard. She invited us to meet with her for more fellowship. Elaine turned out to be a godly woman, who was refreshing to our weary souls. We had just gone through a traumatic experience with one of our friends in Idaho.

This friend of Jeannette's had been supportive of our ministry and had accredited Jeannette for her salvation. She had had two back surgeries, which had caused damage to her spinal column. She was in perpetual pain and bedridden most of the time.

We did all we could to encourage her in her challenging ordeal. One day, she called us on the phone. She told us the Lord had given her a vision concerning our ministry and that she needed to talk to us. We immediately went to her place. When we arrived, we could tell she was greatly shaken. She proceeded to tell us what the Lord showed her.

She said we had four more years of intense afflictions, and then, both Jeannette's art and the ministry would go far. In fact, she admitted that she experienced the intensity of our afflictions and they were so great they made her double over. She saw us losing more friends, which was a surprise since we figured we had lost most of them over the past three years. Finally, she saw that she was actually going to turn on us, but in time, that God would heal her and restore our relationship.

She explained that they were putting her on a new drug and that it would actually take her into the very pit with Satan. She pleaded with us to forgive her beforehand and to continue to love her no matter what.

I must admit, I rejected the idea of four more years of intense affliction. I actually tried to reason it away. However, what was more devastating was the idea of losing her friendship even though it might be for a season. We promised her that we would continue to love her no matter what happened.

When she received her new medication, we held our breath. Nothing seemed to happen. Later, we learned that the pharmacist gave her the wrong prescription and it almost killed her.

We went on a short trip to Washington before she was put on her new medication. It was while we were there that she called us at the place we were staying, regarding an incident that had occurred prior to our trip to Washington. Before we left Idaho, we had a major confrontation with the leadership of a certain church. The Lord had clearly directed our steps as to how to challenge the church, in hopes of exposing the sin of arrogance and heresy to bring much needed correction and repentance. This confrontation had not been pleasant, and even though the church had a bad reputation in the community, the very people who gossiped about it came to its defense. Clear battle lines were drawn in the community.

Our friend had been supportive of our battle and had agreed with us in prayer. As we began to talk to her on the phone in Washington, we could see her vision was indeed true. Because of the drugs, this friend had turned into someone who was now demanding we make a public apology to the church or she would take action. We tried to reason with her, but we could see that she was in Satan's grip.

She did carry out her threat. She wrote a slanderous letter to the editor of the local newspaper against us.[1] There is nothing like being crucified and hung out to dry in front of the whole community. Needless to say, our enemies rejoiced over her slanderous rebuke. According to the rumor mill, Jeannette's former partner even joined in the gathering of the vultures and partook of some carcass as well. I can only imagine what a celebration it must have been for all of them. If only they had known they were all playing into the hands of Satan.

In a way, we felt God was releasing us from Idaho. It was as though our friend had been the only reason we had stayed in our spiritual wilderness. Her attack had cut all of our ties of responsibility to her and Idaho. Now we could leave without looking back.

I began to see how God worked this very same scenario when I left my hometown after my separation from my husband. It had been such a traumatic time that I was quite glad to leave, and I never have been tempted to look back. I am reminded of what Jesus said in Luke 9:62, "No man, having put his hand to the plough, and looking back, is fit for the kingdom of God."

We found consolation over our recent loss and attack in our new friendship with Elaine. At the time, we did not realize how God would use this special saint. She was the first one who sponsored

---

[1] We recently learned that God did miraculously heal this precious saint in some of the areas of her health, but as of this writing our relationship with her has not yet been restored, but we realize it might not happen until we see her in eternity. The editor of the paper who published the slanderous letter was released from his position with the newspaper a couple months after printing the letter.

a *Hidden Manna Seminar* in her home, opening some vital doors for us.[2]

It was also during this time that we learned that one of Jeannette's archenemies in the Seattle area was struck down with a physical ailment. Jeannette had sensed that if we did move to Seattle, we would be on the radio. However, she also knew it would mean destruction to us if this person ever became aware of her presence. This individual had set out to destroy through slander, various ministries, including the one Jeannette had previously been involved with.

Jeannette had told the Lord that as long as this person was on the scene nothing could really happen. When we found out that this person was in a coma and not expected to live, we went to a parking lot and began to cry out for mercy on her. It was almost like witnessing another Ananias and Sapphira in Acts 5. It actually brought tremendous fear upon us. We could see that God was serious, and He was moving everything that stood in the way of what He had designed for us.

This individual eventually died. We prayed that this person had repented of her works of darkness so that she would be assured of waking up in the receptive arms of Jesus.

As the doors of ministry began to open in the Seattle area, Jeannette felt a nudging to come back to her birthplace. Even though God had moved a major obstacle out of the way, she struggled with moving back because she hated the weather in Seattle, and had a wonderful art studio in Idaho. She realized that the transition would be incredible.

As she considered all the options, Jeannette did not see how we could financially survive in the Emerald City.[3] After all, we only had two regular supporters and the cost of living was much higher

---

[2] The Hidden Manna Seminars help you identify your nature, rebellion, and cycle. You can read about this information in the book, *Hidden Manna (Revised)*.

[3] Seattle is also referred to as the Emerald City.

there than in Idaho. She finally threw out her fleece about having someone offer us a house rent-free. Within a week while doing ministry in the Snohomish and Lake Stevens area, a friend walked up to us, and began to tell us about a house he owned in Seattle. He wanted to sell it, but in the meantime, he needed someone to take care of it. He was wondering if we would be willing to move into it rent-free if we maintained it.

The final mountain was moved out of the way. For the next couple of weeks, we spent long hours cleaning and painting the house in Seattle. We were excited, but at the same time concerned. We would be moving into a neighborhood where every house had been broken into and robbed at least once. We didn't have much, but asked God to protect it. I am happy to say that we lived in that house for nine months without any incident, except for an egg being thrown at our screen door and Jeannette hearing some gunshots ring out through the night. Our God who never slumbers did protect us.

After we finished preparing the house in Seattle for occupancy and ministry requirements, we went back to Idaho, and within the week packed up all our belongings. We were wondering how God was going to get all of our household goods over to Seattle. We had two vehicles and had to rent a U-Haul truck. We definitely did not have enough hands to make it in one trip. To our pleasant surprise, another newly acquired friend, Joan Pray, volunteered her service, along with her husband and two daughters to help move us.

Joan had been greatly blessed by the Hidden Manna information. She volunteered to promote us in the Washington area, placing her as one of our team members. She and her family had planned a vacation around the same time that we were packing up our possessions in Idaho. She asked her husband, Mike, if they could take a detour on their way home and help us pack up the U-Haul truck. Bless his heart, he actually agreed to not only help us pack up, but he drove the truck.

When Jeannette went to rent the U-Haul, the sales person looked at her as if she had two heads. People could not assume that they would be able to rent a vehicle with no advance notice in such a small community. They needed to have at least a two-week notice because they didn't always have trucks available. On the day Jeannette and Mike, Joan's husband, had to pick up a truck, they just happened to have one come in. It was a larger truck than Jeannette had reserved, but they gave it to us for the price of the smaller truck.

Between all of us, we had the truck packed up in one night. We left around eight the next morning. Our move was so quick and quiet, that some people we had known were not aware that we were even gone until a couple of years later when we went back for a visit.

God had one more pleasant surprise for us. Jeannette and I had been traveling around in my Ford Ranger pickup. It was the last reminder of my past marriage. We sensed that the pickup would no longer be adequate because it only held two people. There were three members of the team, and it appeared that we would be doing promotion and seminars together.

We posed this challenge to Joan. We found out that Joan had a relative who was a car dealer. Up front, we did not expect anything. We had no real money, but we decided we could go and see what God would do. We wanted a van, but we knew that was shooting too high, so the dealer suggested we consider a station wagon. He had two used ones. God impressed upon Jeannette before we went to the car lot not to be such a redneck because she stubbornly stayed away from all foreign cars.

The first car we looked at was a Nissan station wagon. It was an impressive little car with all of the modern-day conveniences, such as electrical windows and door locks. The other one was a

Ford that paled greatly when compared to the Nissan. The dealer told us that the better of the two was the Nissan. Jeannette remembered the previous impression God had laid on her about foreign cars. She agreed to drive the Nissan.

To his dismay, the dealer found the keys locked in the car. They had to break in. As they were fooling with the door, the alarm went off in the car. It beeped and blinked its lights. Jeannette saw the car's response as possessing personality. This made her begin to appreciate this foreign job.

Driving this car was a luxury for Jeannette. She knew that the car would fit our needs, but the big obstacle was finances. We had no money. Secretly, she asked the Lord how much money we should be willing to pay along with our trade-in. The amount that came to her mind stunned me when she shared her insight with me. It was only $20.00.

We waited for about a half-hour when the dealer came out with the news. He looked at us and said, "You owe us $14.77 for the registration, and the car is yours. "

That day we were in complete awe as we considered the new blessing God had miraculously given us. The car turned out to be beyond our wildest expectations. We knew that God was on the move once again. We could feel the current leading us away from the barren wilderness with all of its storms into new waters and territories. We had no idea where the current would take us. However, we were confident of one truth: God would be with us every inch of the way.

7

BUFFETED

And lest I should be exalted above
measure through the abundance
of the revelations, there was given to me
a thorn in the flesh, the messenger of
Satan to buffet me, lest I should be
exalted above measure.
(2 Corinthians 12:7)

"Oh Lord, help me. Satan, I come against you in the name of Jesus. Get off my ears!" I put my hands over my ears as to try to stop the tormenting sensation that seized the top of my ears and worked its way down to the ear lobe.

The sensation felt like a rat nibbling on my ears. It happened about the same time each day. At times, it was so intense, I thought I would go insane if it did not stop. There were even a couple of times that I would call out to Jeannette to come and pray for me.

It would take anywhere from a couple of minutes to ten minutes of spiritual warfare before the sensation would cease. I remember asking the Lord, how long would this sensation last. His answer was simple, "For a season." I had a feeling I knew it was going to last until I learned the lesson that had opened me up to Satan's oppression.

As I considered my plight, I realized how bizarre the realm of Satan is. It is hard for most Christians to acknowledge that Satan is more than a belief or creed, and that he truly is a powerful enemy of all souls. It is hard for believers to recognize that God uses this enemy to train, test, and develop character and sobriety in them.

The spiritual occurrence I was now encountering was so strange, I wondered how many would consider me a fanatic, a little tilted, or just plain paranoid if they heard about this unseen challenge. I had to admit, I questioned my own sanity at times. I also began to wonder how many Christians were going through strange fiery trials because of Satan, but who were leery of sharing it.

The truth is, most Christian creeds in America allow little or no room for Satan. Most will acknowledge that he does exist, but many are ignorant of his devices.[1] Ignorance may be bliss, but according to Hosea 4:6, such ignorance is destructive.

In my heart, I wanted to learn this particular lesson surrounding my plight quickly, in order to experience relief. However, I sensed that God was not going to let me off the hook that easily.

We had been in Washington almost nine months. We had been running an incredible race to promote the ministry and seminars. We had rented an office to give us a professional front. We also had been on the radio and TV, as well as offering *Hidden Manna Seminars* every Saturday. God did bless some of our attempts. We met key people who spread the word about the ministry after we were used to successfully minister to them.

Not only were we conducting seminars, but I was also teaching a Discipleship Course to some Korean women. They were from the old country and some could barely speak English, so I had to use a translator. We also worked with a Korean youth group for

---

[1] 2 Corinthians 2:11

three months until the church could hire a youth minister. Those three months were quite humbling for us.

The first time we met with the Korean group, we were told all we had to do was teach the Word and they would do praise and worship. Up front, they all appeared to be quiet and respectable, which was quite a contrast to the youth of America. After prayer, they went into praise and worship. I couldn't believe my ears. Their voices were so pure and sweet. It felt like heaven opened up and the angels were actually singing with them.

My mouth fell open in awe. What a difference from the Christian youth of America whose praise and worship is often fleshly, pagan, perverted, and repulsive. I have in the past been appalled at the lack of purity and holiness in, not only our young people's form of worship, but in their conduct and attitudes. However, these young people embodied something that made my spirit soar. It was as though their singing was a sweet fragrance that brought joy and pleasure to God. Their purity humbled me.

It was also an education for me to work with young people who had to struggle between two diverse cultures. I watched them juggle between a culture that demanded total respect for parents and elders and a self-centered, undisciplined and disrespectable society that often displays great rebellion towards all authority. I often wondered how they managed to discipline their American influence enough to successfully live at peace with their Korean culture.

I recalled a concerned young Korean father asking me how he should raise his daughters in America. He felt it was important they know about their Korean heritage, but at the same time learn to effectively live in America. As he was speaking, I felt the Lord give me the answer to his dilemma. I explained to him that both cultures had their good and bad points. What he needed to do was take the best of both worlds and encourage his daughters to abide accordingly.

Our involvement with the multi-cultures found in Seattle made us feel like we were missionaries in a foreign country. It was a rewarding experience. I still remember our last meeting with the Korean youth group after the church had hired a youth minister. I felt we had learned more from them than they had from us. The week before, we had managed to get the group together to attend the Easter production of, *"The Victor."*

It was a live dramatic play that depicted some of the teachings and crucifixion of Jesus. It was a production that came with all the effects that made everything appear to be real. These young people had never seen such a performance before. I heard some sniffling among them as Jesus was in the Garden of Gethsemane, and I saw the handkerchiefs and tissues come out during His crucifixion. The play made a lasting impression on their hearts. As one of their young leaders said the opening prayer in our last meeting together, it was obvious that he was still thinking about the images he had witnessed the week before. He began to pour out his heart to God about what Jesus had to endure to secure our salvation.

Just before this young man ended his prayer, he was thanking God for sending us to them. He acknowledged that if we had not stepped in when we did, there would be no youth group. Needless to say, there was not a dry eye in the place.

Not only did these young people display purity and respect, but they were also grateful. Jeannette and I both felt humbled by these young people's love, and grateful to God for allowing us to touch their lives for a season.

Eventually, we found ourselves on the front lines, which brought us face to face with Satan. Occasionally, we encountered a Christian who was oppressed by him. As we confronted the oppression, we begin to learn how the enemy of man's soul cleverly enslaves people.

One time, we were conducting a seminar for a Christian women's retreat. A certain woman shared with me how much she loved Jesus and wanted to serve Him. I looked into her big brown eyes and could not see any evidence of oppression.

After the final session, she came up for prayer. She shared with Jeannette how she was unable to move forward in her spiritual life. Jeannette pointed her finger at her and declared, "That is a hindering spirit." Just as the last word came out of Jeannette's mouth, the woman was supernaturally lifted up and literally thrown to the floor, barely missing a chair.

I leaned down to straighten out her leg. Just as I stepped back, I watched her back arch, her mouth opened wide, and a blood curdling scream come forth. At that moment, Jeannette began to rebuke the devil as a couple of women tried to climb over each other to get out the door. Out of the corner of my eye, I saw another woman who appeared to be plastered against the wall with fear. Three others seemed to be paralyzed in their chairs.

As for the woman on the floor, I noticed the demon choking her. I leaned down to pull up what I guess to be a 105-pound woman into a sitting position, but found Satan had her glued to the floor. As I started to rebuke Satan's grip on her, two women managed to come out of their shock and help Jeannette and me pull her up to a sitting position while rebuking the entity. (The next day, my arms and shoulders were very sore.)

The battle became intense and the fighting loud. The woman's body contorted in unnatural ways, and she was spitting up a substance that had a sulfuric smell to it. At one time, I looked into her eyes. I was surprised to see that her brown eyes had a greenish tint to them, and were shaped like a lizard's.

Needless to say, all the creeds I had been taught about Christians not being able to have a demon totally went out the back door. I thought about how easy it is for Christian leaders and teachers to sit behind their desks or stand behind a pulpit and advocate certain non-threatening beliefs about such things as Satan. It is also easy to be adamant about it. However, when you are on the front lines battling Satan, you end up throwing away your comfortable creeds in order to survive and be effective.

It reminded me of an engineer who had been a professor at the University of Idaho. He shared how he spent four years learning what the books at the university had to say about his profession, and the next four years disregarding all the theories he had learned in order to actually practice his profession. He acknowledged that what he was taught may have looked workable in theory, but often miserably failed in practical application.

I could see where some accepted Christian beliefs may look good in theory, but fall short in practical application. After encountering Satan a lot, I have learned much about my enemy. He mocks man's creeds, laughs at our ignorance, glories in our fear and indifferences, and plays havoc because we are not prepared or discerning enough to confront him.

I think it is important to explain that Christians cannot be possessed, but they can be oppressed or hindered, just as the daughter of Abraham had been for eighteen years.[2] There are well-known ministers of the Gospel who have discovered this hard, cold truth. They have different names for it, such as demonization or strongholds. I simply call it oppression or demonic influence.

Many Christians are oppressed, but they have nowhere to turn. They fight something they cannot understand or overcome. Often, they fall through the cracks into condemnation and despair.

We ended up fighting Satan's kingdom for two hours before he totally let go of this Christian woman. Afterward, she told us that she had no idea demons were real. She thought demons were like leprechauns.

---

[2] Luke 13:16

This intense battle signaled the beginning of a different ministry for us. We would encounter Satan in many battles for the souls of men. The battle would be fierce at times. In this battle, we watched the same manifestations of Satan you read about in the Bible. Our conclusions about Satan have always been the same. Not only is he evil through and through, but he never plays fair, is terribly gross, and constantly lies to those he has enslaved.

I knew God had been preparing us for this battle in Idaho, but our training intensified in the state of Washington. Both Jeannette and I encountered Satan on a personal level to learn first-hand how he works. Jeannette was the first one to fall into one of Satan's subtle traps.

Jeannette had thought that her flesh was pretty well dead. One day, she met a man who had the ability to stir up every emotional desire a normal woman possesses. She found herself falling into some unseen whirlpool that began to suck her further into it. Intellectually, she knew the man had some real problems, but emotionally, she could not stop herself from falling prey to him.

At first, we both thought it was nice to have a Christian brother. I had no problem that he was attracted to Jeannette, but I began to feel something push against me. This unseen entity began to mock and torment me. It was as though it was declaring that in the end it would own Jeannette and destroy the ministry. It mocked that there was nothing I could do about it. I sensed I had to fight for her, but I was confused as to how.

I tried warning her and she would agree with me. However, as soon as he came around again, she would be pulled back into his grip. I got to the point where I was ready to let this unseen tormentor have my friend and destroy the ministry when God stepped on the scene.

Jeannette felt all kinds of alarms go off concerning this man, but she was in mass confusion. She managed to push through the confusion and investigate his character. She found out that he had quite a reputation with the single women at the church he attended. In fact, he was like a wolf in the hen house. Jeannette also found out that he had committed fornication with a couple of these vulnerable women. The light started to come on. Jeannette was beginning to recognize the culprit that was overshadowing her logic and will. It was a seductive spirit.

The truth started to set Jeannette free and after prayer, the seductive spirit totally let go of her. Jeannette admitted she learned a very important lesson. A person must never think the flesh is dead because when you least suspect it, it will raise its ugly head to entangle you into a destructive web.

I also needed prayer after this situation. I didn't realize it, but Satan had managed to do a number on me. I actually felt spiritually violated. It was as though an intruder had broken into my home and defiled everything that was pure and sacred. I actually came face to face with major fear that I had to overcome.

Exactly a year later we found ourselves in a similar battle, but the roles were switched. I was the one who walked into the trap and Jeannette was the one who had to fight for me as well as the survival of the ministry.

It all started when we tried to help a former jail inmate get on her feet. We had met her while working in jail ministry in one of the county jails. We knew she had many challenges, but I felt we could help her. We allowed her to live with us and took her everywhere we went. She helped out at the office as a receptionist and took care of the book table when we conducted seminars.

One day, while we were at the office, this woman actually encountered a demon. She could see his shadow moving back and forth outside our office. It was so frightening to her, she even refrained from going out to smoke a cigarette.

She told Jeannette about his presence, but Jeannette had already encountered it when she went out to run an errand. Jeannette also encountered him again upon returning. She came in the office with her eyes wide and informed me that the demon appeared to be one of Satan's best. She also informed me that the Lord had shown her that I was an city without walls, and that I better be careful because I was unprotected.[3] I was so busy at the time that I just gave her warning no more than a passing thought.

A short time later, Jeannette and I began to have differences over our new helper who had suddenly become my protégé. I had always felt that with enough time and investment, a new convert would truly change and become a new creation in Christ. I recognized that this individual was still very rough around the edges, but she gave the appearance that she wanted Jesus.

I must admit, at the time I did not understand the criminal element. I didn't know about the mindsets and attitudes these people develop in order to survive in the dark, shadowy, and dangerous world of drugs, prostitution, and crime. I did not realize they almost needed an extra dose of integrity to subdue the criminal thought patterns and habits that were so much ingrained in them in order to become true overcomers in Christ.

My idea of ministry often caused me to go to great lengths to minister to others. I'm sure my so-called "commitment" appeared to be commendable to most people, but to God, it was self-righteous, arrogant, and often inspired by blind ignorance.

First of all, let me make a statement. Our strengths often serve as our greatest weaknesses in ministry. We actually begin to rely on them rather than on God. It is an easy trap for the sincerest ministers to fall into when they are trying to run the race. My commitment was a strength, but my unrealistic and prideful philosophy about ministry made me an unwalled city, ripe for attack and destruction by the enemy.

To try to make a long story short, this con managed to throw an evil covering over my head.[4] This type of covering will keep

---

[3] Proverbs 25:28
[4] Isaiah 25:7; 30:1

you from perceiving what is truly going on around you. I was totally unaware that my protégé was cleverly sowing seeds of discord between Jeannette and me. I did not realize that she knew Jeannette was seeing through her, but she was able to con me. She saw me as a meal ticket for her and her troubled son who was in jail at the time.

I did not realize that there had been an unnatural attachment made between us in the spiritual realm. Those who are involved in deliverance know this unnatural attachment as a "soul tie." An unnatural soul tie is like a bungee cord in the spiritual realm. Every time a person goes to move forward spiritually, it actually pulls them back into the grips of the situation. It is used as a means of control in the spiritual realm, which serves as a type of witchcraft.

Jeannette told me later that she would try to reason with me, but it was obvious that I was not hearing a word she was saying. Nothing was penetrating the demonic covering.

Just before the situation came to a head, the Lord laid it on my heart to fast for three days. At the time, I thought I was fasting for a financial breakthrough. However, the truth was, I was fasting for the survival of our ministry.

Jeannette and I were now in constant conflict. After almost two months of intense battles, Jeanette was ready to walk away from everything. The Sunday before it all was exposed, I had taken this woman to church, leaving Jeannette at home. I felt something actually lift off my head during the praise and worship service. It was at this time that I felt the sensation of a rat nibbling on my ears. I suspected the sensation had something to do with the spiritual realm, but I could not figure it out.

The next day, Jeannette had a dentist appointment. We were hardly talking because of the thick wall of tension that had grown between us. Unbeknown to me, Jeannette had started to make inquiries about jobs and making plans for her exit.

Jeannette seemed relieved to escape the farce she was witnessing. Meanwhile, I was still struggling with the sensation that was plaguing my ears. Just a couple of weeks prior, I had a vision of a rat scurrying around and nibbling on everything in its path. I was trying to wade through a maze of confusion and stress in order to figure out the identity of the rat. Was it Jeannette or could it be someone else?

It was at this point that God stepped on the scene. While Jeannette was praying in the car about the situation, the Lord told her to hold on for a little while longer. Jeannette figured a little while longer probably represented 30 days. She hoped she could hold on for that long.

It was also during this time that Jeannette talked to Elaine Johnson. She not only prayed for Jeannette, but also brought forth some wise instruction. That night, Jeannette and I went out to talk about the future of Gentle Shepherd Ministries. My heart was heavy because I was toying with the idea that maybe it was time for us to go our separate ways. I also was trying to tolerate the burning tingling that was engulfing my ears.

As we sat down, Jeannette firmly reproved me for giving a novice too much responsibility, the very same scriptural counseling she had received from Elaine earlier.[5] As the words came out of her mouth, they penetrated my soul with conviction. All of a sudden, everything became clear. I could see the real identity of the rat and it was not Jeannette, but my protégé.

That night, everything broke loose as we confronted her. She was told she had to abide by certain rules or she needed to leave. In the confrontation, her rebellion and anger came to the forefront. Her demon raised its ugly head, revealing that there was no indication on her part that she wanted to come clean.

---

[5] 1 Timothy 3:6

As I lay in bed that night, the Lord began to deal with me. I realized that I had been proud of my so-called "commitment" to ministry. He also showed me that I was secretly taking credit for the spiritual advancements I thought my protégé was making in her life.

I realized that night that it was all a con game on her part. I also knew that it did not matter how wonderful of a minister a person might be, people still have their own wills. In the end, they will make the final decision regardless of the type of investment they may have received from others.

Intellectually, I knew all these facts, but I had been blind by my naiveté and arrogance. I was shocked to realize that I was close to touching God's glory by being willing to take credit for work that can only be accomplished by God.

The next day the rat left the nest, but the burning sensation that danced around my ears with cleats remained with me for ten more months. Some days it was worse than others. I could sense that in the spiritual realm, Satan wanted to wear me down. He was coming against my ears in hopes that I would once again listen to his lies.

It was all so unbelievable and bizarre, but I knew that God was on the throne, instilling a very important lesson into my spirit. I also knew that the chastisement I was receiving was the greatest evidence that God loved me, and that His mercy was great and His grace unfathomable.

One day, I met a woman who was in the New Age. Her Christian sister brought her to my women's Bible Study at church. I could see that this New Ager had an unclean spirit, and for some reason it took a liking to me. Her Christian sister got excited because she saw me as a means to bring her sister into the kingdom.

Immediately, I could see that it was a test. Before my experience with the former jail mate, my religious pride would have jumped at the opportunity to run and save an individual. I went to the Lord about this New Ager. I knew she had heard the Gospel, not only at my Bible Study, but also from her sister. The Lord showed me that she wanted to possess my knowledge and my soul, and that she was not really interested in salvation.

For the next couple of weeks, I avoided her, but one night, while I was working late in my office, I began to feel the sensation around my ears. In a short time, it intensified to an unbearable pitch. I kept praying against Satan's attacks. As I was praying, the phone rang. It turned out to be the New Ager. She wanted to get together. I began to explain to her that I was busy, but if she was serious about coming to the salvation of Christ, we would be glad to meet with her.

I could tell that I took the air out of her balloon. She was not interested in Jesus Christ. As I hung up the phone, the sensation stopped. Praise the Lord, I had learned my lesson.

Recently, I felt the same sensation around my ears. I knew that it was a form of witchcraft. In prayer, the Lord revealed two different sources who wanted to control me. One source wanted to use me for personal gain, while the other one wanted to silence me as far as the stands I was taking against error in the church.

As I took authority over both attempts of control, I praised God for the school of the Holy Spirit. It is a tough school, but it has trained me to stand against the wiles of the enemy. Needless to say, the sensation around my ears stopped, and Satan was forced to go back to the drawing board

The problem is that Satan will try other avenues. These avenues are subtle and can hit close to home. I know from experience that Satan strikes the hardest by using people, especially Christians, to hinder the work of the true servants of God.

8

MUTINY AND PIRACY
ON THE HIGH SEAS

Yea, mine own familiar friend, in
whom I trusted, which did eat of
my bread, hath lifted up his heel
against me.
(Psalm 41:9)

"Beware of people who put you on a pedestal, for down the line they'll use you as target practice." This statement from Jeannette often summarized our dealings with the people with whom we became closely involved. Many of these people wanted to be in ministry, but were not willing to pay the price. We refer to these people as "wannabe ministers."

Gentle Shepherd Ministries started to be recognized as an upcoming, valid ministry in the Seattle area. We had various people not only flocking to us for ministry, but to help us with our ministry. We had one person tell us that she was the missing key to our ministry. This high opinion that she had of herself not only showed us she was immature, but that she also had a religious spirit that would spell major trouble for us.

As a result of all of our encounters with wannabe ministers, Jeannette and I had often joked about her writing a book called,

So You Want to be in Ministry! (Count the Cost!)[1] Most people start out with this romantic notion about ministry, but if some really do manage to get into full-time ministry, they will find it is anything but romantic. Occasionally, such individuals might have moments of great ecstasy, but most of the time they have to work hard in the midst of drudgery and uncertainty without much appreciation or recognition. It is a life which is unpredictable, and for servants of God, their time is not their own. They find themselves working under unrealistic standards, and the pay can prove to be absolutely lousy, but the rewards are great.

Zealous Christians start out wanting to be ministers with noble visions of turning the world right side up with the Gospel. After many temptations, testings, and trials, these individuals begin to get the reality check that ministering is no picnic. Eventually, all of the religious stuffing, aspirations, and nonsense are knocked out of them. In the end, those who survive simply end up ministering for no other reason than the fact that they love God and want to be obedient.

Looking back, I realize this is the motivation God must develop in each of us if we are going to be worth anything to Him. I know He had to tear up everything in my life so that I would become an open-ended vessel. As He poured in to me, it automatically went out to other people.

There have been many helpers who have tramped through our lives, and this is where I discovered that helpers fit into three categories. The first category includes those who are indeed ministers, and we had the honor of training them for full-time ministry. The second group is made up of those who have been called to help for a season, and then are called elsewhere. The third group are those who put themselves on the team.

---

[1] Jeannette did not have the heart to relive all of our experiences; therefore, I took up the challenge and found myself witnessing the faithfulness of God in greater ways by writing this book.

227

The third group is comprised of people who end up trying to play God by trying to fit themselves into particular positions in the kingdom of God. Sadly, most well-meaning volunteers fit in the third category because they have not been properly prepared. These are the people who can do incredible damage to a ministry because they are not called.

It is important to note that not everyone is called into full-time ministry. Many have a strong desire or a zealous notion to serve God, but neither of these constitutes dropping everything and joining a ministry. Ministry can take place anywhere, including the home where it is greatly lacking, or on the job where you can always find lost, hurting souls.

In one situation, I made the terrible mistake of playing God by impulsively placing a person into the leadership of GSM. Later, God greatly chastised me for it. This is why I still remember it well. We needed another person to fill an officer position on our board. I decided a particular minister would be a good president for GSM. He had allowed us to minister at his church a couple of times, and he appeared to have a pastor's heart. He seemed to be scripturally on; therefore, he seemed to be accountable.

I had it all figured out in my mind that this man could be President; Jeannette, Vice-President; Joan Pray, Secretary, and I could serve as the Treasurer. Without asking God about it or consulting Jeannette, I asked him to pray about being the President. He readily accepted the position on the spot.

At first, it looked like the perfect team, but then a glitch began to appear. This pastor's wife was not in agreement with his participation in the ministry. We also had noticed that she seemed to simply tolerate his position as the pastor of his church, but I also began to see that she thoroughly despised his association with us.

He was spending a lot of time with us as we organized the ministry and tried to pray our way through everything. Eventually, we managed to meet one night a week. During those times, she would call and make a big stink. Looking back, I cannot say that I really blame her. He really enjoyed fellowshipping with us, and did not attempt to go home right after the business meeting.

One night, it got ugly between the two of them and he decided to stay at a friend's house, instead of going home. He never told us his plans, but she called us every two hours to try to locate him. As you can imagine, it was a miserable night.

They did get back together, but I realized there must be agreement between a husband and his wife and not just a surface façade. It was not our goal or desire to allow the ministry to come between them. I began to see the seriousness of the whole matter. Granted, this couple had some real issues to confront and the incident concerning GSM just brought them out to the light, but there must be agreement in spirit.

When I realized my error over the situation, I went to the Lord and asked Him to solve the problem because I had no idea how to right the situation. This is when the Lord began to reprove me. He showed me that I had been flippant about the ministry and the Hidden Manna information He had entrusted to me. He revealed to me that I was the one who needed to be President of GSM in order to maintain the integrity and goals of the ministry, and to protect the Hidden Manna material.

The Lord's hand remained heavy upon me for three weeks. It appeared as if the situation would never be resolved. Finally, the Lord gave me wisdom and within a couple of days the pastor resigned with some hard feelings on his part. It was at that time that I decided I would never take the ministry into my own hands again. It didn't matter how much I liked someone or how qualified they seemed to be God needed to make the final determination.

In many cases, people put themselves in the ministry. They would volunteer to help us and eventually wormed their way into the inner core. The problem with "wannabe ministers" is that they quickly become self-righteous experts about everything. Since they are experts, they can tell you why your ministry is not worldwide, and why you are being plagued with struggles.

As ministers of the Gospel, we are faced with the same dilemma that all ministers contend with when people consider your ministry or calling to be valid. You have to walk a fine line between being transparent, while not really letting anyone in.

The problem with being respected as ministers is that people have certain expectations as to how you should act. These expectations vary according to people. I must state, these standards have nothing to do with blatant sin or heresy, but with personal, petty, unrealistic, and immature ideas of how ministers should act at all times.

For example, you cannot be too human even though you are. You do not have the luxury of having any personal opinions that you dare voice in the wrong way because if your fans disagree with you, they will begin to consider you foolish or judgmental. You cannot display too much frustration or distress because you are to be super spiritual. You cannot be too needy because God supplies all of your needs; therefore, to give any other impression simply means you lack faith. You also have to be careful about the clothes you wear. In other words, you must appear to be poor enough that people will not feel you are being unwise stewards with money, but at the same time, fancy enough that you have credibility.

One of the conclusions you perceive the most is that people are not really looking for ministers, but for God who is the only perfect One. Because I am neither God nor perfect, I have accepted the fact that no matter what I do, I am not going to measure up to man's unrealistic religious standards. However, the problem with being human in ministry is that it is totally unacceptable to those who expect you to conduct yourself a certain way according to their standards. Of course, when you fall short of the people's expectations, you are not allowed to simply become equal with them because of your humanity, but you suddenly become their inferior. After all, you betrayed them and caused them great disappointment. This is usually when all-out mutiny starts.

These very same people you have often supped with, invested in, and worked with turn on you with almost a vengeance that has absolutely no mercy. Since you are clearly not God, you have done the unforgivable in their minds by confirming that you are only human. Admittedly, it is always interesting when you find yourself unexpectedly on the pedestal one minute and end up on the bottom of the totem pole the next. It definitely causes its own kind of rush.

I remember one former friend and supporter who actually got upset with us because we did not treat her children like little gods. One day, God even rebuked me for revolving all of our activities around her rebellious, stiff-necked children to keep them entertained. After all, they couldn't seem to conduct themselves in a reasonable fashion for more than ten minutes; therefore, if we wanted any kind of peace, we had to orchestrate everything around them.

This mother felt, as friends and loving ministers, we simply needed to be quiet when her little darlings acted like the Hatfield's and the McCoy's in our home. Eventually, she came to the end of her rope and attacked us. Even though she had taken issue with other petty things, her biggest complaint surrounded how we treated her children. I must admit, the children were nothing more than the product of their parents, especially the mother. It was obvious that the mother was in great need of a reality check.

Ministers and their spouses learn that there is a big risk every time they let someone into the inner core of their lives. After all, most people do not want to be an island unto themselves. We all would like to be able to trust those we consider to be close friends enough to allow them to walk past the protective walls into our fragile glass houses. And, when we finally work up the nerve to let someone in, there is a tendency to check them out to see if they have a bucket of rocks in their possession.

In most cases, people prove to be like everyone else who secretly is looking to a minister to be God. They have their own unrealistic standards concerning a minister's conduct. They may not initially bring their rocks in with them, but they know how to get to them quickly when you fail their expectations. Such failure now justifies the right to attack your personal life.

Being in the ministry can be a lonely life. Ministers and their spouses are often forced to isolate themselves from others in order to prevent crucifixion from immature and unrealistic sheep. This can take a toll on ministers and their families.

According to a report that came out by James Dobson of Focus on the Family, 80 percent of pastors and 84 percent of their spouses suffer from depression. In the area of burnout, 40 percent of pastors and 47 percent of their spouses experience this emotional state. Around 1,500 pastors leave their assignments each month, due to moral failure, spiritual burnout, or contention within their local congregations.

Ministers and their families are forever struggling with this lonely way of life. They juggle so many issues as they have the added pressure of having to consider every aspect of their life. The questions never cease. Who can they trust? Just exactly what are they allowed to share without causing speculation and gossip, thus, discrediting the effectiveness of their ministry? How can they bring a balance between their personal life and the ministry?

Once these fair-weathered friends try to become the conscience or the Holy Spirit in your life, it is a matter of time before they jump ship. If they have donated anything of substance to your ministry, they usually end up taking it with them, committing not only mutiny, but also piracy. We have lost valuable articles such as a brand new computer and a used car. We could have fought for these objects, but we recognized that they represented an attachment that we no longer desired to have with the individuals involved.

Another area that brings great hindrance to the servants of God is the finances. It is amazing how many Christians in America are totally unrealistic about the needs of the servants of God. Most of this unrealistic perspective has to do with indoctrination and ignorance encouraged by the church system.

Through the years, Satan has robbed our finances in various ways; therefore, greatly hindering us. For example, God told some people to help us financially. These people either chucked the impression up to their own imagination or they found what appeared to be a more noble cause to give too.

Working in the mission field in America, you quickly discover that Christians in this nation are not always giving people. Rather, they can prove to be quite selfish and self-centered. I don't know how many Christians I have ministered to who gave the impression that they could not give a donation for our services, but they could eat out, buy videos, and pay $150 an hour for a secular psychologist.

I remember one time investing much energy into a certain woman. I knew she did not have much money, so I did not expect anything. However, in one of our sessions, she shared how she supported TBN. I guess she thought I was going to be impressed. But, when this woman told me she was making a donation to an organization that was not really helping her personally, and overlooking a ministry that was, I began to get an insight into the blindness that well-meaning Christians operate within. I could see the type of attitude that many Christians have towards small ministries. Small ministries are apparently good enough to use and abuse in times of need, but not legitimate enough to support.

I had a lot of momentum behind me to help this woman, but when she made the statement about supporting TBN, I felt like I had hit a wall, going a hundred miles per hour. All of a sudden, I felt exhausted and old. I realized how viable ministries are often overlooked by those they help because of the mindset of many Christians. The Apostle Paul put it best, "Even so hath the Lord ordained that they which preach the gospel should live of the gospel" (1 Corinthians 9:14). "For the scripture saith, thou shalt not muzzle the ox that treadeth out the corn. And, the labourer is worthy of his reward" (1 Timothy 5:18).

It is amazing how people in America, including Christians, expect to be paid for their services, but when it comes to paying a minister of the Gospel, they seem to operate from a different set of rules. In fact, they often give you the impression that God pays the servant; therefore, it is the servant's privilege to give to the recipient everything free, from services to books to Bible Studies.

Let me make this very clear. God's servants have the same needs everyone else does. They have to pay bills and buy groceries in order to simply live. Now, let me ask you this question, where do you think they get the money to keep on functioning so that they can be free to minister to God's sheep? Well, if you think it falls out of heaven, think again. God actually uses people to financially support His servants. His word is very clear that people who benefit from His servants have a financial obligation to them regardless of how much they have given to their church.

I remember one incident when a woman had come in for ministry. As she was standing in the office, she began to double over and moan. Once she got her voice back, she told us the Holy Spirit was sorrowful about how people had failed to properly support us. She recognized the tremendous hindrance it had caused the ministry. She told us she wanted to apologize on behalf of all those who took advantage of us. Her next action stunned us. She walked out of our office without giving any donation for our services to her. I guess this "rather well" to do woman was apologizing beforehand for her indifference.

In another incident, a friend had been upset because we left the Seattle area. I wrote her a letter and explained that we could not financially survive there. In a way, we had been forced to move because people failed to give. Let me give some advice. If you have greatly benefited from a ministry, be supportive of it as God so directs, so others can benefit from it down the line.

Another area in which Satan has robbed us is vows. Vows are commitments or pledges. I don't know how many people have told us, "When we get the money we are waiting for, we will help you." Just before these people received the money, Satan stirred the pot of self-righteousness and judgmentalism, causing the relationship to break down with us. The people then would renege on their word.

The Word is very clear about paying your vows, even to your own hurt. We see this in the life of Jonah. Apparently, Jonah had made some vows. Perhaps one of his vows was to serve God no matter what. We know he actually disobeyed God when he refused to go to Nineveh to warn them of impending judgment. In his prayer of humility and repentance, we read this in Jonah 2:9, "But I will sacrifice unto thee with the voice of thanksgiving; **I will pay that that I have vowed.** Salvation is of the LORD." (Emphasis added.)

It is important that Christians are not impulsive or flippant about their words. Words determine reputation and respect. If you have neither reputation nor respect, you will not be taken seriously or trusted by those you are ministering to.

Through the years, we have learned not to put a lot of stock into what Christians promise us. I have to admit, it has forced us to lean on God for our needs, but it can be devastating to a new kid on the block. If someone has taken you seriously, and you do not keep your word, it can result in despair, bitterness, and hopelessness.

The problem is, most Christians have been indoctrinated to believe that they must only give tithes to the church and offerings (which are usually nothing more than crumbs) to missionaries or ministries. One of our supporters who felt led to give us all of her tithing was sharing her conviction with another Christian woman. The woman turned around and rebuked her for not giving her tithes to her church, instead of to us. As we have learned from this incident and others, this indoctrination has been so cleverly instilled that well-meaning Christians often give their money amiss.

Let me ask you a simple question. Who should determine where donations should go? Should it be God or man? I'm sure your answer is God. Now, let me ask you this, when was the last time you asked God where He wanted you to give your tithes and donations?

You need to realize that when God set down the rules for giving the offerings, they went to one place, the Temple. According to Ruth Specter Lascelle, the ancient law of the tithe required three main tithes. The first one was for the upkeep of the Temple. The second tithe was for the maintenance of the feasts, but every third year a third tithe was given for the poor. In fact, the faithful Jew never gave less than a fifth of his income, and in some cases, he gave a great deal more.[2]

God was the One who determined where tithes went. They went into the upkeep of one place and took care of God's servants, the Levites and priests, as well as the poor. They also were used for the different feasts that the children of Israel practiced.

Where should our donations go today? We assume they must go to our church, since it serves as our modern-day temple.

[2] Jewish Faith and The New Covenant, pages 18-20

Therefore, it is the church which has the responsibility to distribute the money accordingly, right? Wrong on both assumptions!

Do you realize that God has a temple, but it is not made with the hands of man? Do you realize that Jesus' Church is not a building? Do you understand that the existing priesthood is not simply made up of pastors and leaders? Do you realize that in the first New Testament Church they never gave to any building projects?

Here is another fact to consider. Do you know that the Jews do not practice tithing because it is against the Law, as long as there is no temple; therefore, no established Levitical order of priests? [3] Keep in mind, the required Old Testament tithes were basically animals for sacrifice and the first-fruit of harvest, and had mostly to do with sin and feasts. In essence, Jesus literally once and for all paid this particular tithe for all of us and fulfilled four of the feasts. He was the Lamb of God who took away the sins of the world and serves as the firstfruit. [4]

If you noticed, Jesus never made mention of tithing in His teachings. In fact, Jesus established a higher moral code when it came to giving. By example, He showed us that all acceptable giving begins with the presentation of our own life, which serves as the sacrifice. In other words, you must give it all. This giving must maintain the spiritual quality of the New Testament Temple, which is man. It must lift the burdens of the priesthood that is made up of every Christian. It must be done for the edification of all the Church that is comprised of all the saints. [5] It must be done in order to further the spiritual kingdom of God (souls), and not the physical kingdom of man (buildings, programs, and numbers).

Let me ask you, how much money is being spent on unnecessary building projects and fleshly programs in your

---

[3] The Tithing Fallacy; Ernest L. Martin, pages 1-3
[4] 1 Corinthians 15:20-23
[5] Ephesians 4:11-16; 1 Peter 2:5, 9

church? How much of the money goes to the poor in your church? How much of the finances go to the godly pastors and dynamic teachers in your church? In fact, ask the Lord how He looks at how the leadership in your church handles the finances.

The truth is, you are responsible for where you donate the money you have been entrusted with. If a third of donations are not helping the poor in your own church, you probably need to look for a church that will take care of them. After all, if they are not properly taking care of the sheep in the fold, I can guarantee that if you need any help, they will not take care of you either.

Let me ask you a question, do you attend a dead church? If you do, your donations may keep it from having a proper funeral. After the temple was defiled by idolatry, God not only shut its doors, but He buried it under the fiery debris of Jerusalem. Keep in mind, anything dead that is not buried just causes a stench to God and others.

Are you supporting a pastor who is a hireling? If you are, you are putting innocent sheep in harm's way and supporting an imposter who will eventually throw you to the wolves to protect his own self-interests.

How many servants of God have come your way who have imparted life-changing manna to you, but you have given so much to the church, all you can offer is a few crumbs? I say all of this because you may be pouring your money into a dead hole, while hindering the real work of God. You may be supporting counterfeits, rather than real servants of God. In the end, most of your financial giving may have been done in vain.

The sad truth is, many churches are nothing more than big businesses with CEO's for pastors. These churches have become houses of merchandise, instead of holy sanctuaries.[6] Instead of promoting the heavenly kingdom of Christ, many well-meaning

---

[6] John 2:16

Christians are supporting man's personal kingdoms in the name of Christ.

Let's just be honest for a moment. Why are we willing to blindly entrust our money to religious organizations? Perhaps it is because of what we have been told to do by our religious leaders, but what does the Word tell us? Remember, the Word is your measuring stick, not what you have been taught by man.

James 1:27 states, "Pure religion and undefiled before God and the Father is this, to visit the fatherless and widows in their affliction, and to keep himself unspotted from the world." I quoted this scripture to point out that tithing is not mentioned. However, what it does show us is that we must get personally involved with the real needs of people.

When I consider the practices of giving in churches, I can see where the procedure has become a sick substitute for us to not get personally involved with those around us. We can justify our lack of involvement in people's lives by convincing ourselves that it is the church's responsibility to take care of these problems. After all, that is what we pay them for. In a way, it becomes a form of penance and a means to soothe our conscience. In a sense, this procedure of giving simply alleviates us from our personal scriptural responsibility to those around us, while puffing up our religious pride and giving us a false security about our spiritual well-being before God.

Gentle Shepherd Ministries has passed the 35rd year mark. Through the years, Jeannette and I have witnessed lives that were saved and changed, relationships challenged and restored, the wounded healed, and the oppressed set free. In those years, the Lord has graciously honored us with a handful of faithful supporters who have chosen to love us in spite of our humanness. They have lifted our burdens in ways they will never know. In so many ways, they have been part of miracles, as God has miraculously met our needs and multiplied our finances with their sacrificial, loving prayers and donations in order to keep this ministry going.

These supporters who are valuable, silent partners will in the end be exalted and declared before the heavenly courts. They will share in the heavenly rewards of Gentle Shepherd Ministries because they have provided us with the means to minister to hundreds of people. At this time, I want to thank each of our supporters. You know who you are. Because of your faithful support, you have given us a glimpse into God's love and unwavering devotion to those who serve Him.

9

KEELHAULED

Persecuted, but not forsaken.
(2 Corinthians 4:9a)

"The Lord showed me that you have a blasphemous spirit following you around that lies about you constantly." The statement did not surprise me since speculation and slander seemed to follow Jeannette and me everywhere we went. I was very much aware that one of Satan's greatest tactics to destroy servants of God is slander. After all, the word "devil" means slanderer or accuser of the brethren.

This slander against our ministry and character officially started with Jeannette's former partner. She seemed to manage to arouse various speculations about our character over the years.

Another source that produced slander against us was the suspicious environment that has been created in religious system by self-righteous, small-minded people. This system has a tendency to raise its ugly head when it is confronted over ungodly conduct or doctrinal error. In our encounters with the religious system, I began to get a glimpse into why Jesus caused the reaction He did when He walked this earth. He actually emptied Himself of His sovereignty as God, in order to take on the form of a servant and man. When He hit the scene two thousand years ago, the committed religious people ended up resenting Him instead of acknowledging Him as God Incarnate, the Messiah, the Savior of the world, and the Son of God.

It also amazed me to realize that even after Jesus did the miraculous, people still insisted that He was an imposter. The truth is, people never change when it comes to recognizing the truth. It is hard for them to discern the counterfeit from the original because of their pride.

I remember the day a woman pastor came to Jeannette and me. She told us that she had some people coming to her with certain "concerns" about us. I could easily guess what their concerns were—they suspected that we were lesbians. I assured the pastor that their concern was indeed a false speculation. I also encouraged her to send these concerned people along with any future ones to us. Of course, no one ever came to face us with their *"concerns."*

Gossip and slander are often founded on so-called "concerns" that are nothing more than vain imaginations and speculations. The Word is very clear about bringing such ungodly thoughts to the light in a scriptural manner, to avoid falling into the various traps of Satan. These deceptive and perverted traps are very successful in bringing destruction. They actually succeed in tarnishing an innocent person's character and murdering reputations. Many ministers and ministries are victims of character assassinations by so-called "concerned Christians."

I think it is important to consider Jesus' example in the New Testament. He sent His disciples out in twos, but in today's world, two single women or men who may be a team in ministry immediately arouse suspicion in the Christian realm. This perverted suspicion reveals how much the world has a foothold in how Christians evaluate the things around them.

Jesus made a very interesting statement. He said the children of the world are wiser than the children of the light. It is true the world is quick to recognize those who belong to its perverted ways, but Christians are ignorant about how to discern correctly among themselves. Instead of discerning, they simply speculate which often turns into conjecture, judgment, gossip, slander, and character assassination.

I remember that this same woman pastor was so concerned about our reputation that she suggested I go out with a man much younger than myself. I was a little surprised at her advice. I was a divorced woman and did not feel I had the liberty to pursue any relationship with a man at that time. I felt that such a pursuit would not be within the acceptable will of God. I realized that this woman was willing to encourage hypocrisy and even disobedience to God in order to maintain a religious mask before people.

Through the years, the Lord has managed to get me beyond putting importance in what people think, and focus on what actually pleases Him. After all, people are quick to accept masks, rather than embrace the real thing. God, on the other hand, looks beyond the masks and sees the heart.

Another area that will cause slander is anger. Through the years, pastors have slandered us because we would not play their religious games of control and manipulation. In one incident, the pastor became so angry with us that he went around telling people he suspected we were gay. He knew this was a lie, yet it served his purpose as he threw doubt on our character.

In another situation, we had asked a pastor to visit one of our older friends who was bedridden. We felt this pastor could encourage the man in his new-found Christianity. Later, we learned that this pastor and his wife had indeed paid a visit to our friend just before Christmas. When they were there, they actually badmouthed us. There was also some indication that they were unusually interested in his estate, and to whom he would leave it when his time came to depart this world. We shook our heads as we considered the selfish, unbiblical Christian example they had left with this new Christian.

Jeannette called one of the elders of this pastor's ministry and told him the story. She then insisted on setting up a meeting with the five of us to put an end to the ungodly defamation of our character. The elder assured us that he would take care of it. We never heard another word.

I think it is important to note that both of these pastors soon after the slanderous accusations lost their churches. Our God is just, and irresponsible conduct such as pride, anger, gossip, and slander will not go unnoticed or unpunished.

We were hopeful that such perverted speculations would cease when Krista Dinatale joined our team in 1996. We figured three women ministering together would silence vain imaginations and squelch speculations. However, if Satan cannot bring doubt on you in one area, he will find willing vessels that will draw other conclusions because of jealousy and anger.

In another situation, rumor had it that we had a seducing spirit and were influencing people to follow us. The people who were supposedly being seduced wanted to be part of the ministry, but we recognized that God closed the door to ministering with others who were interested in being part of our ministry, an action we all honored and submitted to. But, of course (according to these "concern' Christians), we had this seducing spirit that was leading these people into "religious foolishness."

One pastor was quite jealous of all the people coming to us for ministry. He made the comment that he could not understand why these individuals sought us out because he could do the same thing. Later, we learned that he had caused us some unwarranted trouble and possibly cost us some support.

Another avenue Satan uses are our financial and physical struggles. I don't know how many people have looked at these two struggles and have passed unmerciful judgments on us. Some of these people have benefited greatly from our ministry, but have become judgmental because we did not live up to their self-righteous, bigoted standards. They see our ongoing struggles and conclude that there must be sin in our life. Of course, this conclusion is not Spirit-inspired, but a product of the board that is in their own eye.

However, the greatest onslaught of slander came from the woman who had been shown that we had a blasphemous spirit following us. This woman and her family had supported our ministry in various ways for nearly two years. She had sent various relatives and friends our way for ministry, as well as promoted our Hidden Manna Seminars.

We had fought hard for her different family members. A couple of them got saved, some rededicated their life to Christ, and in the month of February 1995, I baptized eight members of her family in the cold waters of Lake Ballinger, outside of Mountlake Terrace, Washington.

This woman began to get a taste of the power that was available through the Holy Spirit through our deliverance ministry. I did not realize it at the time, but she was gravitating towards the Hidden Manna information and the power of God because she saw it as a means to control her family.

Another woman, who claimed to be a prophet, brought our former friend's desire for power to the forefront. This so-called "prophet" prophesied over everybody, including our friend. She basically told people what they wanted to hear and gave the impression that our friend had a corner on spiritual power and truth.

When we heard about this so-called "prophet," red flags went up, but we could see that our friend was determined to chase after this so-called "power." Within a short time, others were following her to hear a personal prophecy from this pillow prophet.[1] We

---

[1] See Ezekiel 13:20. A pillow prophet is a person that will put people's spiritual discernment asleep by telling an individual what he or she wants to hear in the name of the Lord.

began to see a change. It was obvious that our friend was coming under the seductive spirit of this false prophet.

Jeannette had felt that our friend could not be trusted when she first met her, but kept her misgivings to herself. She also realized this woman would become an adversary in the end if she did not take heed to our instructions or concerns about this false prophet. One day, I was visiting the sister of our friend. While we were talking, the sister received a phone call. I knew immediately that it was our friend trying to get information from her sister about our conversation.

It was when her sister was talking to her that the Lord gave me a complete picture of the wicked games of control and manipulation this woman actually played. He also showed me how she used me to gain valuable information about family and friends in order to cleverly weave a web of control.

This picture caused my heart to sink. I felt myself actually get sick to my stomach. I knew the Lord also was gently chiding me for my unsuspecting part in her wicked games. We totally pulled back from having any relationship with her. A month went by before there was any contact with her. Then she called and set up an appointment with us.

I knew when she and her husband walked into my office that they were bent on setting us straight. I felt my spirit become agitated as they began to try to set us right about our differences over the Holy Spirit, and reproved Jeannette for supposedly insulting one of their friends four weeks prior. This woman then proceeded to try to instruct me in regards to my counseling, concerning a certain situation. I could tell they wanted us to bow down to their pettiness and come into agreement with them.

Jeannette agreed immediately to apologize to the insulted party, but it was obvious that we had to simply agree to disagree about the other subjects. At the end of our conversation, I looked at her and told her the Lord had convicted me about our phone conversations. I looked straight into her dark brown eyes and pointed my finger at the phone and adamantly declared that all gossip would cease. The message was going over her husband's head, but she was sensing that the statement was being directed at her. I remember that her husband made a remark about my statement, and once again, I stated that the gossip would cease.

We left on what appeared to be good terms, but a few days later it appeared that the battle lines were being established. I sensed that my statement had finally hit its target. The results became obvious as this woman and her husband resorted to one of the most vicious attacks against us.

They went to all their family and friends and declared that we were involved in witchcraft and to stay away from us. Obviously, they were bent on closing down our ministry in Washington. To this day, we have no idea as to the extent they succeeded, but God knows, and simply used it for His purpose.

I remember one night when Jeannette and I sat in our small living room. We were literally hiding in the cleft of the Rock. We felt every gun of hell being aimed at us and fired. We knew the war was raging and the arsenal endless.

I remembered how God had shown the husband of this former friend that we were indeed His handmaidens, and woe to anyone who dared to touch us. I shook my head as I realized that God had confirmed to both of these former friends, now turned adversaries, about our credibility. He had shown her that a blasphemous spirit was following us in an attempt to destroy our character. He had revealed to her husband that we belonged to Him. It was amazing for me to realize how God showed them these truths because He knew they would end up falling into the same sinful trap of trying to destroy GSM. She was now trying to destroy our character with slanderous lies, and he was advocating that we actually belonged to Satan's kingdom.

I could see the awesome handwriting on the wall. God was bringing our ministry to a different spiritual place, and He was using the wickedness of these people to bring about the desired results. But, like Judas Iscariot, woe to any individual who is used in such a way. I began to sense that this couple would eventually come under a terrible judgment if they did not repent.

In situations such as these, you begin to understand what it means to be identified with Christ in His sufferings. He was slandered unfairly and accused of being part of Satan's kingdom. A friend who promoted His ministry betrayed him. He had hell's best come after Him with every weapon in the arsenal. But, unlike us, He could not hide in the cleft of the Rock as He hung on the cross.

It is not easy to drink the bitter dregs of the cup of sorrow caused by the sins of others, but there are many spiritual benefits awaiting those who truly become identified with Jesus in His sufferings.[2] The Apostle Paul understood this truth when he made this declaration in 2 Timothy 2:11 and 12, "… For if we be dead with him, we shall also live with him: If we suffer, we shall also reign with him."

I knew that our present suffering would not last forever. I also realized that it was an honor, and not a disgrace, to become identified with the One who displayed great power as the Lion of Judah, but showed tremendous strength through gentleness and meekness as the Lamb of God who was led to the slaughter by the blind ignorance, jealousy, and hatred of mankind.

---

[2] See Matthew 20:20-23

10

OUTSIDE OF THE CAMP

Let us go forth therefore unto him without
the camp, bearing his reproach. For
here have we no continuing city, but
seek one to come.
(Hebrews 13:13-14)

"Rayola will never help another ministry again!" Those words came to me as I realized God was actually challenging me to help another international ministry. I knew I was open to obey, but it would be according to God's will.

In the beginning of our ministry, Jeannette and I had helped various ministries and ministers. We saw ourselves as co-laborers with them in the harvest field. In some cases, we even abandoned our own ministry for a season to give preference to other organizations, and went out on the limb for ministers. We had zealously been supportive in each case, only to be crucified or left holding the bag by those who displayed scriptural irresponsibility.

I can still vividly recall the scene in my mind when Jeannette made the statement about me not helping a ministry again. We had worked under incredible circumstances, such as illness, to complete a discipleship course in three months for overseas missionaries. We had started the project at the request of a small ministry. Eventually, an international ministry took interest in it.

Jeannette became a humble servant to me, as well as to those we were staying with in the state of Washington, while I undertook the project to write the course. I spent 15 hours a day, seven days a week on a borrowed, (and now an obsolete) word processor, to finish this project.

Everything went pretty smoothly until the president of the smaller ministry took it upon herself to promote the course to those who were involved with the larger organization. This promotion actually started before we officially got involved with its promotion of it to the international ministry, but it seemed to escalate when we made our agreement with the larger ministry for them to use the material to train their missionaries and to be used oversees. Both Jeannette and I tried to put a stop to the prior promotion of it, but the zeal of the head of the smaller ministry drowned out all of our concerns.

When we met with the head of the international ministry to present the project to him, I explained to him how the course had been already promoted. He did not seem upset about it, but the next day, our world came crashing down. Apparently, the extent of the promotion came to the light. The head of the international ministry was furious. I could understand his reaction, but I could not accept his unscriptural response.

This religious leader, who preached that all ministry must start and conclude with love, showed anything but love. Instead of confronting us with the intent of allowing us to explain our actions, he set out to make examples of us. He never gave us any opportunity to right the situation, even though he knew it was the leader of the smaller ministry who had orchestrated it.

A week later, after complete silence from him, we sat in his office, while he pronounced judgment on us. He was unmerciful as he defrocked our ordination with his ministry. It was when I went out to the car to get my license with his organization that Jeannette tearfully proclaimed that I would never help another ministry.

She knew how hard I had worked on the project and understood the toll my hard work and his actions had taken on me. She also knew that I was void of energy and fighting depression that later swallowed me up in a great deluge of self-pity and anger.

The Lord was gracious with me during this time, but I began to learn how much stock people put in a ministry. They actually make it a "sacred cow." I have watched ministers of organizations actually justify illegal, ungodly, and unethical practices for the sake of their sacred cow. I have observed these representatives of Christ sacrifice people as they climb the ladder of power, prestige, and financial success.

I realized that the Lord wanted Jeannette and me to keep Gentle Shepherd Ministries in the right perspective. He wanted us to understand that a ministry is simply an avenue that gives some credibility, but it must never become a sick substitute for our relationship with the Person of Jesus. In other words, we must never do anything for the sake of the ministry, but for the sake of Jesus Christ. I began to understand how, in the race for survival and recognition, ministries leave Jesus behind in their practices.

I also started to see the competition that exists between ministries. Regardless of the humble impressions these religious organizations may display towards each other, the bottom line for many of them is survival. This survival hinges on money, and can prove to be unmerciful to those who may stand in the way of such a pursuit. We also found this same power struggle in the church system. This became apparent when we realized what mission field God was calling us to.

Jeannette and I had attended the mission school that the international ministry was sponsoring. I recall how Jeannette and I were preparing to go overseas. We had hopes of going to Russia where people were actually hungry for the Gospel. Our excitement escalated as we saw a picture of the first evangelistic meeting held in Romania after seven decades of being without God and His Word.

I shall never forget the picture of this meeting. The picture was comprised of three regular sized sheets of paper that were taped together. This meeting had been held outdoors in the dead of winter. If you had held such a meeting in America, there would be no show, but in Romania, 60,000 people showed up. I will never forget the spiritually hungry looks on the faces of the people who stood closest to the camera. Their eyes told volumes. They still haunt me as I write this.

Jeannette and I excitedly dreamed about going to a place where people had such hunger for the Gospel and would cherish the Word of God. It was while we were preparing in missionary school that the Lord showed Jeannette that He was calling us to America, not to a foreign mission field.

I wanted to argue with His choice. To me, America is one of the hardest mission fields in the world. It is full of religion and church buildings; therefore, it gives the impression that it is not in need of the Great Physician. The sad truth is, America has become so religious, while redefining Christianity to be nothing more than a subculture and soft-pedaling sin, causing many people to become Gospel-hardened. Its religion has actually blinded many people to their spiritual depravity. The gospel that is now being preached has been watered down to placate soft palates, while our Righteous Lord and Savior has been demoted to a good guy who will look the other way as people wallow in their sin and rebellion.

I was to learn that America is the third largest mission field in the world. It was interesting for me to note that nations, such as South Korea, were sending missionaries to America. It was also a reality check to realize that these missionaries are not being sent to the unsaved, but to the churches.

The Lord allowed the idea that America was our real mission field to sink in before He showed us the second part of our call. He was not calling us to the byways of America, but to the churches. It was hard for me to imagine why God was actually calling us to minister to the Christian church. After all, aren't those in the Christian realm redeemed and on their way to heaven?

Quietly, I was debating with the Lord over the second part of our calling. I reminded Him that we had three major strikes against us that would hinder our work among the churches. The biggest strike was our gender.

In countries where people are hungry for the Word of God, they will accept whatever vessel God may use, including women. After all, the real issue is not what vessel God uses, but whether the vessel is offering the things of God that will result in eternal life.

The problem with the organized church in America is that it is not desperate enough for the things of God. The church may be suffering from malnutrition, but it has failed to recognize it because many continue to gorge themselves on inept, man-centered, wrong spiritual diet.

So much of the spiritual food presented today in Christianity lacks the pure Word of God and/or the right spirit. It actually dulls spiritual discernment and gives Christians a false security. In essence, the organized church has moved away from basic Christianity: That of the preaching of the cross that calls for repentance from sins and worldly ways to embrace a changed lifestyle.

As women in ministry, we continually encounter ignorance, pride, fear, and prejudice because of our gender. These sins are often cleverly hidden behind a couple of scriptures that are used against us in ministry with silent fervency and vengeance.

I understood the attitude that plagued us concerning our sex. I myself had wrestled with the scriptures found in 1 Corinthians 14 and 1 Timothy 2 when I realized that God was calling me into full-time ministry. I decided I was going to settle the issue once and for all. I asked the Lord to bring material to me that would bring proper understanding to these controversial scriptures.

Over a five-year period, material came my way that began to explain the purpose behind Paul's instructions in both of these texts. I found out that 1 Corinthians 14 was inspired because the Jewish traditions (known as the Oral Law of the Jews) were infiltrating the Church of Corinth. My research showed me that life and death issues were behind the instructions found in 1 Timothy 2. The problem with these scriptures occurred when man made a doctrine of them instead of understanding the circumstances that prompted Paul's particular instruction.

The Word of God shows us that God has used women in leadership positions. Deborah was a judge and a prophetess or counselor. Huldah, a prophetess, had actually counseled the priests of her day. Priscilla taught Apollo. And, Phebe was in leadership in the church of Cenchrea.[1]

My research helped me to make peace with my womanhood and accept my calling. I actually began to see how God often used my gender to test the attitudes of others. I realized that if someone was actually too good or prideful enough to receive the things of God from a woman, then in essence, they were rejecting the author as well, God Himself.

Another strike we had against us is that we were divorced women. In some camps of religious thought, if you are divorced, then you can only go so far in your life of service regardless of what you may have to offer. It does put a black mark on your character, even though you are living a celibate, upright life.

Another area that hindered us greatly was our financial status. I'm afraid this challenge was magnified by erroneous teachings of financial prosperity that are often used as an unfair plumb line as

---

[1] You can read Rayola's findings about women in God's kingdom in her exposition, *Women's Place in the Kingdom of God* in Volume 5 in her foundational series.

to a person's credibility in the kingdom of God. If you don't have money, many misguided people question your character as to why God is not "blessing" you. In fact, ministers who struggle with finances are sometimes cursed by popular heretics who claim that people can know God is blessing them because of their financial well-being. In one case, I read about how a popular evangelist told people to not give to the poor because God will not bless them, rather, give to the rich like him and God will indeed bless them. What a lie from the pit of hell. God tells us to give to the poor, and He also warns us that if we oppress people who are less fortunate, He will bring swift judgment upon us.[2]

As the Lord showed me the condition of the Church, I could understand why He was calling us to contend with His Body. Today, many in the organized church are looking for professional entertainers who look the part whether they have the goods or not. They are looking for temporary worldly blessings to heap upon their lusts, rather than spiritual blessings that will last for eternity. They are looking for ways around tribulation, instead of embracing it, knowing it works godly character. They are looking for short cuts to heavenly bliss without denying themselves, picking up their cross, and walking the narrow path of Calvary.[3]

The results are devastating. Much of the church chooses to remain shallow, while encouraging religious entertainment, which is often nothing more than paganism. Christians in such arenas are surface and carnal, thereby avoiding any reality that may challenge their little religious worlds. Because of this worldly preference, the worship has become fleshly in many churches, the preaching dead, and the religious activities vain.

We watched popular Christianity encourage people to wear the acceptable religious masks, avoid stirring the waters, and blindly worship the leaders and the churches. I began to realize that the

---

[2] Psalm 66:12
[3] Matthew 16:24; Ephesians 1:3; James 1:3-5; 4:1-4; 1 John 2:15-17

vital signs of the church implied it was in grave danger of self-destruction. I knew in spite of my gender, divorced status, and my lack of professionalism that I had to avail myself to God. After all, these obstacles do not signify mission impossible to God. And, according to 1 Corinthians 1:27-29, He uses the foolish, weak, base, and despised things as a means to receive His just glory.

Jeannette and I took heart in the types of vessels God chooses to use. We knew we were often considered foolish because of our gender. We were looked upon as being weak because of our financial condition. We knew we were seen as base because of our inability to change anything, and despised because we were divorced and did not fit people's concept of ministers. In fact, we often challenged the self-righteous concepts, and were used to expose hypocrisy and self-righteous pride.

One time, a woman properly described our ministry after praying for us. She told us that the Lord uses us to make a giant swath everywhere we go. She grinned as she added that we definitely leave an impression in every place we travel, whether we want to or not. Her evaluation was proven right as to the type of effect we have had on those around us.

I have to confess, Jeannette and I tried to look professional in order to have credibility in Washington. We lived in an area that was considered the capital of Yuppie Ville. The rich and elite, with their certain look and cars, created an air that went beyond the ridiculous and became an absolute farce.

The church we attended seemed to attract these people. Jeannette and I had decent clothes from Sears and thrift stores, but they did not match the Nordstrom's brand of clothes and the $80 scarves that seemed to highlight some of the people's expensive suits and blazers.

Here I was, a girl from Idaho who grew up in a small community of loggers and sawmill workers. I never put much stock in the clothes or hairdos that people wore because I knew neither determined the character of a person. In some cases, the fancy clothes and hairdos often cover up miserable, wretched, lonely individuals who were trying to find some real substance to their vain, worldly lifestyle.

One day, Jeannette and I were ministering to one of these yuppies. She told us that our clothes were out of style and if we wanted to have any credibility, we had to dress the part. I knew she was partly right. I could see that unless you appealed up front to the eyes of some of these individuals, they would disregard you like an irritating fly, regardless of what you had to offer them.

I struggled with the obvious shallowness that existed in some Christians. I knew this surface life represented a stony heart that had not been plowed to allow the root of God's truth to establish the real substance of a person. I recognized that I could never financially compete with the fashion show I so often witnessed around me. I also knew that it was not necessary. God reminded me that in this present world, I would always be a girl from Idaho, and that my authority and power did not lie in what I wore or in where I was from. Rather, it came from Him and His Word.

I had suffered my first identity crises in ministry, but I quickly learned that my identity would ultimately be found in Christ. I also was reminded that I am not here for the wolves, swine, or goats that are found within the Body of Christ, but I am here for God's sheep who will be drawn by the cords of God's Spirit and truth.[4]

We also were greatly hindered by what I call built-in mechanisms within the church system that come in the form of doctrines. Many of these doctrines were not scriptural, or they lacked the right spirit because of the emphasis that was put in certain areas of the belief system. However, these doctrines or sacred cows often served as a means to control and manipulate

---

[4] To find out more about the wolves, swine and goats, see Rayola's book, *Battle for the Soul,* chapter 15 or her Bible Study, *"What Are You Doing With Jesus"* in Gentle Shepherd's Supplementations.

people. They actually created a frame of reference that kept people from being able to discern properly. I watched people accept heretics over a true servant of God because the heretical teaching fit within their accepted frame of reference. What is sad is, if these people only took time to study, they would find that this particular teaching was not in the Word of God.

One of the greatest examples of this is the teaching concerning "covering." I cannot tell you how many people have asked us who serves as our covering. If we did not have an "acceptable" covering to their way of thinking, many would turn us off like a light switch.

If you have not heard of this erroneous teaching, let me explain it to you. You must have a person or organization overseeing you or you are considered invalid or a "Lone Ranger." The question is, can this teaching be found in scripture? The answer is no, but many people who have been exposed to it assume that it is scriptural, and are adamant that everyone must comply in order to prove they are godly.

Let us just consider this teaching. First of all, the Bible speaks of three coverings. Isaiah 25:7 speaks of evil coverings which are over men or nations. 1 Corinthians 11 tells us a woman's hair is her covering. Finally, Isaiah 30:1 states that the only acceptable covering is the Holy Ghost. As you consider the other coverings, you will find that the first covering is spiritual, but it is evil. The second covering is physical and has no spiritual significance.

As I consider fallen man, I realize that man and his organizations are incapable of being a spiritual covering for anyone. In fact, man's righteousness is as filthy rags.[5] At best, a man or his organization can only become an evil covering. After all, how can you even begin to determine who could serve as a perfect covering for you among fallen humanity? How many

---

[5] Isaiah 64:6

people have innocently submitted themselves to leadership that is totally self-centered and self-serving? Let's face it; the most righteous people are subject to error, delusion, and failure.

Even the Apostle Paul instructed people to follow him as he followed Christ. Paul never commanded people to consider him as their covering. In fact, Paul told people that Christ is the head of His Church.[6] Let's just put this in perspective. If Christ is the head, and man serves as a covering, who has the final authority? Well man, of course. In this scenario, Christ is not the covering or the overseer. Rather, man is the one who is being exalted over the head *(Christ)*. Therefore, man has the final say.

This precarious teaching puts man's soul in harm's way because man or his organization becomes the final authority as to what a person believes. This allows a man or an organization to control and manipulate people, by conforming them to their own religious image. Keep in mind, the real goal of any godly minister is to make you a follower of Jesus so you can be conformed to His image.[7]

We believe what the Word says about the need for His people to surround themselves with wise counselors.[8] We believe that such counselors can call an individual to accountability and help guide their steps. Through the years, Jeannette and I have sought out such counselors.

However, on the other hand, God must be a person's final authority in all spiritual matters. For example, the Holy Spirit must be your conscience; the Word of God must serve as to what constitutes reality, and the Son of God as your example and mirror.

Over the years, Jeannette and I have fought hard to keep God as our final authority. We have wrestled with all the different issues

---

[6] 1 Corinthians 11:1, 3; Colossians 1:18
[7] Romans 8:29; 2 Corinthians 3:18
[8] Proverbs 11:14

and challenges to maintain our liberty in Christ, instead of coming under the bondage of religion or man. We have sought God's will in all matters, instead of accepting man's will or his interpretation.

Sadly, this liberty has caused us to be labeled as "Lone Rangers" because we do not fit into religious concepts or practices. Some people have accused us of having a "so-called" Jezebel spirit. We have been threatened, slandered and crucified by those who consider themselves discerning in the religious system.

Through it all, we had the Scriptures to fall back on. We recognize that all the godly prophets, including Jesus, would have been labeled as "Lone Rangers" in today's religious system because they would refuse to come under the wickedness of manmade religious systems. They were outcasts, but they made the difference with uncompromised truth. They were threatened and falsely accused because they did not fit, but in the end they were exalted by God. They were persecuted because they served as a convicting example of righteousness, but through it all they left a lasting mark on hearts and minds.

It is easy to say that we want to be identified with Christ, but to actually enter into His sufferings is another story. As Hebrews 13:10-14 states, Jesus went outside of the camp or gate. In other words, He went outside of the confines of man, the world, and religion, to pay the ultimate price.

Through the years, I have come to realize that in order to be identified with Jesus, I must be willing to go outside the camp or gate of what is acceptable, comfortable, and convenient. If I make this decision to follow Jesus outside of the comforts of the world, the conveniences of self, and the control of the religious world, I will suffer reproach.

I will taste the bitter sting of persecution, as people will hail me one moment as a minister because I helped them in some way, and then turn around and demand my crucifixion the next moment because somehow I failed to meet all their requirements. I will be mocked because I am an outcast who no longer fits into a world governed by depravity. I will be rejected because I will not submit to an unfeeling religious system that ultimately fights against the truth of God and demands blind devotion from innocent and deluded followers.

In ministry, I have met four types of ministers. The first group is comprised of deceitful workers. These ministers can be found within the gate. They are teaching that gain is godliness.[9] They use this false teaching to justify their worldly lusts, adulterous ways, and idolatrous practices. They rob widows, oppress strangers, shun the fatherless, and discredit true servants of God. Their end is destruction.

The second group is comprised of those who have walked away from godly service because, in their zeal and innocence, they became victims of the religious system. They saw the hypocrisy of the system, and became hopeless because they felt the system represented their only avenue of service. They saw the games, and recognized that they would end up betraying what dignity they had left if they submitted to them. These individuals became aware that the system did not care about souls, but about advancing personal kingdoms. Ultimately, they realized that this blatant disobedience to Scripture and calling is nothing but a scam.

The problem with this type of person is that, not only does they walk away from the religious system and games, but such an individual will also walk away from their calling. These individuals cannot see how God can work outside of the system. Jeannette and I struggled with this very reality. However, God showed us that He would cut another door for us that would be outside of the system. We have watched Him accomplish such a feat.

---

[9] 2 Corinthians 11:13-15; 1 Timothy 6:3-10

If you are such a person, you need to know that your high calling will never be realized within the confines of a system. You must be willing to walk outside of the camp or gate and become identified with Jesus. It is in this identification that your calling will be brought forth.

The third group of ministers are those who stand at the entrance of the gate. They have not yet made the trek outside of the camp to be identified with Christ. These people can be righteous individuals, but they have been brought to a place where they recognize that they have just encountered limitation in their spiritual life and calling. They sense that there is more, but cannot understand how to pursue it. After all, they are doing everything by the book. They are preaching the Gospel and trying to disciple Christians to be followers of Jesus. They have seen the move of God in their midst. They are operating within the confines of their denomination and doctrines, and yet, they feel like something is missing.

These people can remain at the entrance of the gate. However, if they want more, they must risk what has served as the acceptable, comfortable, normal, and convenient way of doing things. In fact, they must risk it all to obtain a greater height and depth in Christ. It will begin to cost them as they challenge the acceptable, confront the comfortable, expose the fallacy of the normal, and reveal the self-serving motives of the convenient.

Finally, you have those who have traveled outside of the camp, bearing Christ's reproach. They are humble people because the nonsense has been knocked out of them. They are simple people because all they care about is pleasing Christ Jesus. They are focused people because they are only impressed with those things that have been ordained and accomplished by God. They are single-minded because they have one goal, to bring glory to God. They are not caught up with ministry or numbers because their only desire is to fight a good fight, finish the course, and keep the faith. Their vision is heavenward and their hope is found sitting on the right hand of God.

Are you a minister of the Gospel? Which category do you fit in? If you are within the gate, you need to repent of defiling the sacred things of God with the world.

If you have become a victim of the system and have walked away from your call, you need to repent. Your call does not hinge on systems or man, but on Jesus Christ. He is your strength and hope. Go to Him in repentance and humility. He will lift you up and refresh your calling.

Perhaps you are standing in the entrance of the gate, and you need to make the decision to risk it all. There is a greater life outside of the gate. After all, the mark we leave on this world is not determined by whether we have a valid ministry, but on the type of relationship we have with Christ.

Past experiences have taught me that it is easy to get caught up in ministry and leave Christ behind. Ministry can cause an individual to burn out. Always keep in mind, everything that we need in order to be effective ministers is found in Christ. We can only receive sustaining spiritual food as we seek Him out daily.

Perhaps you are in the fourth group. You have come to a point where nothing makes sense but Jesus. Your eyes are heavenward and you are waiting for the day when you will see your precious Lord face to face. The walk has been hard and difficult in many ways, but it has also been glorious in other ways.

If you are a recent follower, keep in mind that Jesus will lead you away from the world and religion. He will lead you to the gate where you must decide to relinquish your rights to your life as you know or desire it. The decision you make at the gate will be determined by how much you are willing to abandon to follow Him all the way.

Jesus does not promise us an easy life. He said that we would have much tribulation, but it is in tribulation that Jesus becomes more precious to an individual.[10] Remember, Christ is your real spiritual reward and promise. Do not leave this world lean in soul and spiritually bankrupt.

---

[10] John 16:33

11

SHIPWRECKED

...cast down, but not destroyed.
(2 Corinthians 4:9b)

"Rayola, do you realize we fervently asked God to put us out to sea and when He did, our ship sunk?" I could not help but think that Jeannette gave a great description of the events that occurred when we were just beginning to feel like Gentle Shepherd Ministries was close to being launched out in greater ways.

In the two years that we were in the Seattle area, Jeannette and I had managed to run the whole gamut of promotional avenues. We had been on Christian TV four times and on the radio nine times. Christians were just starting to show a glint of recognition when they heard the name of this new ministry.

Since moving to Seattle, it seemed as if we were in an incredible whirlwind. We were constantly on the run to make the name of Gentle Shepherd Ministries a household word in the Christian realm. Most of our frantic activities were also motivated by the need to financially survive. In fact, we were so busy that we made a common mistake in ministry: We left behind our first love, Jesus Christ.

Our emphasis to maintain a viable relationship with Jesus was lost in the midst of serving Him. We were doing great things for the kingdom of heaven, but the King was being left out. We were doing good things for others, but in the process, we were missing the best for our spiritual well-being.

On top of the ministry activities, Jeannette was offered the opportunity of a lifetime to prove her talents as a professional artist. This offer came when we knew our free rent was coming to an end. The present funds we were receiving through the ministry barely paid the bills. We both knew that if we were going to financially survive, one of us would have to get a job. It appeared as if God was solving the problem by allowing this project to fall into Jeannette's lap.

Jeannette had been exposed to this project prior to our move to Washington. Due to a personal request of some friends, we had met with their former pastor in Bothell. During our meeting, he discovered Jeannette was a professional artist. He began to share his dream about building a chapel where the life of Christ would be depicted in beautiful paintings. I will never forget how relieved Jeannette was that this pastor's vision was far from reality. She was not sure she could accomplish such a feat if she were presented with the opportunity.

When we moved to Seattle, we began to attend this particular church. To our surprise, the pastor had made incredible moves to make his dream a reality. He was keeping his eyes open for the artists that would undertake the various projects he had in mind.

Needless to say, he approached Jeannette about doing the paintings. It appeared that he first tested her out by commissioning her to paint a wall mural of the baptism of Jesus. She started the project a week before Christmas and was done by New Year's Eve. The congregation was enthusiastic about the results, and the pastor must have approved of it because he hired Jeannette to do fourteen paintings for his chapel.

It was decided that these paintings would be done on a canvas that measured 5½ feet by 10 feet. The pastor also wanted these paintings to have a long life, so he instructed Jeannette to find the type of paint that would endure. She went to great lengths to accommodate the pastor in securing the right type of materials. Jeannette decided to use a mixed medium on her paintings. She started out by using acrylic paint to sketch the picture on the canvas, and under paint it, and then she used oil paint to bring it to life.

Jeannette was to learn that the pastor may have loved art, but he did not understand how artists brought life to their artwork. Great masterpieces are not just automatically produced. Rather, they are a matter of inspiration, as well as an expression of the depths of the artist's soul. This expression is not available at just any whim. Artists must first have the vision as to what they want to portray before they can masterfully express it.

The pastor had a deadline in his mind for each painting. He felt Jeannette could get a painting out every two weeks. His calculation was that she would be done in 28 weeks. Although she did not finish within the pastor's deadline, Jeannette completed all fourteen paintings in eleven months, a record time in the minds of most people who understood the immensity of the project.

This unspoken deadline began to cause Jeannette a lot of pressure. It took her over three weeks to properly portray Pentecost with 120 people. The Triumphal Entry took a great deal of time, as she revealed the scene in detail. Each painting had its own challenges, and some were vandalized by young people in the church (because the project was undertaken in a section of the large foyer) which caused her to have to redo some of her work.

Jeannette felt the pressure to produce, rather than create. She pushed herself as much as she could without compromising the quality of her work. Her goal was to see Jesus lifted up and glorified. She wanted the paintings to not only express a life-changing message, but her own personal love and devotion to

Jesus. She felt no time or expense could do Jesus' life any justice, but she wanted to make sure she did her best.

Sadly, Jeannette's day did not end after standing behind a canvas for hours. She came after work and helped me at the office at night. We were doing seminars on Saturdays, and I was teaching a couple of Bible Studies a week that she participated in.

Looking back, I can see where neither one of us were aware of what we were doing to our bodies, especially Jeannette. Jeannette may have been giving her best to God, but she was also unsuspectingly offering her health up as a sacrifice. She didn't realize it, but she would eventually become a broken, devastated vessel.

The first inkling that her body was beginning to rebel against her strenuous activities occurred within a couple of months into the project. She started seeing flashes of light streak across the vision of her right eye. Jeannette has poor eyesight and is dependent upon glasses. Her left eye has a floater that caused hindrance in seeing, but her right eye functioned properly, until the neon flashes started to appear.

Jeannette went to the pastor and his prayer group for prayer. She then set up an appointment with an optometrist. The optometrist discovered that there was fluid behind her retina, due to a tear. However, the doctor had no idea as to why the fluid had suddenly developed.

The next indication that something was going terribly amiss in Jeannette's body was her energy level. She found herself becoming totally exhausted as she fought through her many aches and pains each morning. She worked, while ignoring the tennis elbow and the depression that seemed to be engulfing her every day. She dragged herself out of bed each morning, only to wonder how long she could keep up the pace.

As time went on, she noticed that she was breaking out with a red rash on her neck. Eventually, the rash, along with boils, engulfed the upper half of her body, including some of her face. She was also being plagued with eczema that had joined ranks with her other skin problems to torment her.

At times, she felt her body internally tremble. She began to sense her physical problems were serious and her body could no longer fight back. While celebrating the Christmas holidays, she was attacked once more. She became sick with the flu and permanently lost the use of most of her voice. Jeannette was beginning to feel more and more trapped in her own body. Her fear and frustration were growing. She sensed that she should not go to a "regular" doctor, and debated about her limited options because we had no insurance or ability to pay medical bills.

In April of 1995, Jeannette finished her last painting, "The Crucifixion," just before the church's Easter program. She was so physically, emotionally, and spiritually exhausted that she could not fully comprehend or celebrate her accomplishments.

It was after she had finished the project that her physical problems escalated into a nightmarish realm. Jeannette began to lose the battle with the rashes, boils, and eczema. At night, her whole body would itch and internally tremble. She silently endured the discomfort, while fighting for sleep. In the morning, still totally exhausted, she would wake up to find blood on her nightgown, sheets, and pillows.

I can remember on numerous occasions hearing Jeannette crying in the bathroom in utter pain and frustration. Showers became a torment as the water seemed to burn her skin, rather than refresh it. Clothes became an enemy to her. They would cause more irritation to her already raw, inflamed skin. She became particular about what type of clothes she wore. She found cotton was the only material that did not cause unbearable discomfort to her. She looked at people, and wondered how they could tolerate wearing clothes of any kind.

One night, I was walking past her bedroom when I sensed the presence of something very cold and foreboding. It made me stop dead in my tracks. The Holy Spirit immediately identified the presence that was lingering in her room. It was a spirit of death.

I walked over to her bed. I could tell she was struggling between life and death. As I rebuked the spirit of death, I could feel warmth come back into the room. Peace came to Jeannette's spirit, allowing her to experience rest for the first time in days. Later, Jeannette confessed to me that she knew how fragile life was. She told me her life was like a small flicker of light, and it would not take much to blow it out.

Not only did Jeannette fight the physical pain, she fought great bouts of depression. Fear became her constant companion, self-pity nipped at her heels, and anger threatened to raise its ugly head. One night, Jeannette hit a crisis. She cried out to God and gave Him three options. She told Him, "Heal me, kill me, or bring a Christian herbalist into my life." God answered her prayer by bringing a Christian herbalist across our path.

We have nine internal body systems, and when the herbalist tested Jeannette, she found that all nine systems were barely functioning. She tested her for food allergies and found out that she was allergic to most foods. After all the tests were completed, the herbalist gave Jeannette the verdict. She had been chemically poisoned from her oil paints due to painting in an enclosed area. Since her colon was totally congested, her kidneys not functioning properly, and she never sweated, the poisons were being forced through her body in a negative manner.

Her body had so many toxins in it that these poisons were finding residence in her muscles, causing great pain and stiffness. As her body became overloaded, it started storing the toxins in her cells. Once the cells were overloaded, the poisons were forced out through her pores, causing what she described to be a burning, acid sensation.

She had parasites and candida, which possibly caused her to have a leaky gut. When you have a leaky gut, food particles seep through your intestinal walls into your blood. The immune system identifies these particles as foreign agents and attacks them, causing a person to become allergic to the particular food. This explained her food allergies.

She had to avoid clothing and bedding that were not 100 percent cotton. She had to wash everything twice, once with natural detergent and the second time with vinegar, to make sure none of the detergent remained in the material.

Since there were chemicals in the water, a friend gave us a filter for our shower. Jeannette had to stay away from foods with preservatives, and give up the luxury of having permanents to avoid overloading her system even more.

The herbalist also tested me. She found that three of my body systems were not functioning. She also discovered that I was a borderline diabetic who was facing some major physical problems down the road if I didn't get my body under control with the right diet and supplements.

The herbalist wrote down a list of things we needed to do according to the urgency of our problems. Jeannette needed to start by cleaning her colon, detoxifying her liver, getting rid of the parasites, and healing her leaky gut. She outlined a strict diet, and suggested supplements that would complement the task. As for me, I had to eat right, stop drinking my much beloved coffee, and take supplements that would help my overworked pancreas to function correctly.

When we got home, Jeannette realized that she was at a crossroad. We knew that this health program would cost us hundreds of dollars. We were almost out of the debt that incurred when we moved to Seattle and started our ministry. Now, we were faced with a life-and-death situation that would plunge us deeper into debt.

Jeannette wondered if her life was worth going into debt for. At that moment, she knew she had to choose life and go all the way with the program or give way to the death that was nipping at her heals. As she weighed her options, she chose life, knowing down the line when she was in the thick of things that she would probably regret her decision.

Once Jeannette made the decision, she tackled her health problems with great tenacity. She totally changed her diet and took all the supplements suggested, which threw her body into a major healing crisis.

A healing crisis occurs when the body begins to dump all the toxins into your system. This can cause flu-like symptoms. This crisis escalates if your body is not able to flush this matter out through the different eliminating systems.

The healing crisis was so extreme that the herbalist told Jeannette to back off of some of the supplements. Jeannette refused because she knew her condition was critical; therefore, she needed to take extreme measures. After about a month, we began to see some improvement in Jeannette. We went back to the herbalist, and she admitted in a subtle way that she was not sure Jeannette was going to live.

This was the beginning of our journey into understanding how our bodies work. These temples of the Holy Spirit are incredible instruments, and we need to understand how they work so we can take control and responsibility for our bodies. We went to classes to learn about the body's systems and the functions of herbs. We also learned about metabolic systems, eating according to our blood type, and the importance of digestive enzymes.

However, Jeannette's struggles went beyond the physical. She had to contend with a bombardment of doubts and questions. Why was this happening to her? Was she in some great sin that brought the heavy hand of God down on her? She examined every nook and cranny of her life, only to encounter silence. There was no conviction or revelation of any sin by the Holy Spirit. She had to trust God with the unseen and the unexplained.

As she walked through the valley of the shadow of death, she had to fight doubt as to God's intention towards her. She clung to promises in the Word, and chose to believe that God was with her in spite of the darkness and despair that swallowed up her soul. She became more isolated as people stared at the disfiguration of her skin due to the rash and boils. She began to feel totally alone because no one could share in her plight. It became obvious to Jeannette that it was a great time of testing, not only for her, but for others as well.

Christians have a hard time with the subject of prolonged suffering. The first initial response to illness is usually compassion. However, if an illness like Jeannette's wears on for a long period of time, the compassion quickly turns into speculation and judgment.

The first inkling of failing this test comes in the form of assumptions. People speculate and conclude that there must be some sin in a person's life because God has not healed them. As they quietly speculate, they begin to look for signs that confirm their suspicions.

A person who is sick with chemical poisoning such as Jeannette can be touchy, fearful. and prone to emotional outbursts. If a person has a congested liver, they will suffer deep depression and panic attacks. These people feel vulnerable, misunderstood, and judged. Their level of energy is unpredictable, and their tolerance level nil because their nerves are shot. They struggle with unbelief and anger towards God. Inevitably, such a person will give judgmental people the necessary ammunition to judge and condemn.

Up to this present time Jeannette has been fighting various battles with her health. In these battles, she has encountered many of "Job's friends." These individuals have judged her, including those who have been closest to us. Like Job, we drew the same conclusion about some of our friends, "I have heard many such things: miserable comforters are ye all" (Job 16:2).

Jeannette admitted one day that she sought isolation from people. She shared how she was scared to death of meeting healthy Christians because very few ever seem to understand her plight. Because of their ignorance, they usually ended up judging her, rather than encouraging or praying for her.

The Lord revealed to both of us the devastation that was befalling us as the means of preparing us for the fast approaching destruction. He showed me that we were going into a watery grave. For Jeannette, He related it as walking through a seemingly endless narrow valley that was surrounded by dark, foreboding mountains. The path was long and difficult, but in the end, she would come out into light and beauty. Jeannette began to push past her own doubts and depression to identify her real enemy. It was Satan, the enemy of the souls of all mankind.

While attending a different church one Sunday, we went forward for prayer. As the pastor began to pray, he stopped to inform us that Satan was trying to kill us. It was a confirmation to both of us as to the real source behind our devastation.

This is when Jeannette started to catch a glimpse of how some people are set apart to bear a testimony to the unseen world. God looks for Individuals who will choose to love and believe Him, regardless of the devastation surrounding their lives. Such an individual in the fiery ovens will silence the mocking and accusations of the kingdom of darkness, and cause the angels to rejoice in the courts of heaven.

Recently Jeannette also lost hearing in her right ear due to an infection. She has come a long way physically, but she daily contends with hearing out of one ear as she struggles with voice loss, which was finally diagnosed as Spasmodic Dysphonia.[1] She has more energy, but she must be careful not to overdo it because once her energy is gone there is none in reserve to help her. She still has to face "Job's friends" along the way, but through it all, Jesus has become precious to her.

One day, Jeannette took our little dog, Angel, for a walk. As she was walking around our driveway, she felt Jesus come alongside of her. He inclined His ear towards her. She knew that she could ask anything of Him and He would give it to her. Oh, how she wanted her voice healed, her life restored, but her desire to have more of Him flooded her soul as she walked in His presence. Everything became dim to her in light of possessing the greatest treasure of all. She gave in to her present overwhelming desire by asking Him to give her more of Him.

Jeannette and I have learned that this world holds nothing for us. Our hope is heavenward, our direction sure, and our life rests in the hands of the One who reached out from a cross on our behalf. Jesus truly became identified with us to embrace the depths of sorrow and tragedy that plagues mankind.

As Job declared in Job 19:25-26, "For I know that my redeemer liveth, and that he shall stand at the latter day upon the earth: And though after my skin worms destroy this body, yet in my flesh shall I see God."

---

[1] Jeannette barely speaks above a whisper. Attempts to speak any louder causes a sore throat and taxes her energy.

12

IN THE WATERY GRAVE

Deep calleth unto deep at the noise
of thy waterspouts: all thy waves and
thy billows are gone over me.
(Psalm 42:7)

"Lord, I don't understand why people make it hard for You to simply step on the scene and make things right." Underneath, I knew the answer to the question, but I just wanted to work through my frustration. The challenges surrounding the people in our lives and the ministry had caused me to experience a weariness that was about to consume me.

We had been in a watery grave for over two years. In that time, we had traveled over 5,000 miles to get to our present destination. Our destination not only proved to be barren, but isolated. We were surrounded by wild country that could give you the impression that you were indeed alone. At night, it proved to be an eerie place that gave the sensation that hundreds of eyes were upon you. The reason for such a perception was that the majority of the inhabitants were wild animals along with many small creatures that seemed to come from another dimension.

Mountains loomed all around us. They were as rugged-looking as the countryside. These great mountains seemed to serve as boundary markers to the Lost River Basin near Arco, Idaho, the closest town to the Craters of the Moon.

According to my understanding, this basin had received its name from the fact that the river that ran through the countryside would actually disappear at times. I don't know if my information was right, but the Lost River had something about it that seemed to be as mysterious as it was beautiful.

The terrain around us was symbolic of the struggles we had been encountering since we started Gentle Shepherd Ministries seven years previously. We had encountered much harshness and were now in a grave. We felt at times like we had almost completely disappeared.

The circumstances that brought us to our present place had all the elements for the making of a good movie. We had a variety of situations that had the ability to arouse almost every known emotion in a person's life. Some of the incidents were funny, while others had enough suspense to keep the audience on the edge of their seats.

Even though it was as though we were hidden in a desolate place where no one could see us, God brought people to us. However, once again, we found ourselves under attack. New challenges, like the surrounding mountains, seemed to be looming up in front of us.

We may have had a change of scenery, but not of challenges. It always seemed like we were swimming upstream against the current. I thought about the day that God finally released us from the Seattle area. I knew our ministry was over in that particular mission field, and it was just a matter of time before we left. We both sensed we would be going to Texas.

If you had told me we would be going to Texas a year prior, I would have laughed at you. I had no desire to go to Texas, but when the vice grip tightens, you are willing to go anywhere, just to get out of the squeeze.

When the opportunity was presented to us the first time about Texas, we were in Rome, Georgia. Jeannette and I had been given a free promotional package to introduce our book, *Hidden Manna,* and her artwork to a greater public spectrum. We felt God wanted us to go, but didn't have the means to fly across country to benefit from it.

Jeannette felt impressed to call a godly man and his wife to pray about the situation. They had commissioned her to do a painting of Mary Magdalene, proclaiming to the disciples that Jesus had risen. Jeannette did an excellent job on the painting. The owner even had an open house so people could come and view the masterpiece.

The wife readily agreed to pray about our Georgia trip. The next morning, as we walked into our office, we were greeted by the phone ringing. I answered it to find the kind man on the other end of the line. His profession required him to do some traveling. He told me that United Airlines had just called him that very morning to inform him that he had 100,000 mileage plus and he was giving 50,000 of them to Jeannette and me, so we could fly to Rome Georgia.

We could see the hand of God in the whole situation. We rejoiced in a shocked state. We sensed that God wanted us to go, but we had no idea why. Everything began to fall into place for our Georgia trip. We did not know what to expect, but we were trusting God with the outcome.

Rome turned out to be a spiritual feast for us, as well as the first vacation we had as a team in ministry. We met authors, artists, and people who loved God. Every time we had a physical meal, Jeannette and I enjoyed a spiritual meal, as we fellowshipped with various people from all walks of life.

Rome turned out to be a beautiful place. We enjoyed southern hospitality and got an insight into its people and rich culture. It was like partaking of one incredible dessert.

The subject of Houston, Texas came up during one of our evening meals in Rome. The president of the Christian promotional company started talking about opening another office in Houston. He was keeping an eye open for people to help him. Somehow, he ended up asking us if we would be interested in moving to Houston to help him start this new office.

Jeannette and I were aware that God was closing doors in Seattle, and we suspected Texas would be our next mission field. We told him we might be interested.

We stayed in Rome for a week, flying out of Atlanta, Georgia, May 2nd. When we arrived in Seattle, at 1 A.M., we were greeted by the news that our place of residence, Kirkland, had experienced an earthquake that evening. It had done damage to some homes. Both Jeannette and I were thankful that we were spared the experience, and we later learned that God had graciously protected our condo from any damage. We clearly saw God's faithfulness to honor us in special ways.

For a month, Jeannette and I felt like we were on a roller coaster. The prospects of Houston seemed more uncertain, leaving us with no prospects or options. One Sunday in church, our friend, Krista, approached us and told us the Lord showed her she would be going with us when we left Seattle. Her statement threw me off balance. I simply told her if God wanted it that way, she would be leaving with us. Admittedly, I never really gave her statement any further consideration.

We had met Krista Dinatale at the church where Jeannette had sacrificed her health to produce 14 masterpieces. Krista was going through a devastating time in her life. A pastor of the church had referred her to me for counseling. I never dreamed that our relationship would extend into a friendship.

When we left the church and started attending another, Krista followed us to our new church. She had volunteered her time, and helped us organize some supplies at our office. She slowly became a big part of our lives and hearts.

There was a point that Krista's vulnerability set her up for a fall. Jeannette and I knew she was involved in an unacceptable relationship with a man. However, we also knew when the time presented itself, that the Lord would direct her back onto the right path.

Sure enough, one night Krista called us and confessed what was going on in her life. We took her under our wings and ministered to her. After she left, we knew she had to make some determinations before she could be totally free of the sin that was besetting her. Praise the Lord, she did make those decisions.

A short time after Krista told us that the Lord had shown her that she would be going with us, God finally confirmed it to me. I was conducting a Thursday night Women's Bible Study when Krista broke down and confessed that she was angry at God because He was taking her two best friends (us) away from her. Admittedly, I was surprised at her outburst.

That night, I told Jeannette that we would have to take Krista. She just looked at me and told me, "I knew that all along." I looked at her and asked her why she had not bothered to share that little piece of information with me. She sort of grinned, and told me she figured God would show me in due time.

The next day, I called Krista at work and told her to get her resume ready, that she was going with us to Houston. Talk about a shocked young lady on the other side of the phone! On Saturday, the next day, we received the much-awaited phone call. Everything was in order for us to come to Houston. I suddenly realized that God had held everything back until Krista was properly placed in our future plans.

On June 13th, 1996 the three of us started our journey to Houston. We had managed to get rid of enough stuff that we could fit both of our households and office furniture in a 24-foot moving truck. We decided that we would pull our Nissan car behind the truck, while all three of us rode in its cab.

I was excited about the new adventure. I knew we were in God's will because all the doors in Seattle had been slammed shut, and through it all, there had only been one door opened to us. I felt Houston could be the launching pad for Gentle Shepherd Ministries that we had been waiting for. We were going to help another ministry, while in turn they would help us. It appeared to be a workable situation.

We spent six days on the road. We had some close calls, but God was faithful to get us through each major city and around some life-threatening obstacles. However, on the sixth day, I found myself praying in the spirit. I sensed something major was coming up that called for lots of prayer, and only time would identify the reason behind the intensity of my prayer.

Five hours outside of Houston, we watched a concrete truck run off the road onto the side embankment. A cloud of dust reached high into the sky and began to float with the air currents over the freeway. I noticed an object lying in the highway. My first calculation was that it was part of a tire. I looked in my side mirror and thought I noticed a car coming up alongside us at a pretty good speed.

The total length of the moving truck we drove along with our car made us the size of a semi-truck. I didn't feel I had the liberty to make any sudden moves. As we came upon the object, I realized it was not part of a tire, but a mechanical part from the cement truck. By this time, I was in a squeeze and knew I could not stop the inevitable.

Our truck straddled the large chunk of metal, but the Nissan on the back of the dolly was too low. The object ended up hitting the undercarriage of our car five times, shredding a full tank of gas. Our car's alarm went off. The car lights were blinking, and the horn was blowing fiercely to let us know the assault was not minor. I managed to pull off the road far enough that we could check out the situation. Krista jumped out of the cab to check the damage.

As she got down to look, gasoline started to run around her hand and managed to cling to some of her hair. We managed to open the car door to finally silence our car alarm. We immediately summed up the situation, and quickly diluted the gasoline on the side of the road with our drinking water. We knew we were big targets on a freeway of determined drivers who wanted to quickly get to their destination.

At the time, all three of us were just responding to the situation. We were in a bit of shock through it all. It didn't hit us until later that God had actually spared our lives. Gas tanks that are hit by flying steel objects cause sparks that will cause an explosion and an inferno of fire. We should have blown up with all of our worldly possessions. However, God had protected us, and I realized that He had prompted me to pray all those miles for our safety. Obviously, He was not yet done with Gentle Shepherd Ministries or us.

I still can see the horrified looks on people's faces after they learned about our experience. They would stare at us as if we were walking miracles, and walk away shaking their heads in disbelief that we had survived.

Houston fell short of my expectations. We were three ladies alone in a big city. The organization we were helping supplied us with an apartment that was in one of the worst sections of Houston. In fact, the color of our skin put us in the minority at our apartment complex.

I remember one day Krista said "Hi" to a black man in a neighborly fashion. He somehow misread it and took offense. He was ready to come after her. In another incident, three boys threw eggs at our window. Krista took out after them barefoot. She managed to catch one, but realized she had no idea what she was going to do with the culprit or what she was getting herself into, so she let him go with a rebuke.

In another situation, Krista was taking a morning run. She spied a brief case in a ditch alongside the road. She brought it home and decided to open it. She found the name of the owner and called him. Apparently, the night before, someone had stolen his pickup with his briefcase in it. The thief threw the briefcase out while cruising our neighborhood.

Later, a policeman came to talk to Krista about the briefcase. At first, he seemed to be hesitant in talking to me, while we both waited for Krista who was frantically trying to get ready for work after such a hectic morning. I started to give him our history, beginning with our move from Seattle. I shared with him about our ministry and our desire to minister Christ to people. He started to relax and took the liberty to inform us that we had no business living in this neighborhood. It was a dangerous place, and we should move as soon as possible. I began to realize why he eyed us with suspicion when he first met us. People can be quickly classified based on the type of neighborhood they live in.

The organization we were helping presented us with a different set of challenges. Although cautious about working with another ministry, I felt God was calling us to Houston to work with this organization. We both knew we had to simply trust the Lord with the outcome. We were told that this organization wanted to simply promote Christian materials. We found ourselves in the capacity of a reviewing committee that was to screen every piece of material.

To our dismay, we found that either the material hinged on New Age philosophy or the author had a personal cause and agenda other than Christ crucified. We ended up rejecting about three-fourths of the material we received in the office. Needless to say, this began to cost the organization money.

Eventually, we discovered that this ministry we were trying to help not only had a different agenda than we had, but was also being motivated by a different spirit. We found ourselves at opposite poles and in major conflict with the main leader.

This difference caused us to challenge the leadership at different times. You could tell there was an outward compliance on the president's part because he could not debate with us without coming across as a hypocrite. But, on the other hand, resentment was growing from within. We knew since the inward man was not changing, our relationship would eventually be severed.

A little over five months after being in Houston and many battles later, the sword came down between us. We breathed a sigh of relief. We had heard rumors that involved legal ramifications because of some of the practices going on within the company. At one point, we were even quietly told that the FBI was being contacted.

At times, we felt we were holding a hot potato, and we had no place to really throw it. We also had the challenge of finding out where God wanted us to go next. I was personally hoping that we would end up in Georgia where some doors even appeared to be opening. I tried to console myself that Houston was a jumping off place to Georgia, and we were over half-way to our final destination.

To make a long story short, all possible doors in Georgia shammed shut. We were now back to "Square One" with no possibilities. As the three of us prayed, the Lord began to show Jeannette and Krista that He was sending us back to the Northwest. The first time they mentioned the idea, I balked at it. I wanted to go to Georgia.

I began to feel the vice-grip close around me in Houston as I held on to the hope of landing in the south. One night, I gave in and told God that I would go back to the Northwest according to His will.

As we pursued God for the place, He once again showed Jeannette and Krista the vicinity. When they shared it with me, I totally rejected the idea. They felt that He was leading us to my home state of Idaho.

When I left Idaho almost four years previously, I didn't look back. I had developed some real battle scars, along with some not-so-pleasant memories. I just couldn't see God sending me back to my home state. But, after stating my objection to the idea, I once again began to feel the vice-grip squeezing me. I suddenly knew that to refuse to do God's will would put me into one of two classifications or both: 1) that of a fool and 2) being on the wrong side. To fight God was a useless exercise in futility. God was going to win, and the quicker I accepted the fact, the faster God could do something in our situation. I submitted and began part of the process of discovering which part of Idaho God wanted to relocate us.

In this type of situation, you have to examine if you heard the Lord right. Why would the Lord take us to Idaho from Seattle via Houston, Texas? It reminded me of how God led Israel out of the way when they were going to the Promised Land. Scripture tells us that He did this to keep their enemies from discouraging them.

As I questioned His route, He began to show me the lives we touched. We had witnessed to some people, and even led a young girl to Christ. We had challenged the leadership of an organization, and ministered to other people along the way. He put Krista on our team for the purpose of training her, and I could see where the challenges in Houston had caused three women to come together as one team. He also showed me something else that revealed to me the type of care and commitment that God has toward us individually.

When we shared with one of our herbalists about going to Houston, she made an incredible statement. She said, "Good, it is a natural sauna that will help Jeannette's skin problems." Jeannette had been plagued by rashes, boils, and eczema for almost a year. She realized she needed to sweat, and Houston could accomplish such a task. While in Houston, Jeannette made a point to go out in the heat of the day and force her body to let go of the toxins in her cells that had been building up for years. The sweat that came out of her pores was so acidic it burned her skin. But, after spending four months in the sun, the skin problems went away.

It amazed me that God had killed so many birds with one stone, but I could see that one of His main goals was to see that Jeannette's skin problems were taken care of. What a wonderful God we serve.

He did lead us to the southeastern part of the state of Idaho. Through circumstances, we found a place outside the small community of Moore, Idaho. We went from a place that housed three million people to a small community of 190 residents.

Almost two years after leaving Houston, I found myself walking around the circular driveway of our home in Idaho, asking God some questions. I never dreamed for one minute that He would sovereignly step on the scene to answer my questions, but He did, calming the storm in my soul!

13

FINDING A HAVEN OF REST

*Then he arose, and
rebuked the winds and the sea; and
there was a great calm.
(Matthew 8:26b)*

"Rayola, I want to step on the scene of people's lives, but they are too caught up doing their religious duties to notice that I am not in their midst. They are too busy going their own way to realize they have left Me behind. All I can do is stand on the outside to observe all of their activities." I could feel Jesus' sorrow. It was gut-wrenching to say the least.

I can remember some of the times I had left Him behind. I was busy doing religious things, but He was not a part of my activities. I had convinced myself that I was spiritually all right, even though I had left the source of my well-being behind a long time before. It wasn't until I ran out of options, and my religious attempts mocked me, that I took stock of my life to discover that I was spiritually bankrupt.

Even in Houston, I had to come face-to-face with the startling fact that I had once again left Jesus behind. In fact, I was very angry at Him for allowing Jeannette to get so sick. I had thought I was handling her illness well, until one night in prayer the Lord began to reveal to me that I had shut Him out of my life because of my anger towards Him.

He showed me that He was patiently waiting for me to turn around and come back to Him. I can still remember how the rebellion and anger in me erupted like a volcano towards Him. I didn't want to go to Him. How could He allow this to happen to Jeannette? She had suffered so, and it still was not over. After all, we had striven hard to serve Him, and we were met with nothing but opposition. A body can only take so much.

A great struggle ensued in my spirit and soul. I wanted to hold on to my right to be angry with Him. But I still can see Him quietly standing there with His arms held out towards me. Finally, after a tremendous wrestling match, I came to the end of my anger. I knew in my heart that I would not be happy until I went to Him.

As I went towards Him, I began to repent of my anger and bitterness. I chose to give my fleshly, arrogant rights up, and once again humble myself before the Lord of lords. As I felt Him enfold me, a sweet comfort came over me. I could tell that it was in His heart all along to bring comfort to my soul during this ordeal, but I was too busy dealing with the situation in my own power. I realized that my attempts to handle it were nothing more than fake nobility.

Now, He was walking beside me around my circular driveway in Idaho. I could feel His comfort once again. His presence was like a sweet balm, soothing my weary soul. His strength was gentle, yet all-powerful. I knew that He had stepped out of the throne room of heaven to walk and commune with me.

It was strange to me, for I knew I was in the presence of God, yet I felt I was talking to an old friend. I was slightly aware of the fact that I was walking with the King of kings, but all I could sense was His meekness and gentleness. I knew He was holy, and no man had a right to stand in His presence, but all I could embrace was His love and grace. In the back of my mind, I knew that He had created everything around me that I enjoyed, but all I could feel was His sorrow at being left out of the lives of men.

We at Gentle Shepherd Ministries had come a long way on a hard road, but He had kept our feet from slipping into the abyss. We battled impossible odds to overcome, only because of His intervention. We had watched mountains move, obstacles fall out of the way, steep paths made level, and raging rivers part. We had been battered by contrary winds and lost in the midst of great storms. However, at the right time, and when we least expected it He would stand up and calm the winds and the waves.

It seemed like most of our years in ministry He was either hidden in obscurity, shrouded in darkness, lost in shadows, or too far away to hear or know our plight. But, through the years, we began to realize that He was with us all the time, even though we often missed Him in our circumstances. For example, sometimes His love and grace became lost in our struggles, and His light actually caused the greatest type of darkness in our souls. This produced confusion about His identity and His commitment to us. Eventually, the shadows would evaporate before our eyes for us to discover that He is indeed a loving, caring Person that is experienced in mysterious and intimate ways that are beyond our comprehension. His silence always seemed to mock us in our struggles, but in the end, it enabled us to learn that we had to walk by faith in Him, and not walk by sight. Through all our challenges, we learned that He was there no matter what was going on.

There are different ways people handle the idea of God never leaving them or forsaking them when they encounter circumstances that would call them a fool for believing such a promise. Some people assume that He will be there, no matter what happens, and then, when the storms come, they actually forget to ask Him to step on the scene and trust Him with the details. Others silently hope that He will meet them in all their plans, regardless of His will. And, when a crisis strikes, they either hold onto their false hope or become disillusioned with Him. Still others become skeptical when He does not show Himself according to their terms. This skepticism grows because His blessings become obscure, due to unbelief, and His darkness becomes consuming due to hopelessness. The shadows that He seems to hide in appear to be a cruel joke as mockery raises its ugly head. His silence seems to verify this type of person's worst fears—that God does not exist or He is deaf and dumb to their plight.

This particular day, Jesus was walking with me, causing the worst storms to subside in my soul. It is in such times as these that you wonder how you could ever doubt Him. However, experience tells you that times such as these can be easily lost in the drudgery of daily survival and overwhelming challenges. In fact, these challenges that had led me up to this point were so overwhelming that they almost seemed as if they were at the stage of being ridiculous, or almost funny.

While we were in Houston, the Lord purged all three of us of different things. It was the usual for Jeannette and me, but a whole new experience for Krista who would eventually lose much.

The first substantial article Jeannette and I were to lose in Houston was our faithful Nissan. The car started to have major problems after hitting the object in the road. Electrical problems prevented us from running the air conditioner, which drained our battery, leaving us stranded a couple of times in the tough July heat of Texas. Our power steering was leaking fluid, but had escalated to a crisis point after the accident.

A friend had been kind enough to send enough money to possibly fix it up, but I began to see that our car was ready to cost us money we would not have down the line. I felt that it was about to nickel-and-dime us to death, even if we did get past some of the major mechanical problems. As we prayed about the situation, we all felt the Lord show us that we needed to get rid of it.

On the very day that our Washington tags expired, the Nissan finally died on Jeannette in one of the entrances to a shopping center. When informed of what was going on, the lady in a car behind Jeannette called our boss on her cell phone. Within a few minutes a tow truck came to Jeannette's rescue, and pulled the car to the garage that was located across the street from our office building.

The death of our car started what we referred to as the car saga. In fact, we had various sagas in our ministry. Our first saga involved washing machines. Jeannette had managed to purchase a beautiful washing machine before God had put us together in ministry. When we moved the washing machine to Seattle, it was destroyed in the moving process.

In our attempt to save money, we bought a second-hand washing machine and dryer. While the man was moving the washing machine into our house, he ruined it, leaving us without any recourse. We then were forced to buy a brand new washer. However, when we moved out a couple months later, we could not take it with us, which resulted in our taking a big financial loss on it.

Houston presented a different challenge for us. The washer seemed to be fine, but the dryer was another story. It actually ruined some of my underwear by throwing grease on them.

In Moore, Idaho, a washer and dryer greeted us, but to our dismay, the washer actually ate our clothes as well as threw black grease on them. I remember Krista had purchased a nice outfit in Houston. She washed it, and as she examined it, it looked like someone had taken a knife to it. There were all kinds of cut marks all over the article of clothing. This was neither the first article nor the last that the machine took revenge on.

Jeannette and I finally conceded to buy a new washer and dryer. The idea of going into debt brought anxiety to Jeannette's spirit, but we had no other choice. I am happy to say up to the writing of this chapter that we still have the same washer and dryer set, and they are paid for. Our friends, Tom and Carol Richardson, who helped us move the last couple of times are the best when it comes to handling furniture. They are a true blessing in many ways. We consider them not only friends, but saints at heart, because there is nothing more trying on relationships than the back-breaking job of moving.

Once our car died in Houston, we were posed with the challenge of transportation. Our boss was generous enough to supply us with a car. In fact, he finally gave us his small Geo that had been parked for a while in Rome, Georgia.

This little car had major problems, but our boss was generous enough to fix it up so it would not leave us stranded. It cost almost $1,000 to get it in decent running order.

We had to admit, the car had character. The seats slanted to the side, leaving both Krista and Jeannette with an oversized backache. It had a bullet hole in the door. Apparently, our boss had used a certain finger gesture to express his disapproval to some troublemakers on the Dallas freeway who took enough offense to take a shot at him, hitting the car door.

When we were ready to move back to Idaho, I knew the fragile little car might not survive the trip. I also knew that it would not do well on the Idaho roads, so we decided to sell it. We figured someone could use it.

We had a few bites, but no cash came forward. On the day we went to pick up the moving truck to pack up and leave, the car was still hanging around our necks. We had made arrangements for another ministry in Houston to sell it, but we had fervently asked God to resolve the problem before we left town.

As we were picking up our moving truck, Jeannette mentioned that we were trying to sell our car. That afternoon, the man who rented us our truck became the new owner of a Geo with character. We could see God's hand in all of it.

We also were contending with another saga, that of animals. It seemed like in every major challenge, Jeannette and I had to contend with some animal crisis at the most inconvenient times. We have many such stories. For example, the morning we moved to Seattle, we were held up from making an earlier departure because we were waiting for an animal rescue organization to pick up a dog we had watched on its behalf. It seemed like animals were used to produce tight squeezes, to not only bring suspense to our lives, but also require some fervent prayers of faith.

In the case of Houston, it was a stray cat that had adopted us. We have no idea where it came from or who it belonged to. We gave it away once, only to discover that the new owner was not even taking care of it. Here we had a responsibility for a cat that did not even belong to us. However, we could not just leave it to fend for itself. Praise God, as we were moving out, the assistant manager of our apartment complex saw the cat, fell in love with the small vagabond and took her home. Talk about something being done at the last minute!

It took all day to move out of our second-floor apartment. We had sporadic help, which hindered our progress and kept us from getting out of our apartment before dark. We had everything loaded up and ready to leave when, to our distress, the gate separating the outside world and unwelcome intruders from our apartment complex would not open to let us out of our prison.

I don't know how many times I backed the 24-foot moving truck up to take a run at the gate with no response. Pretty soon, I noticed that various cars had come along side me and had tried to get out of the gate, but to no avail. These people were basically parked and watching how three women in a big truck were going to handle this situation. I suspected we were the most popular show on the block.

Jeannette got on one side of the truck and Krista on the other. Both guided me between cars, people, and kids to a place where I could manage to turn around in order to escape out the other gate. By the time we were set free from our ghetto prison, it was too late to travel on. Our last night in Houston proved to be anything but restful. In spite of all the obstacles, Houston could no longer hold on to us. The next day, we were heading for Idaho to our new destination.

Even though we were glad to get out of Houston, there were many issues up in the air. We were moving in the first part of December. Roads could be very treacherous, so we went the long way around through Arizona.

The roads were fairly decent until we reached Nevada. Circumstances had forced us to spend an unplanned night in Bullhead City, Arizona for the purpose of ministry. We had a deadline on the truck, and I was nervous about the detour. However, it was obvious that the Lord wanted us to stay with our friends in Bullhead and trust Him with the details. I was to later discover why the Lord planned our schedule. The night we stayed in Bullhead City, we not only ministered to a friend there, but there was a tremendous snowstorm in Nevada. God was making sure we missed it.

Another unsettling issue was that we had not been able to secure a place to move into once we arrived at our destination. All we knew was that we were heading towards Mackay, Idaho. We had tried to find a place where we could land through a real estate agent, but each lead led to a dead-end.

We were a day outside of our destination, and were still without a place to live. This was a little different scenario than our previous adventures. Before, we went out knowing our destination, with very little money. This time, we had some money, but did not know our location.

I remember talking to the Lord about this interesting problem. I also distinctly remember what He told me, "You are not there yet." I couldn't argue with Him on that point.

Not only did we lack a residence to unload all of our furniture into, but we also were minus a vehicle. How could we get around without transportation? When Jeannette and Krista prayed about our future residence, they received what I concluded to be contrary signals. One saw a two-story white house, nestled by a stream. The other saw a log house with mountains looming all around it. However, Krista also saw something else that was quite interesting. She saw that a pickup would go with our house.

The night we arrived at our destination, we had to travel through thick fog, on snow-covered, icy roads. The snow had blanketed the desolate countryside, and towards evening, it began to reflect the beautiful colors of the sunset. It cast a pinkish color across the white barren wasteland that lay before us. We also could see the beautiful ragged edges of the Sawtooth Mountain Range reaching high into the sky. I had to admit it lifted my weary soul, but it did not loosen the white-knuckle grip I had on the steering wheel as I maneuvered the unfamiliar roads.

Some people would say I was home after a four-year absence, and in a way, I felt like I was home again. However, I was going into a remote part of Idaho I had not yet seen. I had been all around Mackay, but never to it. I was about to see some incredible country that would be exciting and strange to me.

While we were in Nevada, my mother gave us the name of a pastor who lived in Arco and used to be the pastor of a church in her community. He was the only lead we had, but you only need one right connection.

It is amazing how God works, because Pastor Bernie Philips and his wife, Rose, turned out to be that one right lead. Bernie met us at a popular cafe in Arco, and escorted three strange women, and the newest member of the family, a puppy called Angel, to his home. They offered us food, beds and the phone.

Angel was a Chihuahua and Shih Tzu combination that we picked up in Phoenix. She was almost six weeks old, and our friend wanted us to have this small five-inch furry bundle for Christmas. She seemed so small, cute, and vulnerable, but Jeannette did everything to ignore her.

Jeannette and I had decided to avoid being tied down with a dog before we moved to Washington. However, I felt that Jeannette was supposed to have this little puppy. We prayed about it, but didn't seem to get a decisive answer. As our friend was driving away with the little creature, Jeannette knew she could not let her go. For some reason, God wanted her to have her, and she needed to trust Him with the details. We managed to stop our friend, and relieve her of one special little puppy.

Later on, Jeannette realized that God used the puppy to give her purpose. She had to get up every two hours to feed her for the first two months. She had to potty train her, and take care of all of her needs. I can see how this little dog was used to bring comfort, purpose, healing, and joy to Jeannette during a crucial time of her life.

The House Saga Continues

The next day, after our arrival at Arco, we were on our way to Moore to check out an empty house. When we came over a small knoll in the road, we looked down at the two-story white house that had originally started out as a log home. At least three sections had been added to the original log house, and all of it had been painted white. This house amazingly fit the description both Krista and Jeannette had been given in prayer. There were mountains surrounding it as well as what appeared to be a creek running alongside of it.

It is funny how God may confirm certain things, but leave out major details. All three of us were excited about the house until we walked into it. It was in bad shape. Much of the tile was off of both the bathroom and kitchen floors. It was filthy inside, and we could tell it would require some muscle to get it cleaned. The carpets were stained by abuse from children and animal's urine. Mice and spiders reigned unchallenged in the house. Obviously, we would have to fight to reclaim it.

Krista balked at the idea that this house was an answer to prayer after she saw its condition. We had another option that we decided to consider in Mackay, before we agreed to take the house in Moore. The second house was in similar shape. I will never forget the scene. Krista was sitting upstairs in the second house with tears coming down her cheeks. I looked at both her and Jeannette and told them, no matter how much we wanted to deny it, the house in Moore was our new home. The price and size were right.

I felt sorry for Krista. Jeannette and I had lived in some pretty tough places. I thought about our first house together that had no wind resistance. The whistling winter wind caused Jeannette's bedroom curtains to bulge.

I remember that our first house in Seattle was sufficient, but the neighborhood was dangerous. And, I will never forget our next home in Brier, WA. Fleas had taken over, and everywhere we stepped, especially Jeannette, they would jump on us leaving their bite marks. For five months we fought a courageous battle with those little rascals. When we left, we were not sure who got the best of whom.

Our next place was the nicest of all our residences. It was a condo in Kirkland. It was clean and very suitable for our needs, but even there we witnessed the selling of drugs at night, spousal abuse in the parking area in broad daylight, and even watched police surrounding our building with guns drawn.

Then, there was the apartment in Houston. We lived in a slum area. The view from our back windows looked onto the carport. We saw everything from discarded dirty diapers on top of the tin roof to various other objects. We could see dumpsters overflowing with garbage, and when we walked outside on hot days, it smelled like the sewer was backing up.

I knew the house in Moore would fit into our saga nicely, but I knew Krista was not used to living in such conditions other than in the slums of Houston. Like Jeannette and me, she eventually learned what it meant to make a home out of an undesirable place. When we moved from there, Krista admitted that she had some fond memories of that place, and actually missed it and the incredible mountain view.

The next day we moved into the house in Moore, only to discover greater challenges. The initial problem we encountered was getting a phone. It took two weeks to finally get our phone. During that time, we were completely isolated. I found out that the phones in our area operated on radio channels, which were limited.

The most serious problem, besides herds of mice, turned out to be the sewer. The toilet would not flush because the drain field was not working properly. I cannot tell you how much prayer we exercised in the bathroom, praying that the wastes in the commode would disappear. It was not unusual to spend 15 minutes in the bathroom in prayer. Talk about praying out of desperation!

We struggled with the sewer problem for six months. We discussed buying a small portable potty, but the Lord nixed that idea and promised He would take care of the situation. The situation became critical in June. The very day we expected out-of-state company, the toilet ceased to flush at all. Jeannette and I had to go to town. On our way home, I began to tell the Lord that the circumstances called for action. I felt a peace come over me. As we came over the knoll of the road on our return trip, we saw a backhoe at our place. To our relief, the man on the backhoe had come down to clear some brush out of the irrigation ditch so their farm could get more water. He heard about our struggle from Krista, and dug a hole to serve as a temporary drainage until the situation could be properly dealt with. What a blessing that temporary solution proved to be. It was another six months later before a new drain field was finally put in.

A couple of months before we moved from Moore, we once again started to have sewer problems. The septic tank started caving in. It was right behind my office, and I had the pleasant experience of smelling sewer until our final exit.

One of our ongoing challenges was with the mice that invaded our house on a continual basis. I would try to get up early and pray in private, only to encounter the scurrying sounds of mice in the wall. One time, our friend put poison around for our little invading force. We later paid dearly for it as smells of decaying bodies floated up from underneath the house and between the walls. We decided after that, that we would stick with traps.

Krista was kind enough to empty the traps. One night, she dumped the trap in her bedroom five times. As a result, Jeannette affectionately stuck her with the official title of "fur trapper." In a period of a few months, she had emptied the mousetraps over 100 times.

Mice were not the only creatures that gave us challenges. Except in the winter, we always had to watch for rattlesnakes. Fortunately, we only encountered a small one on our property all the time we were there. We were aware that God was protecting us because there appeared to be a den of them just across the road.

The other thing that proved interesting for us was the history surrounding the house. Apparently, illegal cockfights had been held on the property. On top of that, a young man had committed suicide at this location, and various characters had lived in the house, giving it a historical value to the community.

I remember when the owner put the house on the market. Many people dropped by and asked to see it. All claimed that they had either lived in it at one time, or some relative or friend had occupied it in the past.

In spite of the condition of the house, it became a great place of ministry. Many people viewed it as a place of refuge. As I look back, it did become a place of refuge for us. The Lord wanted to teach us how to rest in the midst of interesting circumstances.

The Vehicle Saga

Another challenge we were confronted with was transportation. We were 86 miles from the city of Idaho Falls, 15 miles from Arco, 20 miles from Mackay, and eight miles from Moore. Moore had one small store that went out of business while we lived in the area. Obviously, we needed a vehicle.

The man who rented us the house heard about our transportation plight, and offered us the use of his pickup. He told us it had problems, but it worked. Since we did not have any other options, we accepted his offer. We later referred to that beat up pickup as the "Beast."

The inside of the pickup was an absolute mess. The transmission gear had been replaced with a cable that had to be pushed down a certain way to get it in the proper gear. The brakes were non-existent, which caused some excitement when it came to stopping.

Due to the fact that there was no power steering, Krista was the only one who had enough muscle to drive it. She discovered that by shifting the gear down, and aiming at snow banks that it was the safest way of stopping the pickup. We also learned that if all three of us were in the cab, two passengers had to lean to the right in order for Krista to struggle enough with the cable to get it in the right gear. I have to admit, the pickup required a team effort.

It took both Krista and me to get the hood open so we could jump-start the pickup in cold weather. If you asked me who won the most when it came to getting the hood open, I would have to say the pickup. It was persistent in not allowing us to open up its mouth.

Sometimes, the whole scene was quite funny, and at the right time, somebody would rescue us from the endless battle we seemed to have with the "Beast." Some people even admitted that they admired Krista for her willingness to drive that piece of metal. Occasionally, I sensed people who were aware of the "Beast's" condition shaking their heads every time they saw us venture out with this incredible piece of machinery.

We managed to survive the "Beast," thanks to people like Bernie who periodically came out to rescue us. I began to sense that Bernie became an enthusiastic witness of how God constantly intervened on our behalf. It was as though he knew God would do something for His three helpless handmaidens, and he wanted to witness it as much as he could. As a result, I felt that his faith was often encouraged at our expense. (Talk about being a living-walking witness.)

Finally, we were told of a car that would fit both our financial means and our needs. We went to look at the car. Krista drilled the owner about its condition. She asked all the right questions. He assured her that it was in decent condition and that it didn't use oil. We bought it so we could give the "Beast" back to its owner.

To our discouragement, we found out that the car actually drank up oil like it was going out of style. Not only did it like its oil, but it was also liberal about sharing its exhaust fumes with us.

Since Jeannette could not handle toxins at any level, her body would become repulsed at any exposure to the poisons finding their way into the interior of the car.

I asked the Lord what we needed to do. He basically told me that He would take care of it. He did. One of our friends gave us a car, allowing us to sell our oil-guzzling vehicle.

The car that was given to us proved to add some relief, but we discovered that it had some mechanical problems that could cost a lot of money down the line. We had it for over a year when we decided to sell it because we began to watch the mechanical problems escalate. The people who gave us the car saw that we were trying to sell it and asked us to give it back to them. As they say, "easy come, easy go."

The one good note about our car saga is that Krista was able to purchase a Nissan pickup that served us well in various capacities. The major problem with that pickup is that it was uncomfortable for the third person who had to ride in the small cab behind the passenger seat. Long distances became unbearable for the one riding in the cramped space, which usually was me.

The finale of the car saga ended about the same way as it started. We had moved from Moore to a community in south-western Idaho. We needed a car we could rely on. While we were ministering in Washington, we discovered that our friend had a Sable Mercury station wagon. This car appeared to be in good shape, but the transmission had gone out of it. Our friend decided to fix the car up and give it to the ministry. He took the car to a transmission place that guaranteed their work. By February, we were the proud owners of a nice station wagon that served our needs.

On Memorial Day weekend, to our distress, the transmission started acting up. We couldn't believe that it was happening after having the car for about five months, but were thankful that the work was guaranteed. To make a long story short, the closest transmission shop that would honor the guarantee was located in Baker City, Oregon, a 180-mile round trip. We managed to get it to Baker City where the man tested it out. Krista rode with him, and watched him push the car beyond its limits. He blew a rod in the motor.

He brought the car back with the shocking news. We had brought a car that was running fine, except for the fact that it would not shift into first or fourth gear. All of a sudden, we owned a car that not only needed to have work done on the transmission, but also now needed a new motor.

We told them to fix the transmission while we went home to pray about the situation. I tried to convince myself that the motor was all right, but I knew deep in my spirit, the car was no more. We waited for over two weeks before we were told to come to Baker City to pick up our car because they didn't want anything to do with it. In the back of my mind, the Lord began to formulate our next move.

Obviously, we needed a reliable car, and we could not expect Krista to be responsible for our transportation. It was time to step out in faith and buy a new car. At least, we could trade our old car in, which would help defray some cost. At the time, I did not realize that the same type of plan was taking shape in Jeannette's mind.

When we picked up our car, we limped off the lot, and headed for the nearest car dealer. The man who worked in the garage section was a Christian. He had our car checked out, and the mechanics confirmed that a rod had been blown in our engine. When we asked how it happened, they implied that the actions of the man who tested our car out for transmission problems most likely pushed our car to its demise. That's when we asked to see a salesperson. Our new Christian friend and protector made sure we got the salesperson who would do right by us.

Jeannette had great credit, and within two hours we drove out with a new used car. The timing was amazing. The interest rates for used cars were at their lowest, and the car was only two years old. It had been leased out, and was in great shape.

This ended our car saga, but I realized when I was in Moore, that the Lord wanted each of us to learn what it meant to rest in Him. Sometimes, we become so busy with things, that we fail to rest. Ultimately, Jeannette and I became battle-weary soldiers.

I could see that the Lord was slowing our lives down in order to teach us to rest in Him, in spite of the circumstances. It slowly dawned on me how Jesus had become a much needed-haven to us in Moore. I also learned that a haven is not only a place of peace, quiet, and rest, but also one of protection. I was about to get a glimpse into how God used circumstances to protect us from certain destructive forces.

14

IN THE COVE

*I will say of the LORD, He is
my refuge and my fortress; my
God; in him will I trust. Surely
he shall deliver thee from the
snare of the fowler, and from the
noisome pestilence.*
(Psalm 91:2 & 3)

"I see you two like sitting ducks, ready to be shot at and destroyed." These words came from our intercessor, Noreen Walsh. She had known Jeannette when she was in her twenties, when they were both working for the Attorney General's office of the State of Washington. They had lost touch with each other until one day Noreen happened to turn on the TV, just in time to see Jeannette and me being interviewed on a Christian TV talk show.

She immediately contacted us, and an old friendship was renewed. I was blessed with a precious new friend and sister in Jesus Christ. Noreen fondly remembered Jeannette as the sparkly outgoing person in a liberal office, who had been honest about both her religious and conservative beliefs. Noreen actually credited Jeannette as the one who planted the vital seeds of the Gospel in her life that led her to a personal relationship with God through Jesus Christ.

Noreen became excited about our ministry and wanted to financially help us. However, when she sought God out about financially supporting us, He instead instructed her to intercede in prayer on our behalf for at least an hour a day.

I remember when she told us that God wanted her to pray for us instead of giving money; I assured her that her intercession was priceless. At that time, we did not know of anyone else who actually interceded for us. We both knew that without prayer, we would not get anywhere in ministry. Noreen would prove something else to us, that without prayer, we would not survive the onslaught of the enemy.

One week, it seemed like our whole world was caving in. As we struggled with everything, we felt that we were spiritually vulnerable. We called Noreen to find out if something was going on in her world. We learned that her grandson had almost died, causing her to focus all her attention on his precious life that had hung in the balance for a week. We could understand why we felt so vulnerable, learning the lesson of how valuable prayer is in regards to protection.

Over the years, I have become more and more aware of how the prayers of faithful saints have kept us. We could see how the intercession of the obedient servant becomes a valuable hedge between those on the front lines and the demonic realm.

As I was walking around the circular driveway in Moore, talking to Jesus, I became more aware of the unseen protection that many of us take for granted. We do not realize that every breath is a gift from God, and that our life is very fragile and hinges on God's constant watch and care.

Krista, Jeannette, and I realized that Moore was a tough place to be spiritually. We sensed a great spiritual vacuum over the basin. We knew that physically we were quite unprotected where we lived, but spiritually, we felt hidden from all that would harm us. It was like being in a bubble. I was also amazed that even though a great vacuum surrounded us, we lived in a place that proved to be more than satisfying.

As I considered what the Lord did for us in Moore, I became overwhelmed. In the Lost Basin, we were literally hidden, but the Lord brought many people to us. People came from as far away as Virginia, Utah, Montana, Arizona, and Oregon for ministry. It also seemed that we had special times of resting and opportunities to catch up on our many projects in-between the ministering. He also enlarged our ministry when He impressed us to start a home church.

Between the three of us, we had the means to have a home fellowship. Jeannette sharpened and greatly improved her piano skills, while Krista with her singing abilities led the songs and blessed listeners with her singing voice. And, I shared the Word.

When the Lord first showed me that I would be sharing the Word, I was not sure I was capable of imparting the Word every Sunday in such a setting. The Lord assured me that He would give me the subjects He wanted me to share. He never disappointed me. I have learned a lot from having to prepare messages every week.

God used our home fellowship to challenge and minister to many people. Amazingly, most of the people who came to our Sunday gatherings were from outside the area. We had people from Montana, Arizona, Utah, and other parts of Idaho who participated in our time of worship and the ministering of the Word.

Our Sunday fellowship graduated to a tape ministry. We started sending tapes of the messages to other people who were blessed by them. The tapes went to such places as Washington, Arizona, Utah, Montana, other parts of Idaho, and South America.

It was during this time that I rewrote the sequel to the *Hidden Manna* book, and finished two other book projects that had been pending for over a year. I also wrote a complete Bible Course that was later offered as a correspondence course through Gentle

Shepherd Ministries. It was during this time that I also wrote an "End-Times" Bible study that has helped bring some understanding to the events surrounding Jesus' second coming.

Our days proved to be full and satisfying in spite of the fact that we were hidden in a grave. Even though we were in the grave, a few arrows from the enemy found their target. However, the damage was minor compared to what we had suffered in the past.

Idaho was not only proving to be a place of rest, but a place of protection. I realized that the Lord had brought us into the grave to actually keep us from being destroyed. We were like sitting ducks because there seemed to be no deterrents to keep Satan from declaring open hunting season on us, due to the fact that he could easily locate willing partners who were quick to oblige him. It dawned on us that by hiding us God was minimizing the attacks.

He had brought us to a cove of protection in order to become a personal cleft in the Rock for each of us to hide in. It was in Moore where Jesus became our place of refuge, where we did find rest from the battle, and nourishment for the weary soul. We could tell that He was gently teaching us to wait on Him for His salvation and deliverance.

We also sensed that there was a great battle going on around us. I'm not a person who believes that individuals constantly see angels (nor can mere man command them) and demons, but we have sensed unseen activity around us in the past.

There is a consensus that animals, such as dogs, can see unseen entities. Krista had a border collie named Shadow, who seemed to fit in this category. One night, I was standing on the hearth with my back to the wood stove when I heard a low bark. The bark was close to a growl, and it was coming out of Shadow. The bark shocked all of us. When I looked at her, I could tell that her eyes were intensely concentrating on something behind my head. I looked around only to see open air. I quickly reverted back to Shadow. Her eyes seemed to be following the invisible object.

Within a matter of seconds, the object of her attention seemed to exit, and she settled right down.

Another time, Jeannette was relaxing in her chair in the corner of the living room when, once again, something caught Shadow's attention. She sat, staring at an unseen entity right above Jeannette's head. This time she didn't bark at it, but she had a serene look. Her attention and look caught the attention of all of us, but once again, we could see nothing.

As I was walking around the circular driveway with Jesus, I began to sense that there was a greater audience watching us. Suddenly, I became aware that messengers of God surrounded us. I noticed that there were two tall and powerful angels standing by the house with swords drawn, while the rest stood in silent awe of God Almighty. I was surprised that so many angels seemed to surround us.

I knew what Psalm 91:11 stated, "For he shall give his angels charge over thee, to keep thee in all thy ways." I could see that the Lord was graciously allowing me to see the army that was protecting us from the unseen forces that always sought ways to destroy us.

My ability to see this invisible army only lasted a second, as once again, I became aware of Jesus Christ. Everything became dim as Jesus walked beside me. My heart was rejoicing, for it is He alone who deserves our complete devotion and adoration. After all, He is the One who commands this incredible army. He is the cleft in the Rock, the fortress, and refuge. It is He who is the I AM that I AM, who is ever faithful, full of love, mercy, and grace. He overshadows everything, and in His presence everything either becomes lost or transfigured by His glory.

I became aware that I had been walking around the circle with Jesus for a whole hour. Yet, it seemed like only a few minutes. I realized why there is no time in eternity, because time will always become lost in the midst of His precious presence.

I knew our fellowship was coming to an end, but I wanted to hold on. As we came towards the house, Krista came out the door to check on me. I realized I had to let go. I still remember Him leaving my side. I turned to Him and told Him, "I love you." I will never forget His parting words and the wonder they left in my heart, "And, I love you."

15

FAITHFULNESS

*And let us not be weary in well
doing: for in due season we
shall reap, if we faint not.
(Galatians 6:9)*

"Let's just forget this project altogether!" I was weary of the whole scene. We had tried to get four of our manuscripts in book form. Krista had been faithful to take on the project while we were in Moore, but everywhere we turned we ran into another overwhelming obstacle.

We had moved from Moore to New Plymouth, Idaho, on Thanksgiving weekend. We knew that our era in Moore was coming to a close after the septic tank started to cave in, and the spiritual vacuum over the basin began to edge its way into our home once again. Since our time was almost up at Moore, the kingdom of darkness wanted to reclaim its former territory even before we had relocated.

New Plymouth proved to be a place of transition for Gentle Shepherd Ministries. We sensed that God was about to bring some changes on the scene. The main change involved Krista.

After almost three years with us, Krista felt that God was preparing her to leave the nest. Jeannette and I had spent those years training her, and now it was time for her to spread her wings to find out what she was really made of.

Needless to say, she had mixed emotions. The Lord had made us into a family, but our youngest sister had an inward restlessness to find out who she was in Christ. We did not begrudge such discontentment because it was always our hope that she would find her place in Christ, and bring glory and honor to His name.

Cutting and letting go of the ties that bind people can be quite traumatic, but the Lord prepared all of us in different ways. By the time the door opened for Krista, she was ready, although anxious about where her new adventure would lead her.

Meanwhile, Krista was determined to get our four manuscripts in book form before she went on to her next adventure, even if it was the last thing she ever did on this earth. Her determination was commendable, but it brought her to the abyss of total frustration and depression before it was over.

It is hard to prepare an inexperienced person for an upcoming battle. There is no amount of words that can describe the intensity of coming up against hell itself. It is only experience that turns a person's zeal into sobriety and untamed strength into wisdom.

Both Jeannette and I were quite aware of the battle that was about to ensue over our books. We had battle scars from the past that were acquired during the publishing of our first book, *Hidden Manna,* to verify the fact that we were seasoned gladiators in this arena.[1]

I will never forget the history of *Hidden Manna*. It initially started in 1977. I was a brand-new Christian, who had discovered the salvation of Jesus Christ while serving in the United States Navy. After my enlistment was up in July of 1976, I came back

---

[1] We still have copies of the first publication of *Hidden Manna* but it has been revised and updated. The revised version is in Volume 4 of the author's foundational series and has also been made into a separate book.

home to Idaho where I had planned to use my GI benefits to go to Boise State University. My first semester in the fall of "76" seemed to go without too many hitches, but my second semester was a disaster. Everything seemed to go wrong.

I finally sought God about the matter. I will never forget how He told me to go home because He had a book for me to write. I was both amazed and excited about the prospect of writing a book for God.

As a novice, you automatically think the project will be done tomorrow. It is true that once God instructs something to be done, it is already done in heaven. However, to work it out on earth is a whole different matter. I never realized that God had a lot of work to do in me before He could ever entrust me with any project. Looking back, I can see why He had to call me away from the college scene. He wanted a clean slate to work on, and the education of the world would not only feed my oversized conceit, but it would pervert what He wanted to accomplish.

The first thing He had to do was get me into the Word and the Word into me. Since I was saved out of a popular cult, I wanted to know the truth. This desire caused me to dig deep into the Word.

The next step was to do away with my many incorrect notions about God and religion. These notions later translated into compromise and idolatry, which ultimately led to spiritual bankruptcy. After all, there is nothing like spiritual bankruptcy to make you a broken, but a willing vessel.

In the final stage of preparation, God had to deal with my conceit. I saw myself as being wise and smart. However, when I came to the end of myself, I found out that I knew nothing. When I discovered that I had many biblical facts and much theology, but I was spiritually dull to real truth, God was then finally able to educate me in the proper way.

I wish I could say that this process only took a couple of years. The truth is, I found that I was far more obstinate than I ever imagined. It took God seven years to plow up the soil of my heart and life to bring me to this important point.

In 1986, the Lord began to give me insight into the human natures of people. It started as a small seed that quickly bloomed into life-changing information. At the time, I was teaching a women's Bible study. Each time God gave me insight into the rebellion, attitudes, and behavior of people, I would share it with the women at the study. They, in turn would go home and test it out on their husbands and children. The results not only confirmed what I was being shown, but it changed how the women looked at their family members.

A year after God started to give me the human nature information, I was standing in my home meditating on it, when the Lord spoke to me. He told me, "This is the book I want you to write." It struck me that it had been nine years previously that God had told me that I was to write a book. It took seven years to plow up the soil of my heart, a year to prepare it, and another year for the seed of this information to be tested before He revealed it as the source of the book that He had called me to write.

I was excited. Now that I understood what the book was about, I could write it and fulfill my calling. Once again, I was about to discover my level of immaturity and inability to do anything for God.

Most of my teenage years, I had the simple desire to write, but my use of the English language was atrocious. I could successfully mutilate this language in such a way that I'm sure my high school English teacher shook his head in despair. I was also aware that my language challenges caused Jeannette to almost have a nervous breakdown.

The first three years that Jeannette and I were together, I wrote all kinds of Bible studies because I had a lot of time on my hands. Jeannette was the one who edited them. Each time, she became frustrated over my text. As she grew increasingly frustrated over my English, I became upset and had to battle hopelessness.

I examined my text as best as I could in order to avoid all of Jeannette's red marks, but I always failed to see the many errors that she quickly discovered. I tried to remember the rules of English, only to become confused due to the fact some of the rules had exceptions.

I encountered some great obstacles in my writings. However, through it all, I somehow pushed through my frustration and confusion to write the book about the different natures. We both decided that we needed someone who could totally revamp the information to get the desired effect.

Through a series of events, we met a young Christian teacher who was in between jobs. We had a meeting with him, and he told us that he would revamp the book for $1,000.00. Even though we didn't have the money, we agreed to pay the amount.

We started using our imagination to earn the appropriate funds. We immediately went home, had a yard sale, and sent him the money. We tightened our belts as much as we could, and always sent him the small amount we had left over.

At first, this young man seemed to show some initiative and signs that he was diligently working on the book. But, eventually, communication with him fell by the wayside. We had managed to pay him over half the amount when we became suspicious that his zeal for the book had quickly died out. Jeannette cautioned me not to send him any more money until we saw some definite results.

We began to send out inquiries to publishers about the book to no avail. We quickly learned that the Christian publishing market is not only political, but it is very closed to newcomers. You must already have a name or some big-time money or promoter to get you past their form letters for any kind of personal consideration.

However, in spite of the numerous rejections we received from publishing companies, we kept knocking on doors. Finally, we got one publishing company that showed some interest in some of our material. It was at this time that I asked for his copy of my book with his corrections. To my dismay, our suspicions proved correct. In spite of the fact that the whole venture had sacrificially cost us, we were left holding an empty bag.

We found ourselves dead in the water. I told the Lord that if He wanted this information in book form, He had to do it because it was an impossible task for two handmaidens. The book project went back on the shelf for another year.

During the time of inactivity with the book, some amazing things occurred in the spiritual realm for me. I was asked to write a Discipleship Course for short-term missionaries going overseas. I was aware of my writing handicaps. I knew that the Lord wanted me to write this course, but I could not see how it could be done.

One day, we visited a powerful servant of God. We asked him to pray for us. I will never forget what transpired. He got on his knees and lifted his hands towards heaven. As He called upon the name of the Lord, the room was filled with God's presence and glory. I was unable to move as I bathed in His wonderful presence. When he ceased to pray, and the presence lifted, I felt like something had been broken over me in the spiritual realm.

The next day, I started to write the Discipleship Course. Suddenly, I was aware that I could begin to understand the proper sentence structure. It was as if a light came on, and I could finally see the error of my ways. Not only did my writing skills change, but my speech also greatly improved.

A couple of months later, we met with another missionary. She also prayed over us. In her prayer, she said something that caught my attention, "God is bringing greater freedom to your writing."

(This woman had no idea about my history or challenges in writing.)

I began to ponder my newfound freedom in my English skills. It occurred to me that the great hindrance to my writing was due to spiritual oppression. I realized that I had been under the oppression of a deaf and dumb spirit. I also was aware that my freedom was not complete, and that there were still struggles ahead of me.

This is when I took the book off the shelf and totally rewrote it. Once again, we pursued getting the book published. Through our inquiries, we contacted Chuck and Athena Dean of Winepress Publishing Company. They were relatively new to the publishing business, but they had enough experience that they were able to bring some much-needed counsel to our lives. Jeannette and I could not help but respect their goal to provide an avenue for Christian authors to get their works self-published. We talked about the pros and cons of self-publishing, and I began to see the advantages of publishing the book ourselves. However, one big obstacle stood in our way, money!

The amount to get our book published along with 2,000 copies would cost us $6,000. Jeannette and I had no idea where we could get this amount of money. For many people, this amount would be a drop in the bucket, but for two struggling missionaries, who lived by faith, it could only be classified as "mission impossible."

One day, we were at a friend's place helping him with his housework. Jeannette had first met this man after she was commissioned by his son to do a painting of his boat for him. He liked the painting so much that he agreed to meet with Jeannette. She went over to his house where she met with both his wife and him and later led him to the Lord.

This couple owned a marina in Everett, Washington. They had been a very private couple, and were very careful as to whom they allowed into their world. Jeannette's art not only opened up a way for her to witness to both of them, but also provided a way for us to become close to them. They were both in sad physical condition and needed some help. Once a week, Jeannette and I would travel over 40 miles round-trip to clean their house and take the wife to a medical appointment.

Later, the wife passed away and the man asked us to conduct her funeral. This was a new experience for both us, but with God's help we managed to not only minister to the family, but Jeannette was able to share Christ with many nervous mourners who did not personally know Him.

We began to share with our different friends, including this man, the desire to get the book published. I will never forget how he looked at us and told us to get the book published because he would loan us the money at 4% interest. What a miracle!

We quickly discovered that money was just one of many obstacles standing in front of us. Chuck Dean had edited my book, but had not been brutal enough because he feared undermining the content of it. A group of our friends met with us to try to figure out how to remedy this situation. Eventually, a stout-hearted soul by the name of Lynne Humphreys agreed to take on the project. The editing was extensive, and between her work, home, and other demands, Lynne had a hard time accomplishing the task.

We were being pressured to get the edited version of the book to the Deans who wanted it to be in book form by April. We could tell that Lynne was having her challenges, and we made a decision to pick up the book, and Jeannette would finish editing it.

Lynne was informed on a Friday night that we would pick up the book the following week. On Sunday night, she called us to tell us that she had finished editing the book. When we got the book back, we began to realize what a monumental task it had been for her. Obviously, I had not been totally set free from my oppression, but my writing was understandable enough for her to get through the project.

We handed the edited book over to the Deans first thing Monday morning. Athena admitted that she had never encountered so many challenges as she did with my book. First of all, the corrections were numerous, and while she was making them, her computer totally shut down on her. She ended up going to a copier place to finish editing my book on a rented computer. There were other challenges she encountered, but she made the deadline to ensure the book would be out by April.

The Deans had set up a book signing party for me, along with two other authors, for April 8, 1995 at the Nippon Theater in Seattle, Washington. She informed me that each of us had 20 minutes to explain our books to those who attended.

As I stood in the condo in Kirkland, Washington meditating on what I needed to share, I was reminded of the history of *Hidden Manna*. I realized that the Lord had called me out of college to write this book exactly 18 years before. He had spent the first nine years preparing me, while the rest of the remaining nine years represented the gestation period for the purpose of developing the information to full term.

I also realized that it was God's faithfulness, not mine, that made the book a reality. I thought of all the times I just wanted to give the project up, but He kept it alive. I was reminded of the times I lay the project on the altar for God to consume, only to have it handed back to me in a greater form.

It was God who orchestrated the events, and gave us favor with various individuals who helped us each step of the way. And, it was because of God that I was about to hold the finished product in my hand. As I realized how faithful God was to bring about this incredible reality, I felt His presence come down into the condo. I became overwhelmed by the preciousness of His faithfulness. All I could do was praise Him.

I will never forget the night of April 8th, 1995. Many of our friends who had travailed with us through this project were there to celebrate this awesome event. As I held *Hidden Manna* in my hands for the first time, I was once again awed by the faithfulness of God. When I walked up on the stage to introduce the book, I felt God meet me. As I spoke about the book, I had to share that the real story behind the book was not the information that was changing lives, but the faithfulness of our great God. I will never forget how overwhelming His sweet presence was, not only on me, but also on the group as I shared the history of a book that was almost aborted or forgotten on various occasions for 18 long years. As I finished, I realized there were very few people who had dry eyes, including me.

That night, the crowd almost stampeded our table to get a copy of the *Hidden Manna* book. I knew that God was honoring us, but I also knew who deserved all the credit.

Now, three years later, we once again were faced with the challenge of getting raw manuscripts into book form. Now, it was Krista's turn to realize that there is a great cost to seeing any project through that presents any threat to Satan.

New Books, Old Script

As I made the declaration to abort the project of trying to get four new manuscripts into book form, Krista became silent. She had banged her head against every wall to make these four books a reality. She not only had a headache, but she was stressed out from an intense battle that had officially started nine months prior. She had carried this great burden with great vitality, but now she was exhausted. She had pursued every known angle and avenue only to have plans thwarted by the irresponsibility or unprofessional practices of others.

We all wanted to see each project reach its maturity. Some of these books represented both sacrifices and victories for Jeannette and me. Jeannette had written *Interview in Hell,* while she was sick from chemical poisoning. The Lord had given her the vision for this book back in 1993 when we still lived in Idaho. She was always too busy to write it, but when her illness knocked her out of commission, she not only found the time to write it, but it gave her purpose to live.[2]

I had managed to write the sequel to *Hidden Manna*, called, *Bring Down the Sacred Cows* before leaving Seattle. This book proved to be quite a long, drawn-out project, because I discarded my first draft and totally rewrote it in Moore. My second version showed that I not only had greater liberty in my writing skills, but I had made some real progress in fine-tuning them.[3] I started to write both books, *In Search of Real Faith* and *Revelation of the Cross* in Houston, Texas, and also finished them while in Moore. All four books had valid and timely messages for the present. It was our heart to make them available to others.[4]

We felt that we had discovered a business that could help us. We even purchased a program called "Pagemaker" to format our books for their benefit. Krista was the one who had to pioneer the program in order to teach us the ropes. After much time and money, we discovered that the business fell very short of their promises and our expectations. Other pursuits missed the mark, and we found ourselves back at "Square One." Poor Krista had no more options.

I knew I had to release her from the great burden she was carrying. I could tell that my statement let her off the hook, but she was not willing to concede defeat.

Jeannette and I had some business to do in town so we left Krista with her thoughts. When we arrived home, Krista was ecstatic. She had gone to the Lord in prayer, and He simply asked

---

[2] Note, Jeannette's book on hell is the first book of this volume.

[3] *Bring Down the Sacred Cows* is located in Volume 4 of Rayola's foundational series.

[4] The books on faith and the cross can be found in Volume 2 of the author's foundational series. Due to its popularity, *In Search of Real Faith,* has been put in a separate book.

her if we were willing to pay more money to get these projects done. She saw no obstacles for us to take such a step of faith.

She decided at that point to contact a business in Ontario, Oregon that she was referred to as a last means. The manager ensured her on the phone that they had the means to produce the quality product that we had envisioned. In three weeks time, we held all four books in our hands. What a miracle! Once again, we could see how God smoothly worked out the details after we ran out of options, time, and energy. He also proved His faithfulness.

Lamentations 3:21-26 says it best,

> This I recall to my mind, therefore have I hope. It is of the LORD'S mercies that we are not consumed, because his compassions fail not. They are new every morning: **great is thy faithfulness**. The LORD is my portion, saith my soul; therefore will I hope in him. The LORD is good unto them that wait for him, to the soul that seeketh him. It is good that a man should both hope and quietly wait for the salvation of the LORD. (Emphasis added.)

It is hard to believe that God's mercies and compassion, which are products of His unwavering faithfulness, are new every day. To understand that His mercy and compassion are not limited, nor are they a carryover from yesterday brings tremendous hope to the weary soul. Instead of being overwhelmed by the impossible, each of us can live with an expectancy that God is there to meet us at every turn with mercies that subdue hopelessness, and compassion that overcomes defeat.

The reality of God's faithfulness sustained each of us in the following days. The transition that occurred on the heels of the victory surrounding the four books proved to be not only challenging for each of us, but would test our own faithfulness towards God.

For Krista, her adventure would lead her into a trying situation that not only showed her what she was made of, but also fine-tuned her faith and relationship with God. It would prove to each of us that the Holy Spirit had been faithful to do some deep work in her that would serve to enlarge her in her struggles, instead of destroy her.

For Jeannette and me, we found that the transition not only caused us to graduate to a different realm of ministry, but we found ourselves being brought somewhat out of the grave. I wish I could say that we graduated into His full glorious light from the grave we had been in for over three years.

We were aware that God was raising us up, but we found ourselves in a cave, instead of in the warmth of His complete resurrection. It was not a traumatic disappointment, because we were mindful that we were now only one step from experiencing His glorious resurrection power. However, we had to settle for peering out the small opening to observe His inviting light. It was from this perspective that we had to choose to be faithful to what He was calling us to do in our dark little hole. We were about to experience another intense battle, only this time, we would not be the main targets of Satan.

16

IN THE CAVE

*Jesus therefore again groaning
in himself cometh to the grave.
It was a cave, and a stone lay
upon it.
(John 11:38)*

"Jeannette there is one advantage to being in the cave, we are closer to being resurrected." I was trying to find a positive side to our new situation. It seemed like we were not only in a spiritual cave, but in a physical one as well.

The transition of Gentle Shepherd Ministries led Jeannette and me from New Plymouth, Idaho, to a smaller community in Idaho located one and a half hours away. The house we rented was like a cave. It was small and dark. We had to cram all or our office equipment into our small bedrooms.

We were trying to keep a Christian perspective about this change. My parents lived in the community, so we felt that we were not completely alone. The house rent was cheap enough that we could maintain car payments with some ease, along with our other financial responsibilities.

We were trying to figure out why God brought us to this place because it did not take long for us to discover that this tight community was like so many others that we had encountered. The people were comfortable with their little worlds and did not want to be stirred up beyond their comfort zone. The problem with maintaining a private world is that it inhibits constructive growth. You usually discover that the byproducts of small worlds are ignorance and fear.

Our cave turned out to be so dark and depressing that it overshadowed God's purpose. It reminded me of the caves I read about in the Bible. Many of these caves served as tombs. The only ingredient required to turn a cave into a grave was to roll a big stone across its opening. Likewise, we felt there was a boulder in front of our cave hemming us in.

Like Lazarus in John 11, we sensed that we were actually wrapped in grave clothes, unable to move forward into ministry. Regardless, of the situation we had to be faithful with whatever mission the Lord was entrusting to us. We had to look beyond the hindrance of the cave and find out what God had in mind for us.

Our real mission in our cave was clearly revealed to us in October. We suddenly realized that God was calling us to a different type of ministry. He was calling us to be intercessors. God was asking us to be co-laborers with Him in a different way. In the past we had co-laborer with Him by planting and watering spiritual seeds in the hearts of many. Now we were being called to labor with Him in prayer to tear up the fallow ground of hardened hearts, shake faulty foundations, push back darkness over heirs of salvation, and snatch people out of the grasp of hell.

This would prove to be a different arena, since for the last six years we had been on the front lines while others had been called to be intercessors on our behalf. Now we were no longer on the front lines, but being called to intercede.

I always knew that intense intercession was hard work, but I was about to find out first-hand. I have to admit intercession drains you in indescribable ways. You must be willing to patiently pray without seeing quick results. You must cling to Christ and His promises, even when everything seems hopeless and impossible.

You must believe, even when all hope has almost completely disappeared.

Obviously, God was serious about our next assignment. He took away the entire clamor that was left in our lives, along with busy activities and most of ministry by putting us in this dark cave so we could clearly hear His next call for intercession. When we were called into intercession, we had no idea as to the seriousness of our mission and the people whose very well-being were dependent upon it. One of those people turned out to be Krista.

The three of us knew that God had called Krista to her next position. She was to work for an international ministry. We had been introduced to this ministry because some very close friends promoted it. We trusted the judgment of our friends (a married couple), that the leader of the ministry was a true minister of the Gospel.

When we first met the leader, we did not spiritually discern anything that would cause us to doubt our friends' support of him. We both developed some minor concerns that did not call for us to send up red flags to caution others' involvement with his ministry.

The doors to help this ministry seemed to open up wide for all three of us. Jeannette and I were being enticed to help this ministry in exchange for some so-called "security" and "credibility." We also could clearly see that God was giving Krista the go ahead to be part of this man's ministry. In fact, we watched Him open the doors mightily for her to become a part of this organization. However, in the end when it came to Jeannette and myself actually becoming a part of this ministry in any form, God seemed to turn around and quickly closed vital doors, thus preventing us from becoming personally involved.

At first, we could not understand why the doors had abruptly closed until we began to hear some alarming reports. Admittedly, our concerns started out minor, but they eventually escalated into giant red flags.

The first warning we had was the fact that the leader showed no regard for the personal time of others. It appeared that he put great demands on those involved with him in the name of "ministry." The second indication that the man was not all he claimed to be was that his newsletters lacked anointing and promoted questionable and confusing doctrine.

Over a period of time, we began to receive various complaints from other friends about his newsletters. They shared how the messages in his bi-monthly letter caused fear and darkness, instead of edification, leaving them confused.

The real implication that the man had problems was his need to control the lives of people involved with him. This was made obvious to us when we were considering helping his ministry. He attempted to tell us through our friend that we could not promote our ministry in any way while helping him. His demand forced us to run in the opposite direction from helping him in any way.

This need to control others was confirmed by Krista. He proved to be an unmerciful tyrant to his volunteers. There were numerous expectations that were constantly being heaped upon sincere and well-meaning people who wanted to serve God by helping him. Obviously, he knew how to use people to the fullest.

He also gave the impression that his ministry was the only legitimate ministry on earth. His claims were backed with the subtle threat that if anyone left his ministry, they would find themselves in danger of damnation.

Eventually, after intense intercession one of his pastors graciously resigned. The fallout over this situation proved that this leader not only had a fragile ego, but was also not willing to let anyone of importance leave his organization unscathed.

As the information filtered to us concerning this man's practices, we could begin to see that his organization was a bona fide cult. This man indoctrinated his people with the precision of an expert cult leader. Not only did he bombard them with questionable teachings, he consumed their time, leaving them with no personal time or energy to discern or evaluate what was really happening. Their undivided loyalty was expected, and anyone who displayed inconsistencies towards his cause or individual thinking contrary to his agenda was immediately put down with twisted scriptures and intimidation.

We were not aware that this man was really scripturally off until Krista had been part of the organization for a couple of months. It became obvious that this leader was a wolf in sheep's clothing when he openly promoted the antichrist doctrine of the Manifest Sons of God in his newsletters.

He had cleverly avoided being associated with heresy, but a wolf cannot keep his identity hidden for long. He started to promote a kingdom theology rather than the Gospel of Jesus Christ. He was subtly trying to bring people under the Law, instead of bringing a clear understanding of Jesus' redemption. He ignored the real problem with people and their heart condition, while encouraging them to accept a substitute or cosmetic surgery for the real surgery that needed to be done by the Spirit of God. He did this by putting down the organized church, and exalting the Law, the Sabbath, and other forms of outward conformity.

We noted that our friends were getting caught up with the Law instead of the Gospel. They were busy trying to clean up outward actions, rather than pursuing an inward transformation through submission to the Holy Ghost. We witnessed confusion on their part as they struggled to bring two opposite covenants together, that of Law and grace.

Jeannette and I were a little surprised that God had sent Krista into the clutches of this cult leader. We later realized that God was answering Krista's prayer to grow up in Him. Krista had sat under sound doctrinal teaching for three years, unhindered and protected from deception. She was taught that a Christian's main commission is to preach the Gospel and that believers have a responsibility to make people followers of Christ. She had been constantly instructed on the basic principles that were upheld by Jesus.

It never dawned on us that the Lord would establish her mightily in the faith that was first delivered to her by exposing her to the counterfeit. The wolf she found herself under was promoting another gospel, preaching another Jesus, and adhering to another spirit. Krista began to see the contrast between the liberty that comes with the light of truth, and the bondage that comes with the destructive power of darkness and delusion. It caused her to dig deeper into the Word, as she strove to find refuge in Jesus.

Meanwhile, the Lord called us to intercede on Krista's behalf, as well as for our friends and other unsuspecting people who were being quickly sucked into his delusion. This intercession proved to be intense, as well as exhausting.

We were involved in concentrated intercession for three months before we saw any results. As previously stated, one of the pastors of the ministry was led out of the organization. His basis for the departure was that the leader was preaching another Gospel. This man realized that he could not walk in agreement with the leader and his self-serving agendas.

We continued to fiercely pray for our friends. The Lord gave us a vision of them riding a white-water raft down a rushing river. You could tell that the husband especially was enjoying the excitement of his ride, but the Lord showed us that they were heading for falls that would bring utter devastation to their lives.

We did everything we could to constructively challenge our friends regarding their leader's teachings and procedures. Jeannette sent them valuable material that had the potential to shake their foundation, but the evil covering over them kept the light from penetrating.[1] We even had a confrontation with them, where I verbally shared my concerns about this man's practices and doctrine, but to no avail. We found ourselves at a standstill. I could tell that they fervently believed the credibility of this man.

Jesus said that He did not come to bring peace but a sword.[2] The sword He was referring to is truth. Truth will separate and divide. It will bring people to make decisions one way or the other.

In the past, I would have started an all-out crusade to prove I was right. However, I have learned that such a crusade comes from pride and only leaves victims. Once a person makes a decision of the will, it takes the penetrating conviction of the Holy Spirit to change the individual's mind.

After our final confrontation with our male friend, he emailed us, showing us that he had made a final decision to stick with his leader. We knew that there was nothing more we could say or do to change his mind. It was also at that time that God released us from interceding for both him and his wife.

In a case like this, one always hopes that their evaluation is wrong. We knew that our friends were sincere in their commitment and support of this man. Even though our discernment and confirmations from various sources had verified our concerns, we knew that we had to respect their choice and drop it.

The problem with intense intercession is that there is a lot of momentum behind it. Our friends' obvious decision not only brought an abrupt end to our momentum, but emotionally, we felt we hit a brick wall. Both Jeannette and I had to wade through sorrow and disappointment. We had fought so hard, only to watch our friends become more sucked into this man's deception.

We felt that God had given us a promise that He would snatch them out of the grips of destruction, but not until they drank the last drops of the bitter cup of delusion and betrayal. We wanted

---

[1] Isaiah 25:7; 30:1
[2] Matthew 10:34

them to be spared of this cup for we know the devastation it yields. The bitterness of this cup will eventually bring people to a point of total despair and destruction because they have put their whole heart and trust in a man, rather than in Jesus.

When you helplessly watch people being seduced and indoctrinated into heresy and delusion, you begin to realize that people are prone to deception. Many who fall into this trap are sincere, and claim that they want the truth.

The fact that we are prone to deception makes each of us feel vulnerable. When this truth begins to dawn on you, it is not unusual for some to begin to examine why we humans are susceptible to the works of darkness. You can find yourself asking hard questions and wonder what is in the character of man that causes him to prefer darkness to light.

After many years of dealing with people, I have discovered this character flaw. Every human being possesses it, which makes each of us candidates for delusion. It is called pride.

It is easy to see pride in others, but it happens to serve as the biggest blind spot in a person's personal life. In fact, it is usually the last blatant sin that people identify in their own lives. Even though pride is arrogant and demands independence, it is this same flaw that makes man susceptible to delusion.

This delusion becomes a powerful avenue that any clever, wicked leader can use to manipulate and control people. Wicked leaders know that all they have to do to gain this type of control is to feed pride's ego, pamper its needs, and exalt its self-importance. This is how a person who has never faced their pride is set up to innocently fall into the spider web of delusion and destruction.

Cleverly, wicked leaders use pride at every level to control their followers. These false leaders not only subtly use pride to ensnare a person, but they also use it to quench any doubts and independent thinking. If a person shows any independence outside of the leader's control, the individual is accused of having pride. They are then intimidated and shamed for having such blatant sin. Thus, pride is not only a snare, but it becomes a vicious cycle for the individual who has never been broken by the harsh reality of its control and darkness in their personal life.

The people who are often deceived are sincere in their desires towards God. Many want to serve Him. They have a zeal that has never been realized or fulfilled. The problem with such people is that their desire may be noble, but in reality, it is misleading because it is often motivated by pride.

The Word of God is clear. Man's greatest pursuit should not be one of service, but of knowing God. His ultimate sacrifice should not be money, time, or energy, but that of self-denial and becoming a sacrifice that is in line with the acceptable will of God. Man should not be caught up with ways to impress God, but rather his agenda should be to obey God's will in every area of his life.

The problem with zealous ministry, misguided sacrifices, and agendas is that they can become a matter of duty, while being indifferent to the heart, mind, and will of God. They become substitutes that focus on religion, doctrines, and works, while being disloyal to God. They have forms of righteousness, while harboring idolatry and betraying Christ.

The key to avoiding deception is to have enough integrity to face pride and to make a determination to love the truth enough to own up when wrong. Then, humble yourself enough to repent of wicked ways and confess dishonorable pursuits, loyalties, and agendas.

I have learned that the only shame in deception is not the fact that a person has been deceived, but that the individual is too proud to face it, confess it, and gracefully learn the lessons that can produce true humility.

At this time, if you asked our friends how they viewed our response to their leader, they would probably be gracious, but give you a typical reply. They would probably stress that we are greatly mistaken about this man, for he is of God. After all, we do not know him as they do. This gives them the ability to rightfully judge. They might add that we have heard biased claims and that one day, we will come to our senses and see how wrong we are.

Do I care if I am wrong about this individual? The answer is no. The Holy Spirit has not convicted me otherwise, and mere man has long lost his glamour in my eyes. I realize that the only thing I am impressed with in a person's life is the life of Christ.

Like our friends, many people follow leaders on the basis of flattery, false promises, power, and miracles. Flattery and false promises are lies. Power and miracles based on faulty foundations of darkness must be properly discerned and not serve as a gauge to blindly confirm the validity of a person's ministry. People must remember that man possesses nothing outside of the spiritual realm. He is merely a tool to be used for the work of either God or Satan. It is the one who is behind the power that must be discerned and recognized.

Some would be concerned that I am not supporting one of God's "anointed." "Anointed" simply means that a person has been set apart for a special work. However, it does not automatically make a person right, nor does it demand blind loyalty or support. For example, King Saul was anointed of God, and he was wrong about many things. God even pronounced judgment on him. David recognized that Saul was anointed king, but he did not always submit to his leadership because it would have meant his death.

My main responsibility towards this leader was to guard my heart. I hold no grudges nor anger towards him. I also have put him in God's hands. He is the One who will separate the wheat from the tares. If this man is of God, God will confirm his ministry, but if he is not, God will be the One who brings him down.

The other reason that I am not concerned about my opinion of this man is because my well-being does not hinge on agreeing with him or supporting him, but on my relationship with Jesus Christ. There is great liberty in knowing what is really important as far as my spiritual life is concerned. I have learned long ago that man will fail, and doctrines leave one empty, but Christ is the only One who ultimately stands when all of these substitutes fade away or are judge.

My question will always be the same to those whose claims of importance in the kingdom of God are based on denomination, doctrines, or spiritual leaders, "That's nice,...but what are you doing with Jesus?" I believe this one question not only determines a person's present spiritual condition, but their eternal destination.

17

DELIVERED?

Jesus said, "Take ye away
the stone."
(John 11:39)

"You get out of there right now!" It was as though Jeannette was trying to pull Krista through the phone lines. I could tell that Krista's final day working for the international ministry had arrived sooner than planned. It had only been a week-and-half since the conversation with Krista that showed all three of us that it was time for her to leave the cultist clutches and heretical influences of the international ministry that she had been helping for the past nine months. I could tell that Krista was at a critical breaking point, and if she did not leave soon, she would explode. Her anger for the tyrannical leader was hitting a crisis point. He had not only lost her respect and trust, but he was now deemed an enemy of the cross and an absolute fool in her eyes.

For months, we had watched this emotional momentum build up in Krista. We were aware that Krista would not remain with the organization for long, but timing was everything. God had to be the one orchestrating the events to ensure her spiritual well-being and provide a place for her to run to.

We had all prayed on the phone to receive confirmation as to the right timing. The three of us came out knowing that it was time for Krista to give her official notice. Krista knew that the remaining three weeks were going to be a nightmare. Her goal was to leave gracefully, but past examples implied that she would not be allowed to leave without being intimidated, harassed, and demeaned.

Secretly, I was hoping that she was wrong about her evaluation, but underneath, I knew she was in for it. I wanted to protect her, but I was aware that it was not my job. God had ordained this situation to test and train Krista. The results would be a credit to the unseen work and sustaining power of the Holy Spirit.

No one knows what they are made of until the person is tried in the fire. We had trained Krista for three years, but could never measure the depth or strength of her foundation. God used this false leader to not only reveal the quality of her foundation, but to perfect it. It pleasantly surprised and blessed all three of us.

I suddenly realized that for three years we had been preparing Krista to stand in and through her testing. Sadly, Christians do test people's spiritual life on the basis of ministry, positions, and number of people influenced; but the real test of a person's spiritual life is the quality of their foundation. If a person is unable to stand in times of testing, the rest is nothing more than rubbish.

Krista not only stood sure on her foundation, but I could also sense that she was maturing. First of all, I sensed an attitude change. Krista is a very serious and intense person, but she needed to learn to laugh at her situation. She began to develop a sense of humor about her challenges, which brought much needed release and laughter during some of our phone conversations.

Krista had been restless and discontent about her quality of life before she moved to Seattle. In time, sobriety took hold of her spirit and appreciation took root in her life. Her restlessness turned into quiet confidence and her discontentment into peace.

The present phone conversation showed that the situation had hit a crisis point. I was not surprised to see how quickly everything was deteriorating. The night before, we had received a phone call from Krista. She was emotionally on edge. The leader had set up a meeting with her to supposedly discuss how they were going to handle her departure.

Krista had rightfully stated in her resignation that she was leaving because God was moving her on. She told our friends first because she was living with them. When she informed the leader, he was not gracious. He told her that she could not hear from God, and he went one step further by insulting Jeannette and me for having any part in her decision.

Krista survived round one and agreed to meet with him to discuss the handling of her departure in regards to preparing the rest of the staff members. The meeting turned out to be more like an FBI criminal investigation.

For three hours five people interrogated her. Apparently, no one could graciously accept the idea that God was moving her on. They prodded her until she admitted that she did not agree with the leader's teachings, but she maintained that God was leading her into new waters.

I was not surprised that the leader made a federal case out of Krista's decision to leave his so-called "elite ministry", but the idea that people had ganged up on her made me irate. I personally wanted to nail the leader's arrogant, self-righteous, insidious hide to the nearest wall. Such procedures may be acceptable in the criminal system as a means to get at the truth from guilty parties, but not in Christianity. There is no place in Scripture where such a procedure was ever established.

In fact, I steamed all night over the unscriptural and demeaning practices of a man who dared to call himself a loving, Christian leader. How dare a man take one of God's sheep and abuse her in the name of ministry. The next morning, my emotional momentum had reached such fervor that I was ready to go to Washington and clean house.

Fortunately, God had better plans. The former leader who had left the organization a few months before, telephoned us. He asked me what was going on because the Lord had kept him awake all night. Needless to say, it did not take me long to inform him of the ridiculous charades that had taken place the night before.

He immediately made a decision to stand between Krista and the wolf. He already was aware of this man's methods, and had previously survived the onslaught of his attacks. The next thing we knew, Krista called us from her new protector's home. She had been in a third meeting with this cult leader who seemed to be relentless in trying to bring her under his control. This time, the roles changed, Jeannette became irate and told Krista to get out of there immediately.

Before the day was over, Krista's worldly possessions were packed up in less than two hours, and she was relocated to another place. Although the fallout was just beginning for those involved with Krista's departure, she was spared the full impact of it.

That night, Jeannette and I rested more easily. We knew that we had to face the fallout, which lasted for three weeks, but Krista was free from the jaws of her predator. As we rejoiced over Krista's deliverance, we began to wonder if our deliverance from the cave was not around the bend. We could only hope and pray.

What About the Grave Clothes?

Our cave was becoming more oppressive. We had done a lot of intercession in our small prison, but our creative juices were stifled by the thick oppression that had proved to be suffocating.

Our answered prayer for deliverance came in the form of an unlikely individual. I had met this individual a couple of years before. He had various problems that eventually brought him to the end of himself. He sought me out for ministry.

I was aware that he was involved with mortgages and even owned a couple of homes. On my upcoming second ministry session with him, the Lord impressed me that he was the key to getting us into the Boise area. Jeannette and I had been drawn to Boise for a couple of years, but could not see how we could afford to live there. As I turned the idea over in my mind, I finally verbalized it to Jeannette. Immediately, she became excited because the Lord had shown her the same thing a couple of days before.

During our meeting, I presented the idea to him. He readily agreed that we needed to be in Boise, and he could help us. In fact, he owned four homes altogether. One was his personal home, another was his cabin, the third was a rental, but the fourth was a new home he had recently purchased. I could tell he wanted to reserve the fourth home for other purposes, so, on our first visit, we agreed to look at his personal home in Boise and the rental. Jeannette and I did not feel comfortable about his personal home, and we didn't feel right about kicking the renters out in the third home. We went home without any real prospects, but trusting God to work something out.

On our second trip to Boise, we not only went there to see homes, but pick up Krista at the airport for a week of much needed rest and recreation. On our second trip, we looked at his brand-new home. It was beautiful, and Jeannette fell in love with it. Secretly, Jeannette had given the qualifications of her next home to God. She wanted it to be brand new home, along with possessing a wonderful kitchen and enough room to function. It had to be in a nice, safe location with ample light and a fenced yard for Angel. This house fit her criteria.

I knew this man was reluctant to rent the brand-new house to us, but I felt there were no other options. I took the situation to the Lord in prayer. The Lord showed me that this man had dedicated the house to Him and His work. Because of this dedication, the Lord had set it aside for us. Upon questioning the man about what the Lord had shown me, he admitted that he had dedicated it to Him.

Even though we had financially struggled in our cave and lost some valuable support, we started renting the new house for $50.00 more a month. Even though this man was nervous and reluctant to rent the house to us at such a low price, he kept his word. We could see God's faithfulness in the whole situation to provide a home along with the finances.

Almost a year to the day that Krista left for Washington to help the international ministry, she moved back to Idaho to once again become part of Gentle Shepherd Ministries. Our family was again complete. We started to make headway towards setting up a Web page for the ministry. We were excited about the prospect of finally going online. A Christian woman had volunteered to be our Webmaster for free.

We knew this woman had some real mental and spiritual problems. She was judgmental and opinionated, causing her to be unpredictable and dangerous. We sensed that she could turn on us at any minute, but prayed that she would finish the Website before she went off on one of her religious tangents and causes.

Sadly, she started one of her religious crusades against us before she finished the Website. She not only dropped the ball on us, but she also began a hate campaign, especially against me, that split the Internet e-group she was overseeing. It was obvious to many that she was bent on destroying me. I knew she was dangerous, but her vindictiveness even exceeded my expectations of her capabilities to destroy anyone who did not agree with her. We later discovered that she was a practicing astrologist.

The woman's vicious attack lasted for a week. Then, God miraculously interceded on our behalf and abruptly stopped it. We could breathe more easily because the assault was over, but we now had an incomplete Website that needed to be finished. A trustworthy friend stepped in to help, but we knew his time was limited, so we decided that Jeannette and Krista would have to take the necessary classes to finish it.

Our creative juices once again began to flow. I was able to finish some old projects and get on top of new ones. Jeannette started working on her new book. But, even in the midst of all the new prospects, I was aware that we still did not have total freedom to move forward. I knew that God had rolled back the stone and delivered us from the cave, but something was still hindering us. I suddenly realized that we were still wrapped up in grave clothes.

I was reminded of Lazarus in John 11. He had been dead for four days. Jesus had the stone rolled away from the entrance of his tomb and called him forth in resurrection life. Lazarus walked out of the tomb alive, but still enfolded in the grave clothes. It was then that Jesus instructed others to take the grave clothes off of him.

This new house represented a new life to all three of us, but we also realized that the face of Gentle Shepherd Ministries would have to change. The ministry, as well as the three of us, had the mark of death upon us, or, in other words, the grave clothes. The truth is, all resurrection life has a mark of death upon it. After all, it is the mark of death that sets something apart for the glory of God.

In the years of ministry, I learned that a dedicated Christian's life has many marks of death. If a person really chooses the Christian life, they are choosing the road of Calvary, that of self-denial and the cross. In retrospect, I can see where, many times, my preparation for victory came by way of self-denial, and my preparation for greater life came by way of death to some dream, idea, vision, and way of thinking and doing.

I knew that God had called us forth from the grave after four years of tasting its bittersweet reality, but now we must wait for Him to bring the right people who would loose us from our grave clothes. Meanwhile, what is one to do but trust the One who is ever faithful? I knew He would soon bring the right people to loose us. Until it happened, we continued to pray that our lives would be prepared to shine with the brightness of the glory of the Son of the Living God in this dark world.

In his devotional book, Oswald Chambers shared how God takes years to prepare his saints to shine brightly, but the bright light only lasts a short season. The truth is, all lights will give way to greater lights. I can see where God has been preparing me for decades to shine, whether it is for a minute, hour, day, or season. It is my heart's desire to reflect the unhindered glory of the Bright and Morning Star. This is my simple prayer, for I have realized the value of my life. As the Apostle Paul concluded in Philippians 3, life means nothing unless a person lives it for one main purpose, and that is to die in order to gain the greatest possession of all— the Person of Jesus Christ.

18

THE EPITAPH

"...he was not; for God
took him."
(Genesis 5:24b)

"What would I like my epitaph to read when everything is said and done in this present life?" This is a question I occasionally ask myself to get some bearing on my spiritual life. I realize that thinking about eulogizing your life in order to write an epitaph in the prime of it, is something that few people probably ever really think about. Most people put off the prospects of death, but for Jeannette and me, the walk of faith and our grave clothes brought this subject to the forefront for both of us.

In the midst of the many limitations we have faced over the years, it is hard to ignore how fragile life is, and how dependent we are on God. When you read Genesis about how God created life, you cannot help but notice how the book of new beginnings ends with a coffin. As stated previously, real life is always marked with death. The Apostle Paul confirmed this truth when he made this declaration in Romans 8:36, "As it is written, For thy sake we are killed all the day long; we are accounted as sheep for the slaughter."

Jeannette and I had to face death in various ways. We had to face death to self, rights, personal goals, health, and the normal life. Our many projects that had been offered to God, along with the ministry, experienced a form of death every time we put them on the altar as a offering to God for His use and glory.

It amazed us to realize how death is not finality, but a beginning. In fact, death serves as a door to a greater life. Therefore, I believe an epitaph should clearly commemorate the characteristics of a person's life that will be carried through the door of death, into their next existence.

I have often taken stock of, not only my present life, but also the goal I wanted to obtain before I left this world by writing the one line that could honestly be put on my stone. I did not want my life to be glamorous like Hollywood with all of its flattery, fantasy, hypocrisy, and foolishness. I had long ago left the idea behind of ever making a political statement that would memorialize me in some history book. I forgot about prestige, popularity, and importance when all of my romantic notions about ministry fell to the wayside. Truthfully, I found each pursuit to be as vain as the world that inspired it.

My search to write my epitaph caused me to consider what I really wanted my life to say about my relationship with God and my service to Him. Each stage of growth brought me closer to fine-tune the statement that would hopefully define a life that was given as a sacrifice in total abandonment to God.

The first thing I wanted people to remember about my life is that it was obvious that I had been with Jesus, like Peter and John in Acts 4:13 where people noted they had been with Jesus. To me this would be one of the greatest compliments anyone could pay me.

Like the Apostle Paul, I wanted Christ to be an unquestionable reality in me and through me. Paul knew that Christ was the great prize he wanted to possess. Not only did He want to seize the reality of Christ, but he also wanted to be possessed by Him. As he said in Philippians 3:12: "...if that I may apprehend that for which also I am apprehended of Christ Jesus."

As I look back over my life, I see how Jesus became more and more real to me in different stages of spiritual growth. I first started out as a zealous Christian who found out that I was ignorant about Jesus and had substituted religion in His place. This harsh reality brought me to the feet of Jesus, seeking Him out.

The next great level of growth found me at His table, learning of Him and growing in my spiritual life with leaps and bounds. At the next place of enlargement, I found my romantic concepts about Jesus and ministry giving way to the fiery trials of faith. In the following stage, I found myself being exalted into ministry, only to be humbled by the grave. From the grave, I found Christ becoming more real as He became rest to my weary soul. At the next level, I discovered what it meant to be a co-laborer with Him.

My ultimate desire was for the life of Christ to consume me so much that I could declare with Paul, "…nevertheless I live; yet not I but Christ liveth in me." Like Enoch, I wanted to come to a place in my life where I could not be found because I had been so taken up by the reality of my God that nothing else was left of me.

The next virtue I wanted to be evident in my life was spiritual character. Oswald Chambers said it best, "My spiritual character determines the revelation of God to me."[1] I always wanted a greater knowledge of Christ, but I realized that my character had to be enlarged to embrace greater revelation. I also knew that a person is never born with character, but that it has to be forged in their life.

Spiritual character is often carved out of granite with a chisel, established in fiery ovens of tribulation, and unveiled by a cross. I realized that the price to establish spiritual character could be great, but I already knew it would be well worth the cost.

I summarized through my travels that godly character is the only quality that validates a person's claims and gives them

---

[1] Oswald Chambers; Approved Unto God *with* Facing Reality; pg. 48

authority and discernment. Oswald Chambers brings perspective to this truth. He stated that the Lord cannot meet us until there is character. He goes on to say: "The discernment of God's truth and the development of character go together."[2]

One of the mottos from my High School senior year that often came to me in my challenges and trials was, "I dare you!" Jeannette and I had to dare to take chances and be willing to be wrong in order to get things right. We dared to take some unusual risks so that we could live by faith. Even though we didn't work at a regular job, we found ourselves working harder doing odd jobs. We watched God prepare unusual means for us to financially survive. The key is, we had to be flexible and willing to do things that were unpleasant and seemingly impossible. For example, around Christmas, we painted windows in freezing, miserable weather, but God multiplied the money we received, and we were able to pay our debts.

During the Desert Storm War, the Lord gave Jeannette the idea to paint yellow ribbons on windows in three different communities. It gave us a much-needed financial boost. Before she lost the use of most of her voice, she also taught painting classes at different times to bring in money during some of the greatest crises and physical struggles of her life. The money that came through these jobs seemed to meet our immediate needs.

Another odd job that we found ourselves doing was cleaning houses, and later, washing windows. Some of the challenges we encountered in our cleaning projects proved overwhelming at times, but God got us through each project.

Various challenges in ministry dared us to step into uncharted territories. The Lord showed us that our office space in Woodinville, Washington would enlarge to include another section of the building, along with growth in the ministry. We initially rented

---

[2] Ibid; page 37

a section of offices in the back of a beautiful building. Then, the Lord showed me that we would also end up with the section of offices located in front. When the renters moved out, we were offered the front section, but the rent amount for both the front and back offices was too expensive.

I reminded the Lord that He told us that we were to have the front offices as well. He gave me an idea for presenting a counter rent proposal. It would save us over $350, even though it would triple our rent. To my surprise, our landlord agreed to our proposal. Even though our rent had tripled, the Lord always brought in enough money to pay it. This experience was a miracle and a faith-builder.

Each step of faith was a dare. We accepted the challenge because we had nowhere else to go. The rewards for accepting these challenges were that our faith, character, and life in God were enlarged.

Another area that proved trying was going back to "Square One" to get something right. I cannot tell you how many times I had to redo the "Hidden Manna Workbooks" for our different seminars. I had to repeatedly go back to the drawing board to get the workbooks right.

On my last try, I was ready to give up on the idea of revising the basic workbook. In fact, I was throwing a fit. My pride was greatly suffering because redoing something more than twice affected my fragile ego. I was beginning to feel like a failure. Jeannette silently watched me, as I threw a major tantrum. I was tired of trying to get it right, only to find after much time and energy that I had failed to accomplish my task.

After my tantrum, Jeannette quietly spoke volumes as she gave me her knowing look. She knew that I would get it right because it had nothing to do with my pride or weariness, but with giving my best for God's work. I had learned that the secret of failure or success in the kingdom of God has nothing to do with getting it wrong or right. It actually comes down to doing the best you can, until you feel that the only thing left is for God to touch and sanctify it for His use and glory.

I realized that the trials and failures enlarged my spiritual character. Sadly, most Christians want the things of God, but they don't want to pay the price. I wanted the things of God to be evident in my character, and God honored my desire, even when I kicked and screamed along the way.

Jeannette once said that she saw three tracks in the sand when it came to her relationship with Jesus. She was able to distinguish the two faithful footsteps of Jesus, but the third track didn't make sense until she realized that it represented her being dragged behind Him. Our Lord will always honor our sincere desires to follow Him, even though He has to occasionally drag us, while our unwilling flesh loudly protests and our pride refuses to go gracefully.

In reminiscing about the hard route we had traveled, Jeannette summarized it in this statement, "Rayola, we may have looked like fools to those around us and to the Church, but we have the promise of a greater resurrection."

Hebrews 11 talks about those who dared to possess the life God made available to them by walking by faith. Some appear as total failures as they were mocked, persecuted, imprisoned, and silenced through death. However, the writer of Hebrews made two statements that express how God views these isolated renegades in 11:35 and 38, "…that they might obtain a better resurrection" and "of whom the world was not worthy."

Obviously, the people mentioned in the Hall of Fame of Faith in Hebrews 11 had spiritual character that served as a bright shining light in the midst of great darkness. Today, these silent witnesses challenge every succeeding generation of Christians to take up the torch that has been handed down to them, and run the great race. Unlike our Olympics, this spiritual race is not about winning, but about finishing the course. This lifelong marathon is not about medals that will lose their importance and luster with time, but gaining an eternal prize, Jesus Christ. It is not about entertaining great crowds, but about gaining the attention of lost souls that need to be stirred by the light of Christ. This race is not about speed, but about faithful runners who have not only abandoned everything, but have also endured great hardships to apprehend the greatest prize of all--their high calling of God in Christ Jesus.

The final statement I wanted on my epitaph was that I was a restless pilgrim. The Word refers to Christians as pilgrims or sojourners. When you look up the meaning of these two words, you realize that there are three qualifications for being a spiritual pilgrim.[3]

The first requirement to be a spiritual pilgrim is that you do not belong to the world. In fact, you don't fit into the world, and as a result, you have probably become a great irritant to those who are of the world. The reason a spiritual pilgrim does not belong to the world is due to the fact they have no real root system in the world. Such pilgrims are not aimless wanderers, but travelers who have a definite destination. Since they do not have any ties with the world, they can pursue this destination without having any regret about what they have left behind.

The second qualification of a pilgrim is a restlessness or discontentment until they arrive at their destination. Jeannette and I have recognized a growing restlessness in our lives for the past couple of years. This restlessness is not because we are miserable in our present situation, but because the desire to arrive at our final destination has escalated.

Many people look heavenward because they desire relief from the bombardment of worldly struggles and sorrows. Jeannette and

---

[3] 1 Peter 2:11

I look heavenward because we have become very homesick. Relief and being homesick spring from different sources. Relief is a desire to find alleviation from the struggles of this world that are often born out of weariness and disillusionment.

Homesickness is a longing in your heart to be home in order to fellowship with loved ones. It is the place where you belong and where you are reminded of your real identity and inheritance. Being homesick for the Christian pilgrim simply means that they miss being with Jesus, sitting in His presence, and worshipping Him, unhindered by the flesh, the world, and Satan.

Great spiritual giants suffered this homesickness. The Apostle Paul made this statement in 2 Corinthians 5:8, "We are confident, I say, and willing rather to be absent from the body, and to be present with the Lord." Paul would rather be home with his Lord, but was willing to remain a sojourner in the world, if he could bring glory to God by continuing to be an asset to those he served.

I saw this same restlessness in the life of David Brainerd. David was a missionary to the Indians during the 1700s. God used him to make great inroads into the spiritual darkness that enfolded them. In spite of bringing light into great darkness, you could tell that David was homesick. He was a restless pilgrim who accepted his calling, but was forever looking heavenward. The more the world became distasteful and unacceptable to him, the more precious his Lord Jesus became to him.

It was obvious by David's writings that he was being consumed with the desire to see and be with his Lord. At the age of 29, David Brainerd got his desire. He entered into eternal glory, to never again be hindered from loving, worshipping, and sitting in his Lord's presence.

Jeannette and I developed this homesickness as the world became more repulsive and the reality of Jesus Christ began to fill up every vacant area of our lives. As we have traveled this route since 1989, we have discovered that the world has nothing to offer us. At best, it brings total ruin to people's lives. It is designed to entangle its victims in order to rob them of hope. It enslaves people for the purpose of killing any possible life of Jesus in them, and entices its patrons in order to destroy that which is pure.

As the world has become less attractive to us, our citizenship in heaven has become more precious. As we have watched the systems of the world, like the claws of a vulture, sweeping down on unsuspecting humanity to usher them into hell, the arms of Jesus have become a desired haven to us.

We have also watched delusion spread over the whole world, as a dark covering. It makes minds dull, hearts hard, and exalts pride as an aggressive, unmerciful and relentless god. As we have watched this wicked covering engulf lives, we cherish the light of our soul, Jesus Christ, and we look forward to the day when we will see the unveiled majesty of this same glorious light in heaven.

The final qualification of spiritual pilgrims is that their vision is always beyond the world. Like Abraham, spiritual pilgrims may have great promises that have not yet been fulfilled, but they are not interested because they are looking for a city whose foundations have been established by God.[4]

For the past three decades, our vision has changed. We have become more focused on our real home and inheritance, making us restless to arrive at our destination. Everything of the world, no matter how great, becomes pale in light of our Lord, heavenly destination, inheritance, and residence.

I had asked Jeannette she wanted on their epitaph. After thinking about it for a short time Jeannette gave me this simple answer, "A sinner, saved by grace!"

The question remains, what do I want on my epitaph? I kept coming back to the epitaph that marked Enoch's life. But, do I dare desire such an epitaph as his? Why not, all things are

---

[4] Hebrews 11:10

possible with God. And, who knows, when it is all said and done, maybe people will be able to say of me, "She is not; for God took her."

The question now is, what would you want your epitaph to say about your spiritual life? Are you ready to do whatever it takes for the final statement about your life on earth to be forever echoed in the courts of heaven?

19

THE JOURNEY CONTINUES

And God shall wipe away all tears from their
eyes; and their shall be no more death,
neither sorrow, nor crying, neither shall
there be any more pain; for the former
things are passed away.
(Revelation 21:4)

As I have already mentioned, it has been over three decades since Jeannette and I started this incredible journey. This book has been on the shelf at different times. It has been taken off the shelf a couple of times, once to be edited to be made into an e-book, another time to be formatted to be put into a volume as a book and once again in 2023 to be reedited.

In those years, there have been many more challenges along the way, but the Rock of Ages has always stood sure and immovable in our midst. The storms have continued to rage, but we have always found a safe haven in our Creator. We have tasted the depths of the grave in different ways, but continue to discover that each aspect of the grave is a greater revelation of our real Ark, Jesus Christ. After all, He is the place of rest and safety for every struggling soul. We have felt the entanglement of grave clothes, only to find the liberty of His life, setting us free to know the abundant satisfaction of having Him as our source. We have felt the bitterness of the north wind halting our advancement, only to watch it give way to the healing breezes of His south wind.

People have come and gone in our lives. God still continues to bring people alongside of us who will support and encourage us, even though after a season most of them are led elsewhere. He is however, establishing a core leadership in Gentle Shepherd Ministries. These committed individuals feel the burden to come under the same yoke, to fulfill the vision of this ministry according to their different callings and gifts.

The vision of this ministry to preach the Gospel and make disciples of Jesus has never changed, but it has been redefined, as God directs our steps down different paths. After being prompted by the Lord, we have closed various fellowships after working to establish the life of Christ in people that walked through our doors. During our time in Nampa, Idaho we embraced and worked among the Hispanic community. Once again, we felt that we were indeed missionaries embarking on foreign soil.

We certainly discovered the bondage of culture while working with the Hispanics. These people have been kept in the dark clutches of ignorance and fear. Many are hungry and thirsty, but fear is prevalent. However, the love of Christ continues to reach through the veil of cultural bondage to bring life and hope. Like others who are entangled by the world, the truth is capable of helping these people to understand their place in Christ, as well as discover their calling, accept their gifts, and become true servants in the kingdom of God.

On an international level, we have sent various discipleship courses to Africa, as well as receiving requests from India and the Philippines for similar support.

The Lord continues to work on each of us, constantly challenging us to consecrate ourselves to Him. Faithful to His working, He has taken us through some fiery tests to establish our spiritual foundation in greater ways. He provided us with nice homes along the way that have become, not only a sanctuary for us, but others as well.. Regardless of where we land, we all know we will always be in some type of transition because our real home is not of this earth.

Our latest transition led us to Northern Idaho, and our prayer is that the next one will be our ultimate destination, but regardless of where He sets us He is on the move. We are aware that time is short as we watch events escalate towards the time Jesus spoke about just prior to His crucifixion. It will be a time of great darkness, opening the way for the life of Jesus to shine brightly in the lives of His people.

Such times remind us that everything of this world is temporary and is in constant flux. Likewise, changes are forever occurring in life and ministry as we go through the seasons of our spiritual lives. We hold things of this world lightly, so that when God asks us to let go of the present, in order to give way to something new, our hands immediately open in sweet surrender.

Landing

We have had some sagas in our final transition. Praise the Lord we have a reliable car, a 2006 Honda CRV that I have asked the Lord to maintain until He comes. Transportation has ceased to be an issue.

Our washing machine ordeal has hit a few snags along the way. The dial was broken on the washing machine we had and we bought one of those water-saving machines. Jeannette's opinion is it is a poor excuse for a washing machine and a black eye to the principle of a washing machine that saves water while leaving clothes dirty.

When we moved up to North Idaho, we found one hindrance after another trying to get out of Nampa, Idaho. It was a clear night in February and it was not until 9 p.m. by the time our caravan of two U-Haul trucks and vehicles escaped. Instead of taking us 2 ½ hours to get to the mid-point of where we would spend the night, it took us over four hours because we hit one of the biggest snow storms recorded at that time in 100 years.

The storm closed roads and gave us another day of rest at our half-way point before having to drive the rest of the way. When we arrived at our new location, it proved to be the coldest day they had had in years. We lost some of our stuff because it cracked and broke.

We agreed to move into a house sight unseen. It had potential but, in the end, we called it the "Sewer House." There were electrical problems, black mold in the house, and evidence of abuse from former residents who were known by the cops for being involved with drugs. In fact, Krista found some weed, but the final straw was when the sewer backed up into the downstairs because the septic tank was overflowing.

We knew we had to get out of the six month lease we had with the landowners and the mold problem became a good excuse. However, we had to find another house. When it came to houses, we discovered Jeannette had faith God would supply.

She felt led to go into a real estate office and tearfully asked if there were any rentals. The real estate agent told her about a vacation house that had just come up for rent. It only had two bedrooms but it was furnished for 12 people to stay there and that the owners allowed dogs, which, at that time, included our dear little Angel and another adorable Chihuahua, Bell.

I must say it was a beautiful place located alongside of Priest River. It was an almost two-acre lot that had over 40 trees on it that included Douglas Fir, Yellow Pine, Bull Pine, Walnut, Maple and fruit trees. The house was adequate due to a basement for the three of us but Jeannette and I had to share the only bedroom upstairs that we not only had to fit twin beds into but our office desks as well.

The setting of the river along with the deer, moose, osprey, and eagles brought such inspiration to us. We not only finished up some books but due to the constant problems we were having in getting our books published, we were forced to become our own publisher. It was another time of great learning with much trial and error but today we can see a manuscript through the process from formatting it into a book to creating a cover for it.

It was here that another transition took place. Krista found a job in Sandpoint. At the time we were involved with training another person, Carrie Seaney. Carrie was a school teacher and lived in Sandpoint, but got a job with the school district in Priest River. They simply changed places. Carrie came to live with us while Krista moved to Sandpoint. Jeannette asked Carrie why she wanted to live with the Baldwin sisters (From Walton's Mountain). Carrie and I still laugh about the statement while Jeannette shares a knowing smile.

After three years in the house by Priest River where many lessons were learned about pruning trees along with cleaning up and burning the slash, using a snow blower and meeting considerate neighbors, we felt it was time to buy our own place. Jeannette had been looking for a place on the internet. There were very few places but she found one house that fit our criteria five miles away in the community of Oldtown, Idaho. She later showed it to us and declared that is our house.

We made our move on it by faith. We prayed about how much to offer for the house which was a repo and got a specific amount. The process was started, a loan was sought out by Carrie, the bank holding the title agreed to our amount and Carrie for the most part was approved for the loan and we were given different closing dates by the loan officer. The dates passed and we began hearing from what I called "Job's friends" who questioned if we were on the right track and really heard from the Lord. We were also looking at the possibility of losing our earnest money after almost three months of excuses from our loan officer. Finally, our real estate agent had us talk to another loan officer who stated something was not right.

The next day Carrie called the bank branch that was overseeing the bank in our particular region to find out what the hold up was on finalizing our loan. A woman kindly put her in contact with an individual who turned out to be the main guy over the region and the next day the loan went through and we were ushered into our new home within two days. The only casualty in it was the inept loan officer. He lost his job.

We moved into our present house in 2013 and it proved to be interesting as we had to address neglect since the house had been in repo for three years. After ten years of projects and remodeling, we finally have the house that has reached its potential.

Jeannette and I continue to remain busy in ministry. We have a Bible Study and fellowship. Jeannette turned 80 in 2023 which also marked our 35th year since we formed Gentle Shepherd Ministries. She still does not have the full use of her voice, but ministers through the Internet and our monthly newsletters. Although ministry can prove to be difficult for Jeannette, she quietly shares her experiences and lessons in our different Bible Studies. She will not be silenced by the loss of her voice. Her heart is to reach out to people in any capacity that is available. She has faithfully walked a hard path, in spite of her many physical challenges. But there is a quiet confidence and strength in her, even settling to my spirit. There have been numerous times during her many struggles that she could have given up, but she continues to cling to the One who will never let her go. As a result, her testimony of God's faithfulness, as well as her authority in Christ, continue to grow.

Through the years I have had some medical challenges, but I see where the Lord has made me more pliable. I would like to say

I have handled all times of challenges graciously, but I have not but our Lord continues to be faithful.

My writing is slowing down and I think I see an end to writing anymore books. Between Jeannette and me, we have written close to 70 books. Years ago, the Lord gave me a vision of integrating these books into the Discipleship Course. The course is helpful to those seeking to grow in their life in Christ to advance beyond the fundamental understandings of the Christian life. We have placed these books on the altar. I have learned that my responsibility is to surrender all to God. From that point on, it is God's affair, and it is His responsibility to work out the details in accordance with His will and glory.

Through the years, we lost some dear friends. One was Carol Sue Haskins who was part of the unique group of ladies in Kirkland, Washington. I had the honor of teaching our Discipleship Course to these ladies. Every Thursday night for about a year, we laughed, shared, and at times cried together. For most people, the life of Carol Sue will have no meaning. She is a faceless name to the world. Needless to say, most people never crossed paths with her. They have no memories of her laughter or her concern for the souls of people. If Jesus tarries, in a matter of three generations, she will be forgotten, except for her name being mentioned on some family tree.

Life is short and fragile. Most pass into eternity without even a thought, except by family and friends. After all, death is part of life. What did Carol Sue leave behind her in her short time on this earth? As her pastor stated, she left "stuff" and relationships behind. Stuff will pass away, but the impressions and investments we make in others will continue. And, the only investment into people's lives that will make it past this present world into eternity is Jesus Christ.

The death of a close friend makes me rethink the values of my life. As stated, I gave up the idea of worldly fame, success, and importance a long time ago. In so doing, I no longer worry about if I leave an impression on the world. I have become too sober-minded and realistic to be caught up with the glamour of ministry or greatness. My main concern has been reduced to being faithful to seek out God's will for my life, to uphold the calling He has given me for His kingdom, and to maintain the gifts He has entrusted me with for the edification of His Body.

Recently, I once again changed my epitaph. The older I get, the more I appreciate simplicity. Getting down to the bottom of the matter cuts out a lot of nonsense that takes people on rabbit trails for the proverbial carrot. A particular gravestone came to my attention. It was simple and plain in appearance. The one whose life it marked remained anonymous as their name was missing. There was only one word written on this unassuming gravestone: *Forgiven*.

This simple word reminded me of the whole purpose of Jesus' redemption. No one can make it to heaven unless God has forgiven them for their sins, and Jesus was able to secure such forgiveness through His redemption. In light of this simple truth, nothing else really matters. I want my life to declare to everyone that God has indeed forgiven me. A gravestone may not even mark my present life when all is said and done, but my future life is a certainty in light of God's forgiveness.

Meanwhile, I continue to strive to be faithful with what is in front of me. I am one year away from hitting the milestone of my 70th birthday. I no longer harbor romantic notions, but I have not become skeptical about what I see. I am gaining more of a realistic perception about life, but avoiding becoming cynical about what I discover. As I close in on another year of Christian life, my expectancy is growing. The realization has hit me that I am getting closer to my real destination and home. The expectation sometimes is heightened by the events taking place in the world.

The events remind me of how hopelessly loss the world is. Clearly, time is short, no matter from which direction I approach this life.

My heavenly perspective has become more focused as I look up knowing my redemption draws near. However, I must always come down to earth and continue to face the reality of this present life. The realization of this present life is that until my redemption is fully realized, my spiritual journey on this earth continues up foreboding mountains, through stormy waters, across impossible terrain, through harsh valleys, and the uncharted territories of my own human soul and spirit. But no matter how challenging the journey is on earth, I stand assured that, in the end, I will see Jesus in His power and majesty. Like Paul, I can declare: "For the which cause I also suffer these things; nevertheless, I am not ashamed: for I know whom I have believed, and am persuaded that he is able to keep that which I have committed unto him against that day" (2 Timothy 1:12).

Epilogue

One of the many realizations I have had to accept is that this book will not be completed until I meet my Lord face to face. In fact, every book I have written will only reflect a partial revelation or understanding of Him and His Word in light of His eternal truths. As a result, I have decided to do my best to complete each book and offer it up as a sacrifice for His glory and purpose. And, thanks to modern technology, each book had been offered through the Internet via e-books, and now they can be digitally printed.

It will only be from the point of meeting Jesus in His unhindered glory, that completion will come to my life and the work that has been set before me. It will be from the point of His glory that true worship and praise will rightfully lift Him up in His majesty and greatness. It will be from such a perspective that the endless volumes that have been written about Him and His redemption will finally stand completed, for He is the Alpha and Omega. Up until then, there is always greater territory to seek in regards to His infinite character and ways. There are always greater revelations to be unveiled to the seeking heart. There is always that need to seek out and find Jesus in the midst of His Word, as well as in the fiery ovens of faith, and in the trials of spiritual growth.

In my perception, my present life is winding down, but in the scheme of eternity, I realize I am always being called higher. When we were still in Nampa, we asked the Lord where we were as far as the ministry was concerned. He showed us an aircraft carrier going out to sea. At the time, I had to shake my head at the prospect. Here I thought my life, and this ministry, were winding down, when in reality He was sending us out on an aircraft carrier.

Obviously, the aircraft carrier pointed to the intense war that was confronting us. After all, we have been living in precarious days for some time. This is not a time to sit on our laurels, and hope all goes well as we enjoy what time we have left. Instead, it is a time to go to war for the souls of those who are still being weighed in the balance of eternity.

Eventually the aircraft carrier was rendered incapacitated, causing us to once again take to the high seas in a rowboat. That is when we finally landed in our house in Oldtown, Idaho, far away from any boats and ships. We are still fighting a war but it is a ground war for souls. People still come and go, while there are always a few who remain in the boat. The latest picture we have received is coming around the bend in a river that will bring us to a larger place. It points to transition and greater liberty.

The ministry's face has changed. Carrie is a Gospel soloist and is about to make her seventh CD. She carries the burden of ministry as she often shares her life and testimony with her beautiful singing voice. Krista married in 2019 and is busy with her new family and being part of the worship team in her church.

My hope remains the same. At the end of this incredible journey, I pray that I will be able to declare what Paul said when his life was about to be offered up for the sake of His Lord:

> I have fought a good fight, I have finished my course, I have kept the faith; Henceforth there is laid up for me a crown of righteousness, which the Lord, the righteous judge, shall give me at that day; and not to me only, but unto all them also that love his appearing (2 Timothy 4:7-8).

Bibliography

Strong's Exhaustive Concordance of the Bible; James Strong, ©
1986 assigned to World Bible Publishers, Inc.

Webster's New Collegiate Dictionary; © 1976 by G. & C.
Merriam Co.

Daily Thought for Disciples; © 1990 by Oswald Chambers
Publications Association

Women in Today's Church, George Watkins, © 1984

Shade of His Hand; © 1991 by Oswald Chambers Publications
Association Limited

Jewish Faith and The New Covenant; Ruth Specter Lascelle ©
1980

My Utmost For His Highest, © 1935 by Dodd, Mead & Company,
Inc. Copyright renewed 1963 by Oswald Chamber Plications
Association, Ltd.

The Tithing Fallacy; Ernest L. Martin, © 1979 by The Foundation
for Biblical Research

Oswald Chambers; Approved Unto God with Facing Reality;
Approved Unto God © 1936 Oswald Chambers Publications
Association. *Facing Reality* © 1939 Oswald Chamber
Publications Association. Combined volume © 1946 Oswald
Chambers Publications Association. This edition © 1997
Oswald Chambers Publications Association Limited.

Other books by Rayola Kelley:

Hidden Manna (Original)
Battle for the Soul
Stories of the Heart
Transforming Love & Beyond
The Great Debate
Post to Post: (1) Establishing the Way
Post to Post: (2) Walking in the Way
Post to Post: (3) Meditations Along the Way
Post to Post: (4) Inspirations Along the Way

Volume One: Establishing Our Life in Christ

My Words are Spirit and Life
The Anatomy of Sin
The Principles of the Abundant Life
The Place of Covenant
Unmasking the Cult Mentality

Volume Two: Putting on the Life of Christ

He Actually Thought it Not Robbery
Revelation of the Cross
In Search of Real Faith
Think on These Things
Follow the Pattern

Volume Three: Developing a Godly Environment

Godly Discipline
Prayer and Worship
Don't Touch That Dial
Face of Thankfulness
ABC's of Christianity

Volume Four: Issues of the Heart

Hidden Manna (Revised)
Bring Down the Sacred Cows
The Manual for the Single Christian Life
Parents are People Too

Volume Five: Challenging the Christian Life

The Issues of Life
Presentation of the Gospel
For the Purpose of Edification
Whatever Happened to the Church?
Women's Place in the Kingdom of God

Volume Six: Developing Our Christian Life

The Many Faces of Christianity

Possessing Our Souls
Experiencing the Christian Life
The Power of Our Testimonies
The Victorious Journey

Devotions
Devotions of the Heart: Books One and Two
Daily Food for the Soul: Books One and Two

Gentle Shepherd Ministries Devotion Series:
Being a Child of God
Disciplining the Strength of our Youth
Coming to Full Age

Nugget Books:
Nuggets From Heaven
More Nuggets From Heaven
Heavenly Gems
More Heavenly Gems
Heavenly Treasures
More Heavenly Treasures

Gentle Shepherd Ministries Series:

The Christian Life Series
What Matter Is This?
The Challenge of It
The Reality of It

The Leadership Series
Overcoming
A Matter of Authority and Power
The Dynamics of True Leadership

Other Books By:
Jeannette Haley
Books co-authored with Rayola Kelley:
Hidden Manna (original)
The Many Faces of Christianity (Volume 6)
Post to Post 3: Meditations Along the Way
Post to Post 4: Inspirations Along the Way

Other Books:
Rose of Light, Thorn of Darkness
Interview In Hell
Interview On Earth
The Pig and I
Reflections of Wonder (Devotional)

Children's Books:
Little Stories for Little People
Traveler's Tales
The Adventures of Zack and Mira
The Adventures of Paul and Dana
(A House on the Beach)
The Monster of Mystery Valley

www.ingramcontent.com/pod-product-compliance
Lightning Source LLC
Chambersburg PA
CBHW062359090426
42740CB00010B/1335